To Make The Run

To Make the Run
A Seafarer's Memoir

By
J.E. "Joe" Gladstone

Carquinez Press
Crockett, California

147 INKWORKS

First Printing 2005

ISBN: 0-9744124-2-2
LCCN: 2004115654

Printing by: Inkworks Press, Berkeley CA 94710
Design by: Design Action, Oakland CA 94609

To order additional copies please contact:
Carquinez Press
P.O. Box 571
Crockett, CA 94525
Carquinezpress.com

Table of Contents

This memoir is affectionately dedicated to:

The memory of Carl and Rose Koster who made
the first suggestion;
The memory of Morris Weisberger who gave me the chance;
Ann, Irene, Rick and Laura who asked me when was I coming
home; and all those who helped me make the run.

Foreword

Some years after I left the sea, the idea germinated in my mind that someday I might like to write about it. It was only after I retired from all gainful employment that the opportunity presented itself to sit down and do it. There are certain writers who held down full time jobs and wrote after work far into the night, like Herman Melville, Edward Gibbon, and Anthony Trollope. I don't pretend to bat in their league. Another league I don't bat in is that of Jack London or Joseph Conrad.

This book is about those who sailed American merchant ships during the Great War of 1939-1945 and the lives they led. This era is gone; it is part of our past. But if it is ever in the political cards to revive the American Merchant Marine, the testimony I offer may be of value in picking up the narrative and going from there.

This story would never have seen the light of day had it not been for the encouragement of friends and family. My many thanks go out to: Maria Brooks of Waterfront Soundings who was good enough to show my manuscript to Archie Green of the Fund for Labor Culture & History who has been instrumental in bringing it all to fruition; Maria Hetherton whose editorial talent did wonders; to Lisa and John Robinson of Carquinez Press who will publish it; and finally, to my only living Sailors' Union of the Pacific buddy and friend, Jim Cunningham, whose knowledge of ships and the sea is downright encyclopedic. And one final caveat: all the opinions I express are my own. After all, it all happened on my watch.

Joe Gladstone
October 2004

Preface

Three millennia ago, the blind poet Homer heard a story about a mariner who had made his last voyage. Leaving sea duty behind, he marched inland with an oar on his shoulder. When he reached a village where no one recognized the oar, he settled down.

Despite centuries of scholarship we do not know the circumstance of origin of this narrative, now titled "The Sailor Who Went Inland." Nor have we learned whether a seafarer or landlubber related it to Homer. In these days of instant communication and internet searches, ancient yarns continue to circulate. We hear of a retired armed-guard crewman whose sailor buddy from upstate Michigan finally gave up on fierce winters. Mounting a battered snow shovel on his Ford, he headed south. In Arizona a gas station attendant asked him, "What's that gizmo on your car?" The traveler settled down.

Joe Gladstone, a retired merchant seaman, appreciates Homer and uses a computer. In *To Make the Run*, he reflects on his years at sea, 1940-1952, and his activity as a rank-and-file member of the Sailors' Union of the Pacific (SUP).

Unlike the Odyssey's wanderer and the Arizona sun-seeker, Joe chose to "plant his oar" a stone's throw from the sea in Santa Cruz, California. There, as a senior citizen, he participates in community affairs, and attempts to distill his life experience for use by present-day workers.

Joe Gladstone began writing his memoir in the late 1980s as a present to his children and grandchildren. For a decade, he made minor revisions to the text without serious consideration of book publication.

As is often the case, a writer who completes an autobiographical manuscript has little energy left for promotion.

Fortunately, Maria Brooks—then filming a documentary on Liberty Ship sailors during World War Two—encountered Joe's typescript. She shared it with me, attesting to its substance. Upon initial reading, I sensed Joe's natural gifts as a storyteller, affection for shipmates, and his sophisticated treatment of turbulent maritime-labor history.

An opportunity to publish *To Make the Run* arose after the chartering in the summer of 2000 of the Fund for Labor Culture & History. Among its educational goals, the FLCH had undertaken to print various books in conjunction with the Carquinez Press as well as other academic institutions. Sea literature is immense; books and articles seem to appear with every tide. Hence, publishers must be convinced that their volumes will supply new voices to the field. We in the FLCH remain confident that Joe Gladstone's memoir will delight sea enthusiasts. Beyond the existing audience of maritime buffs, we anticipate that *To Make the Run* will be especially useful to present-day sailors and their peers on merchant vessels.

The first generation of West Coast sailors who banded together in the SUP included many self-educated men—fluent in diverse tongues, skilled in putting pen to paper, and aware of print's potential in trade-union causes. Contrary to the popular image of the seaman as a hulking brute buffeted both by cruel bucko mates and inhuman conditions, leaders like Andrew Furuseth and Walter Macarthur were worker-intellectuals of the first rank. Although Joe Gladstone served on twentieth century steam or motorships, in his book he reminds us of the early SUP tradition of the literate sailor, one who reads and writes of "cabbages and kings."

Current union educators and labor historians have long disagreed on how to treat radicalism on the waterfront and at sea. Are members of the Industrial Workers of the World (Wobblies), or subsequent Marxist-influenced unions and left sectarians to be treated as heroes or villains in their conflict with "official" labor organizations? Joe Gladstone participated in SUP struggles against enemies: internal and external, perceived and real. Yet he does not write as a political partisan justifying a rigid "line." Instead, his voice is calm; his message complex.

Each reader will find special areas of interest in *To Make the Run*: Great Depression memories, shipping out, World War Two danger, trade unionism's ambivalent course, technological shifts, rustbucket routines, a crew's companionship. I am particularly drawn to the author's ear for tradition. He recalls a time-tested tale's details; he knows that vernacular speech decorates a yarn; he hints at the hidden or complex messages within sea stories.

I select but one of Joe Gladstone's anecdotes to illustrate his combination of reportage and interpretation. He describes his first coming ashore on San Francisco's Embarcadero to purchase a West Coast sailor's "uniform"—Harry Lundeberg Stetson (white cloth cap), grey hickory shirt, black Frisco jeans, black shoes, white sox. Walking out of the shop in splendid gear, Joe became "a transformed person, a member of an exclusive fraternity, identified outwardly as a West Coast man, and inwardly as one who is playing a certain unique role on the stage of history." Today, we can accept Joe's account as that of a young man simply buying new clothes on payday, or as a powerful belief that his fellow maritime unionists were destined to act decisively on the "stage of history." We ask: What animated Joe's vision of an Embarcadero shop or an antiquated freighter as a stage? Who were the actors? How did they learn their roles? Who in the audience could see the drama's ending? These questions, and many others, will occur to readers as they discover *To Make the Run*.

I conclude my preface by acknowledging the colleagues who have shepherded this book through its respective stages: Maria Hetherton, FLCH editor, read the typescript, exercising her skills in editorial matters.

John Robinson, proprietor of the Carquinez Press, ably handled the myriad publication details. The staffs at Inkworks Press, Berkeley, and Design Action, Oakland, together actually produced this book. Tom Carey translated metaphor into several sketches for our book.

Additionally, Gunnar Lundeberg and Dave Connolly, principal officers of the Sailors' Union of the Pacific, encouraged me at every turn in our voyage. Finally, my thanks go to Joe Gladstone for permitting the Fund for Labor Culture & History to issue *To Make the Run*.

At this juncture, I'll not reveal the meaning of his title. However, I view the phrase "to make the run" as a metaphor for an entire life voyage. Joe tells us only a portion of his story. Will he offer additional chapters? Unlike Homer's legendary sailor, Joe Gladstone has planted his oar at the Pacific's edge. There, he has reflected on his sea experience.

We salute his contribution to maritime literature amid his continued faith in working people. We look ahead to other old timers' stories of their life runs.

Archie Green

"Here Is The Great Immeasurable Sea,
In Which Move Creatures Beyond Number.
Here Ships To and Fro,
Here is the Leviathan Whom Thou Hast
Made Thy Plything."
Psalms 104:26
New English Bible

"Yet a sailor's life is at best a mixture of a little
good with much evil and a little pleasure with
much pain. The beautful is linked with the
revolting, the sublime with the commonplace
and the solemn with the ludicrous."
Richard Henry Dana
"Two Years Before The Mast"

Chapter One
First Things First

The brig *Pilgrim* on which Richard Henry Dana shipped as ordinary seaman took 150 days from Boston, Massachusetts to Santa Barbara, California via Cape Horn sometime around the year 1835. George Washington was inaugurated in 1789; the Republic was not quite fifty years of age.

This is a story of a portion of a life. It concerns a young man of approximately Dana's age who ships aboard an American merchant ship during an era in our history that came to be known as the Great Depression. The story seeks the light of day in an effort to contribute some information and knowledge about life on American merchant ships, for the most part freighters, whose general physical condition may be described by a popular waterfront phrase of the day as a "rustbucket."

Though many seafaring men found gainful employment in dockside jobs and short coastal runs which took them away from home for very short periods of time, from a few nights to a few weeks, this narrative plays itself out on offshore deep-water ships whose trips lasted minimally from three to six months. The time-span encompassed twelve years; from two years before Pearl Harbor to a year before the end of the Korean War; from the spring of 1940 to the spring of 1952.

❈❈❈❈❈❈❈❈❈❈❈

... and as the gang were being assigned their respective jobs by the bosn, an old timer detached himself and took me aside, the bosn nodding and saying, "You go with Duffy and he'll show you what to do."

1

Duffy, it turned out, was his last name and the one by which he was universally known. He was a "Downeaster" or a "State-of-Mainer." He had a full head of snow-white hair and a sprinkling of tattoos on both fore and upper arms. Much later, when we got to know each other, he told me he was a former Wobbly, that is, a member of the Industrial Workers of the World (IWW) about which he promised to tell me more some day. At the moment, the crew needed me to perform a most serious and demanding task. This, my very first job, would be my baptism under fire, and will have to be executed with a certain degree of judicious aplomb. It all sounded much like Hemingway talking about grace under pressure. The substance of the problem was that I had "to make the run."

He explained very seriously and in a fatherly tone that the crew was "hanging over the stern on their tails" repainting the ship's name and port of registry, and were pretty thirsty, desperately in need of "a heave ahead." Though I recognized immediately what he meant, it was sometime later that I discovered the original meaning of that phrase. When a ship is being maneuvered into the dock, the pilot sometimes calls on the forward capstan to give a slight shove ahead. It is synonymous with taking a drink, as in "one for the road."

"Officially only the master is permitted to bring liquor aboard ship," Duffy went on, "and sailors are positively not permitted to drink on the job. The bosn dare not ask anyone to go ashore, and the mate on watch must not allow the stuff to be brought aboard. So, if you want to learn to be a real sailor from the bottom up, the first thing you must learn is "to make the run."" He then turned over some well-worn dollar bills, the meager result of a "tarpaulin muster" (that is, he took up a collection) and with the admonition to get "the best for the money," he saw me off at the gangway, pointing me in the right direction.

The "gin mills" and "grog shops," as sailors call saloons and retail stores respectively, were close by, and I stopped at the first one up the street from the dock, bought a bottle of Jack Daniels and hurried back. It was really no problem secreting the bottle under my jacket, and no mate was to be found anywhere near the gangway whereby Duffy escorted me back to the poop deck where he was supposed to be sitting on the stage over the side and painting. However, he had one last thing for me to do—learn to lower a bottle over the side. I have used that knot many times and remember it well to this day. In our lexicon, it's called a jug sling.

It was only then that I officially met the crew and, after being thanked profusely for a job well done, was assigned a watch. And as my career unfolded and the years passed, I became convinced that in life, "first things first." In order to learn a trade or profession, you must first, if you will, learn "to make the run." Then the teaching and learning can begin.

Chapter Two
Shipping Out

In those days, there was a well-worn route from the subway stop in Lower Manhattan to Broad Street. It took you past an enclave of hole-in-the-wall shops and stores, small seedy-looking restaurants and bars, all superimposed by two- and three-story tenements where entire generations of people from drifters to whole families probably lived out their lives. Tucked away off the corner of the 100 block, sandwiched in between a bar on one side and a hash joint on the other, was a narrow opening, which led to a walk-up. On the street door was a small sign, easily missed by those who weren't specifically looking for it. In block letters it said:

SAILORS' UNION OF THE PACIFIC - AFL
PORT OF NEW YORK OFFICE

For three solid months, day in and day out, Monday through Friday, I had dutifully appeared at the union hall, answering the job call every hour on the hour from 8:00 a.m. to 5:00 p.m. The ritual never changed and became downright monotonous. The job I was looking for was an entry-level berth on a merchant ship, known as an "ordinary seaman." And the rule was very strict. At the end of the day, if no member had claimed the job on the board, the port agent picked a likely candidate from a list of registered newcomers he kept hidden in his desk. And the only way to get on the list was not only to know about it, but also to know somebody who knew somebody. As luck would have it, I knew somebody who knew the port agent.

It was some time around Easter of 1940 after a number of years on the bum, unemployed and holding odd jobs intermittently, when the declared war in Europe was as far from us as the miles of ocean separating us from them, that the fortuitous circumstances finally came together to make it possible for a young man just past his teens, to ship out on a merchant ship for places as far away as one could imagine.

The day finally came when my luck turned. Just before closing one evening, the port agent, Morris Weisberger, called me over and told me that there was an "Ordinary's" job open and there weren't any members around who wanted it. It was scheduled to leave the very next day and was "signing on tomorrow morning." Handing me a piece of paper that he signed, and filling in my name, the ship's name, MV *Willmoto,* and pier number, he bade me God-speed with a short admonition:

Remember: listen to the AB's; they know more than you do. Pitch in when there's work to be done. Show that you're willing to learn. Don't talk too much and keep your nose clean and you'll be all right.

Destinations and ports of call are germane to the life of the merchant sailor, since they somehow flavor the narrative. Shipping in the focsle[1] as an ordinary seaman on a short coastwise run means that you can get off in a few days or a week if you or the crew have a change of heart. But a trip requiring thirty to forty days at sea is another matter. You not only can't get off anywhere, but you also have to get back. A lot of time is spent in a routine existence of working regular hours, sleeping, standing night watches, pursuing hobbies and sharing lots of talk on anticipated shore leave usually involving new sexual conquests, mostly exaggerated. Overriding all this, one requires a special psychological propensity in order to cope with the forced confinement of forty or so other men, since there is no place to hide. And most people learn to cope in spite of the fact that it calls for an expertise a young man doesn't ordinarily possess.

Sleep that night was out of the question. Tossing and turning on the living room couch of my gracious friends, the thought of a steady job, a chance to learn a trade, some square meals for the next four months, an opportunity to see another part of the world, the possibility of breaking out of a demoralized rut into which I was cast by a combination of inner tensions and outer pressures that much of my generation was experiencing; as I say, these thoughts brought me up to a fever pitch. Although the ship was about two hours from where I was staying, I was there at 8:00 a.m. ready to do whatever it took to turn my life around.

There was a sign at the head of the gangway, which I later learned was called the "Sailing Board," saying rather tersely:

MV *Willmoto*
Signing On: 9:00 a.m. Today
Departure: 6:00 p.m. Today
Destination: Cape Town, South Africa

The United States Shipping Commissioner, whose office was then attached to the Department of Commerce and who acts as an intermediary between the seaman and his employer, the shipping company, signs you on. That is to say, a ritual takes place wherein the Commissioner tells you your pay per month and you sign what is known as "The Articles of Sea," whereby you promise to stay with the ship for a given length of time, perform the necessary labor as directed by the master or his designated representative, and upon your return you will be paid a certain amount of coin of the realm. When you sign this document in front of the Shipping Commissioner, it becomes a binding legal contract whose origins go back to the days when the commercial maritime powers of the West tried to abandon impressments at sea and other such niceties as practiced, for instance, by the British Navy.

Having signed on with the rest of the crew, all hands adjourned to the mess room since it was now "coffee time." It seems that our union contract states that there shall be two fifteen minute breaks, one in the morning and one in the afternoon, both in port and at sea. In port as well as at sea, these breaks are at 10:00 a.m. and 3:00 p.m. and the coffee, though not compulsory, had better be ready. This introduction to seafaring life struck me as quite civilized, since to this day there are many shoreside trades that have yet to incorporate such a feature.

When the gang stood up to "turn to," as the bosn (a contraction of the word boatswain) requested, I couldn't help but notice that the fifteen minutes had now stretched to thirty. As time went on, I realized that one of the criteria for judging a good bosn was his ability to stretch coffee time to thirty minutes. As I expected, my first real job started me at the bottom. I was introduced to the not-so-glamorous task of cleaning the focsle and latrines. And most important of all, as my new mentor and watch partner, Duffy, instructed, the next most important thing to learn was to make a real cup of coffee. It was impressed on me that no ship's cook or Steward knows how to make coffee. In fact, the best coffee made is in the jungle, he said, and when I told him that I had spent a little time "jungling up," my credentials were complete. "The jungle," for the uninitiated, is where men of the road or hobos gather, usually under a railroad trestle, to put a meal together and/or spend the night, weather permitting.

Chapter Three
Seaworthy

But ships are but boards,
Sailors but men: there be land rats
And water rats, water-thieves and land thieves;
I mean pirates; and then there is the peril of
waters, wind and rocks.
William Shakespeare, *The Merchant of Venice*

The first few days were a blur—rolling, pitching, seasick and wretched. You wonder how and why you ever let yourself into this. But then around the third day the sun started appearing and things began clearing up a bit; the rolling and pitching stopped; the hangovers diminished and normal conversations were starting up; and the bosn started me working on some scaling and chipping of accumulated rust on the bulkhead. This entailed application of a little elbow grease to a scraper and chipping hammer, and is an important part of the seagoing job that many sailors refer to as "sea-going janitorial work."

While diligently working away at a specific piece of rust, I apparently got carried away and my chipping hammer went right through the bulkhead, and there I was, looking at the open sea! Needless to say, at that point I was terrified, and it didn't help my peace of mind that the Chief mate, who was sauntering along, happened to stop by at that very moment. Sizing up the situation and catching the look on my face, he burst out laughing. Telling me not to worry, he walked up the forward storeroom and came back with a roll of electrical friction tape. He proceeded to cover over the hole I made, and after telling me to ask the bosn for some paint, kiddingly admonished me to save my strength for Cape Town. When I told the crew about it at coffee break, one of them said, "Lucky you weren't chipping below the water line."

I would venture to say that Shylock's voiced skepticism towards the end of the sixteenth century was not too far off the mark. It's all a matter of degree.

The MV *Willmoto* was the only ship left in the fleet of a shoestring operator in the 1930s known as the Williams Line. The sea historians tell us that originally she was known as the SS *Seaconk*, but a diesel engine of a very early variety was retrofitted to her in 1924—hence the designation MV for motor vessel. The old timers referred to her as a "Hog Islander." That means it was of a certain basic design built for World War I usage at the Hog Island Shipyards on the Schuykill River in Philadelphia (more on this later). Like all "Hog Islanders," she was a loyal workhorse on and off through the years, much like the Liberty Ships of World War II. The engine required tender, loving care to even start up.

When we got out to sea, as the saying had it, "with all sails set, a following sea and an egg beater off the stern," she made about eight knots. We broke down at sea at least a dozen times in the forty days it took us to get to Cape Town. We had an excellent crew on deck and they worked feverishly to overhaul all the rigging, both standing and running, so we would be ready for discharging and reloading. And we must have had an equally excellent black gang (engine room crew) to have been able to nurse the antiquated power plant half way around the East African coast and back.

A question that comes up over and again is seaworthiness. When is a vessel seaworthy? After all, if you can punch a hole in the bulkhead on the main deck is it seaworthy? If it isn't, the underwriters will not insure it. Sailors, since the beginning of time have contended that safety in any or all its ramifications are not a requirement from the ship owner's point of view. A famous Draft Board joke of World War II illustrates the point. When you come up before the examining physician, he feels your body and if it's warm, you're drafted. It is the same with the underwriter/insurer. If it floats, it's seaworthy. Having had the opportunity to sail on ships both in peacetime as well as during the last war, I can safely say that the overwhelming weight of the evidence testifies to the general truthfulness of the sailor's view.

Chapter Four
Battening Down the Hatches

Sailing day is the hardest working day aboard a ship. It is also usually the longest. The last of the cargo is being stowed; the ship stores are brought aboard and must be stored in the reefers (refrigeration units) and storerooms for perishables and dry stores, respectively. And as each hatch is finished and topped-off by the longshoremen, it must be battened down by the sailors. This entails lifting three rolled-up, heavy canvas tarpaulins that, when unrolled, measure forty feet square, spreading them over the hatch-top and tucking their ends into steel cleats welded into the hatch combings approximately eighteen inches apart. A strip of steel one-quarter inch thick by three inches wide and as long as one side of the hatch, called a batten, is then lifted up and placed inside the cleats on the combing. The ship's carpenter, known as Chips, walks around the hatch and hammers wooden wedges, one in each cleat, thereby securing the steel firmly against the canvas tarp. This process is known universally as "battening down the hatch." It is of supreme importance and if done correctly, secures the hatch as waterproof; an incorrectly-battened hatch could spell disaster for ship, cargo and crew.

In the years that I sailed merchant ships, and that includes hearing lots of stories, I never heard of a single mishap involving waterlogged cargo, if the hatches were battened down correctly. I have seen my share of dirty weather and typhoons; I have experienced big green ones from every side washing over the battened hatches, and they've all held.

The battening down process must be done almost immediately after the hatches are loaded because in all probability a deckload will be carried.

This means that the ship is still not loaded to capacity, in spite of the fact that the available space in the holds is now exhausted. The rest of the cargo is now distributed over the decks and hatches as much as another twenty feet high from stem to stern. The governing principle of the lawful submergence limit is known as the "Plimsoll marks" named for Samuel Plimsoll, the author of the legislation in England in 1876 that codified these limits into law. In the United States, it was not quite that easy. It actually took until March 1929 for similar legislation to become law. The American Bureau of Shipping determines the freeboard and load lines, and it is so indicated in the middle of the hull by a series of markings and lines showing load capacities for various seasons and waters. The master of the vessel must also record in the logbook the draft, fore and aft, before leaving each port.

Having said all this, is it true? Are the load limits observed? This subject comes up repeatedly in many mess room and focsle conversations. One must employ a little bit of faith and a great deal of experience in answering the question. By and large, I can only say that I was on various ships in which I remember looking over the side and not seeing the Plimsoll marks; that is, they were out of sight. Many others have said the same.

So, technically, when the relevant Plimsoll mark is reached and the deckload is correctly distributed, it must also be secured for sea—a process the sailors call "lashing down." Huge lengths of chain as much as forty feet long, are dragged aboard. Their bitter ends, that is, the very last link on either end, are shackled to a welded padeye on deck, and a huge turnbuckle is attached to the center of the chain and cinched up "as tight as a drum." (A padeye is a one-inch thick steel ring in the shape of an upside down letter "D", its flat side welded to the deck, so as to receive a shackle, chain, line or cargo block.)

If good luck is going our way, the company will send some carpenters aboard and build us a walkway from the focsle to the midship house over the top of the cargo known as a catwalk. This is one of those little things that make life a little more bearable out to sea. Just imagine yourself in the dead of night with the ship running in blackout, the weather foul, rolling and pitching, and you're stepping and dodging over chain lashings and other elements of cargo, praying that the lashings hold at least long enough for you to pass them—all this so you can relieve the watch on time. It is only the rare ship owner who considers the crew's safety as an important element of cost. Usually, the "there isn't any time, so do it at sea" excuse is given, and that's the end of it. The fact of the matter is that there is no way the crew out to sea has either the time or wherewithal to do such a job and if they did, they would have arrived at their destination before completing it. All told, I can safely say maybe two or possibly three of the ships I worked carrying a deckload included a catwalk for the crew.

With the hatches battened and the deck cargo lashed, the gear and equipment must be secured. This entails all the equipment used to bring the cargo aboard and, by the same token, discharge it at its destination. What shoreside people call derricks and cranes, seafaring men call booms. These are mounted on the lower part of the mast and fitted into a gooseneck arrangement thereby providing a universal joint-support, which allows it freedom of movement in a 180-degree arc. When not in use, the booms are lowered into cradles from a vertical to a horizontal position and lashed down against the weather. It is also a standard part of the sailor's job to clean, service and paint them out at sea as well as overhaul and service all the running equipment associated with the booms.

It is in the nature of the job that all hatches are completed at the same time, give or take an hour or so. This makes sense in that loading a ship is a science, sometimes referred to as "trimming the cargo." The hatches have to be loaded uniformly so that the ship goes down into the water uniformly. This implies that the hatches will all be loaded and ready at or about the same time—on sailing day, "everything has to be done yesterday." So, when the long-awaited order comes to pick up the gangway and take in the lines, the sailor is more than ready. However, it's not over yet. Many a departure for sea has been marred by the rude awakening that there are a number or more hatches that have yet to be secured, as well as all the lines that must be stowed down below deck where they remain until a day before we reach our first port of call. The answer is that you keep working until it's all done.

A deep-rooted attitude among seafaring men is that the real place to be is out to sea. Life ashore is a "battle" and all things get straightened out once you're out at sea. The madness and chaos of shoreside life gives way to peace and quiet once you leave it in your wake. So, when sailors are faced with real problems ashore, they feel deep down inside that pretty soon "all this too will pass" and the problems will disappear out to sea. Regardless of the truth or fiction of this feeling, with the setting of sea watches as soon as you cast off the lines, this much sought-after solution to all problems materializes. It could easily be seen how the three-watch system, as it is called, could feed into this feeling and lend credence to the serenity of the anticipated trip.

By the same token, sailors have a certain feeling that possesses them on their return from a trip, especially their homeport. It's called "channel fever" and usually starts up a few days before arrival. It's marked by an air of anticipation; a heightened sense of awareness. Work assignments get done a little quicker; there is a nervousness on lookout. Shoreside clothes are laid out and contemplated. It is most pronounced the last day before arrival when the mooring lines are brought up from the storeroom; the ship's booms are being raised in readiness for discharging the cargo. Invariably, someone starts singing Gene Autry's "Back In The Saddle Again," and the whole crew cracks up.

When the ship finally comes alongside the dock (sailors usually refer to this as "coming alongside"), it then becomes a semi-race as to who gets to the shower first, the requirement being to "shit, shave and shower" in record time. In most instances, the older men usually defer to the younger ones, the jadedness having set in rather early.

Chapter Five

Able-Bodied Seamen

A watch, by law, comprises four hours and is stood twice daily, thereby covering eight hours of the twenty-four. Hence, three watches make up the total day:

Midnight to 4:00 a.m.

4 :00 a.m. to 8:00 a.m.

8:00 a.m. to noon

The sequence is then repeated from noon to midnight and applies to all offshore deepwater ships. Watches are stood around the clock, four on eight off, day in day out, in repetitive monotony and are broken only when the next port is reached. In point of fact, everyone stands a watch, and one is always on watch. The prescribed hours are your watch on deck and all other times you're on your watch below. Then there are those who work during the normal working day, say 8:00 a.m. to 5:00 p.m., such as the bosn, carpenter and maintenance/day man. Their watch on deck is from 8:00 a.m. to 5:00 p.m. and all other time is their watch below.

An important element in the operation of a West Coast ship in those days was the relieving of the watch at least three minutes before eight bells. That is to say, when the watch on deck is to be relieved at 4:00, 8:00 and 12:00 respectively, (the three times that eight bells are struck) it is incumbent on the new watch to relieve both the wheel and the lookout some three minutes before the bell. This was a courtesy to avoid a "bell to bell" operation. A "bell-to-bell" operation was looked down on and discouraged as smacking too much of assembly-line efficiency as opposed to a more humane working environment. Usually the few minutes were used at the wheel, to give the course, say a few words about how the wheel is responding in the existing weather, etc., and on lookout, if any lights are visible and/or whether the night is conducive to romance. From the very first day I stepped aboard a ship to the very last, I, together with every crew I sailed with, observed this practice, and hopefully crews still do.

Everything said until now about deck hands or sailors can also apply to the engine room. Oilers, water tenders, firemen and wipers, known collectively as the "Black Gang," inhabit what sailors euphemistically refer to (tongue in cheek) as the subterranean depths, or underground world of the engine room. It must be said that though there is always a friendly antagonism and joshful kidding between the two, the "seagoing janitors" and the "underground savages"—deck gangs and black gangs—for the most part they get along. Since the writer's experience is informed only by life on deck, he cannot comment authoritatively on life in the engine room. Suffice to say that the work in both areas consists of the same mix of easy and hard, tolerable and obnoxious. The picture is rounded out by a third department, the Steward's Department, which is responsible for the cooking, handling and serving of the food and the linen supply.

In shipboard society, there are two classes, the officers and the crew. The crew, distributed over the aforementioned three departments, carry certificates or "Z" numbers, that is to say the letter "Z" followed by a four or five digit number, as for instance my own, Z 4210. This was your ID for life unless revoked or recalled. To this day, I have never met anyone who could give me a logical explanation for the designation "Z." (Years later I saw the Costa-Gavras movie in which the letter "Z" was banned in Greece during a particularly reactionary time known as the "Era of the Colonels," when almost all intelligent discourse was eliminated from public life. If it weren't for the time warp, I could almost believe a connection.) The U.S. Shipping Commissioner, the authority who signed me on to begin with, issued these numbers, which testifies to the strictly civilian status of the "Z" number. However, by the time of the Korean War, all these functions were transferred over to the U.S. Coast Guard.

"Z" numbers, or shipping papers as we called them, were comparatively easy to obtain on either coast. For most Americans it required a birth or baptismal certificate, or any other legitimate affidavit of a relative present at your creation. As for naturalized citizens, naturalization papers were accepted. Foreign seamen found their "country of origin" papers accepted especially during the war. A lesser-known fact was that at one time, before pictures and fingerprints were demanded, there was an active underground traffic in dead seamen's papers obtainable for a fee. For all those who wanted their past shielded for whatever reason, this became a way of going to sea. I have been shipmates with a number of such people; one, a deserter from the French Foreign Legion, another with a price on his head from his country of origin and, still another, a Socialist refugee from Hitler's Germany. More on this later.

The ship's officers are subdivided into two groups: mates, designating those sailing on deck, and engineers, sailing below. Over all is the master, who comes from the Deck Department and is in command. All officers are licensed, a special designation which puts them in the chain of command, and this license is also subject to recall or revocation by the same authority who issued it, the U.S. Shipping Commissioner.

It is worth stopping for a moment to reflect on the position of the master, referred at various times to as captain, skipper, or "the old man," the last mentioned name used most and the first one used least. In point of law he is responsible, regardless of who is on or off watch, for the conduct and welfare of the ship. That includes cargo, be it freight and/or passengers and crew. He can also pay the supreme price by losing his license and livelihood. The master cannot say, "It didn't happen on my watch." It's all his watch. By the same token, an officer or certificated man "can have his papers yanked," as seafaring people refer to it. It can rationally be argued that it is one and the same thing, except that it's a matter of degree. The sailor in the focsle and the officer on the bridge live in mortal fear of losing their papers. It is tantamount to any professional losing his or her license to practice. And if it happens to the master, he can never sail in that capacity again, since the underwriters will not insure his ship. This has happened many times but the penalty is not always permanent. It all depends on his standing in the company. There are many instances where, if he has the proper connections, he is asked to take a short vacation or given a job as chief mate and after a decent interval of time passes, is then returned as skipper, albeit to another ship. And furthermore, I am reliably told that this happens constantly in the upper echelons of the Fortune 500 world.

The master/captain has other extraordinary powers. In maritime law, he has the power of life and death, literally, over the entire ship and its contents. There is no other power like it. This does not mean that he will use it, that like Captain Vere, who had Billy Budd court-martialed in an hour-and-a-half in the evening and hung at sunrise the next morning, he can do the same anytime he pleases. Furthermore, the maritime laws do not permit it. Rather, he will act more judiciously by handing over the accused to shoreside authorities. Through the years, I have seen many instances of the use of such powers, abusive and rational, sometimes arbitrary and capricious and as many times gutsy and commendable.

As a case in point of petty tyranny, I offer the following. A ship I was on, the SS *West Celeron*, was scheduled for a trip to Dutch Harbor and the Aleutians via the Alaska Inland Passage. Much to our chagrin, we discovered an overwhelming problem as soon as we left San Francisco and got past the Golden Gate. We were carrying a full load of cockroaches. As we came to dinner the first night out, it was a veritable Grand Central Station during the rush hour. We immediately started a campaign with the skipper, Captain Neuman, to fumigate the ship before we left the mainland. He absolutely refused, saying that he saw no cockroaches where he was, that is, in the midship house. We kept after him up the coast and up and down the Columbia River, but to no avail.

Captain Neuman was known as "Geronimo." On some rare occasion, such as speaking to a superior, he would use a normal tone. At all other times he would scream. He came here from Germany after World War I and never forgot his early Reichsmarine training. His was a wiry, weather bitten little guy whose skin was like tanned leather. He walked around with a permanent scowl; he never smiled. Whatever frustrations and/or disappointments he had in the intervening years after the 1934 and 1936 strikes, the world changed for him and I guessed he devised this form of conduct and behavior as a defense against what formerly would be considered downright insubordination.

The next day, halfway up the Puget Sound, at 2:00 a.m. (during the 12:00 to 4:00 watch), one of the sailors put a number of live cockroaches into an empty match box, and on the way up to the bridge to relieve the wheel watch, surreptitiously emptied the contents of the box as he passed the open porthole of the captain's cabin. When the captain was called at 6:00 a.m., all hell broke loose. "Where did all these cockroaches come from?" he screamed. Approximately an hour after we tied up, the fumigators came aboard and that night we were lodged in a local hotel. In our parlance, that went down as a successful job action that made a believer out of Captain Neuman.

There is a postscript to this story. Soon after we returned, the U.S. Government gave the Soviet Union fifty ships to help them in their logistics problems and guess which ship was among the first to make the Hit Parade? In so doing, this transfer has added a new strain to the already full entomological life of the Soviet Union, and as anyone knowledgeable in this area will tell you, cockroaches are one of the oldest living creatures on earth; they are indestructible and will survive a nuclear holocaust.

﹡﹡﹡﹡﹡﹡﹡﹡﹡﹡﹡

Sometimes enormous risks must be taken for the safety of the ship and crew. The tradition of self-preservation has been, since the first ship ever put out to sea: "One hand for the ship and one hand for yourself, and when all looks lost, both hands for yourself." There are many examples in a sea-going career that speak to this attitude, some demonstrating true bravery and others purely self-serving. On the SS *San Clemente* out of Portland, Oregon, we topped off with a full deckload of lumber and about 500 fifty-five gallon drums of gasoline and kerosene. The deckload was lashed down as well as could be when in crossing the Gulf of Tehuantepec off the southwest coast of Mexico—a dangerous area well known to seafarers—we ran into a tropical storm that soon turned into a major typhoon, about at least a ten on the Beaufort Scale of twelve. (This mechanism measures wind velocity in knots and was devised by and named after a British oceanographer, Sir Francis Beaufort, first published in 1805). While being whip-lashed back and forth for a few hours, hoping we could ride it out, the deckload began to shift perceptively. This is always a dangerous sign, since there is the possibility of losing control of the ship. It is one of those crises that one reads and hears about but hopes never to have to face; however, face it you must or the entire complement could go down.

The skipper was a young man in his forties, a former Puget Sound and Alaska fisherman. He left the bridge and asked the bosn to get some sailors on deck and, together, we systematically let go the chain lashings and allowed the entire deckload to go over the side. It must be appreciated that this was a most dangerous maneuver: the turnbuckles had to be unhooked and you had better not be in the way as the chains flew off. The way this was accomplished was to first bring the ship around and create a partial lee. (The weather side is the side exposed to the directional force of the wind and the lee side is the opposite side, hence calmer—usually . . . but not always.) Each turnbuckle, and there were two each, fore and aft of the midship house, both port and starboard sides, has a hooked contraption on its end called a pelican hook which can be tripped by standing a little distance from it and prodding it with a stick. This we did and the sea did the rest.

As soon as the deckload went, we began to ride a little more easily and by the next morning, the storm was gone. Later in the day, we salvaged some of the chains that were still attached to their padeyes on deck. The skipper sent down a quart of Johnny Walker and told us, "I know that I wasn't supposed to leave the bridge, but I just couldn't see sending any man out there to do what I wouldn't do." When the conversation veers around to "profiles in courage," I think of him. And I hope the company realized that although he sacrificed the deckload, he saved their ship. And one more thing: when he came down and told us what he wanted done, he asked the bosn for volunteers. All hands volunteered.

As a matter of fact, from the moment you step aboard a ship, danger is your constant companion. And as in all shoreside situations, both at home and at work, accidents must be avoided and prevented. Dangerous situations go along with the territory, as with the "act of God" just described on the SS *San Clemente*. There are still other examples of how dangerous situations are brought down on you by man-made forces not of your making. This time the cargo was down in the hold rather than on deck.

All cargo, regardless of where it is, must be lashed down and secured against the sea. When this is not done and any sort of bad weather ensues, the cargo begins to move and shift, thereby threatening the very stability of the ship, not to speak of the crew's welfare.

On the SS *Pacific Bear*, stopping over in Pusan, Korea, at the beginning of the Korean War, we took on a consignment of steel battens, the same as we described in battening down earlier, forty feet in length which means the entire length of the hatch. They came aboard, packaged some ten to a bundle and tied with a thin strip of wire every ten feet. They were stowed down in the hold, lying fore-and-aft, that is longitudinally, all across the hatch from side to side, row on row, reaching our capacity at approximately the halfway mark. According to proper cargo stowage procedures, at the very least it should have been lashed down and properly secured with the same type of turnbuckle and chain arrangement as in the previous incident on the SS *San Clemente*. Homeward bound across the North Pacific in mid-winter, one must be prepared for the worst. But such precautions had not been taken.

Before we left, the old man protested vehemently to the company port agent, who, as you might expect, told him to "take care of it at sea;" an almost impossible task for a handful of sailors. So, sure enough, we weren't out three days when the barometer started dropping precipitously and the big green ones started coming over the bow soon after. And it didn't take very long before we started hearing the clanging; first short rumbles, then louder; first some inches and then some feet with each roll of the ship.

The call came down soon after midnight, and all hands, not in the best of humor, made their way down into the hold. What greeted us was a study in chaos. Widely and wildly scattered were an army of long steel battens, moving with each roll of the ship, any of which should they hit you just right, could send you to your maker or maim you for life.

By now, the old man had slowed speed and turned us around so as to create a lee, and using the opportunity, we dragged down some chains and turnbuckles, a job much easier said than done since alongside the dock the ship's machinery and winches usually do this kind of work. Using the padeyes on the ship's side we stretched the chains and hooked them into the turnbuckles, cinching down on them and thereby securing the cargo from any further movement and came home without any further incident. You can well imagine the looks of the longshoremen as they opened the hatch after we got home. They couldn't stop talking about the mess that greeted them.

Under ordinary circumstances, this would have been a cause for a job action. No authority could possibly argue that lashing down the cargo in the hold was not necessary for the safety of the ship at sea. But, as we were soon made aware, the company requirements dovetailed very readily into the plans of the U.S. Army, now fully engaged in yet another war, and we were told in no uncertain terms whose orders we were to follow. And the crowning indignity came when we paid off. The chief mate sent word down that " whereas under ordinary circumstances, working on your watch below would be considered overtime we cannot show it in this particular case, since it was a requirement for the safety of the ship at sea caused by an act of God." However, after a few drinks with our union business agent, he made it good to us under another job!

Some day the book *Profiles in Humility* will also be written, and for that I will nominate another skipper, named McMillan, whom I was with on a tanker in the South Pacific. After our first boat drill one day out to sea, a common and intelligent practice, he decided to make a little speech now that he had a captive audience on the boat deck. It could be paraphrased somewhat as follows: When and if we have to take to the boats for whatever reason, please leave a seat for me. They can always get another tanker but they will never get another skipper like McMillan.

He was another of these wiry little guys about five-foot-four from somewhere in the West Texas panhandle, and he ate, slept and talked oil and cattle all day long. The three mates were all over six feet tall and were scared to death of him. In Honolulu, before we were outward bound for the Solomon Islands, he personally went down to the store rooms and reefers to see to it that we had at least six months' supply of food aboard. Though there were many skippers who took a paternalistic interest in their crew, he was the only one I ever met who went to that extent. He did not trust any of the mates or the steward. In fact he appeared on the bridge at noon daily and took his own sight regardless of what the Mate on watch did or said. As luck would have it, we also had a fine cook and baker, and that made up in no small part for the particular dislike offshore sailors have for tankers. Of this more anon.

It was stated above that the master of a merchant ship usually takes a paternalistic interest in his crew. And the older he is the more paternalistic he becomes. This is understandable. In many societies and cultures, the work place being one of them, the leader or elder of the group is akin to the head of a family. Most skippers never get to exercise or enjoy this feeling of responsibility at home since they're almost never there. Hence, they have this one opportunity to behave "like a father," as one of them put it to me. Chances are that the first ship that ever crossed a body of water, way back at the fording of the first river, the master looked to his crew, and it's been that way ever since. And so it will be as long as we will need organization. And a master there has to be. In that great Commonwealth of Toil in the sky, whenever a crew is assembled, if there is no master they will elect one.

We round out our picture of the ruling class at sea, with two more licensed categories: the purser and the radio operator, the latter commonly referred to as "Sparks." The purser was an invention taken over from passenger ships. On such ships, he had the dubious honor of dealing with passengers and their money, and in so doing, had lots of work. Somehow or other, we woke up one day and there was a purser on freighters. Nobody to this day knows how it came about. Surely, some ship owner's front office saw a need to employ pursers who became technologically unemployed when the big passenger ships were all converted to troop transports. The purser's reason for being, so the argument went, was that the mates and engineers were swamped with paper work and so the purser took all that off their backs. Well, as most of us saw it, the only thing they ever did other than hokey jobs thought up by the old man or the mates was to take sunbaths.

The radio operator was a different story. He was our link to civilization. Out at sea he filed and received weather reports and positions. He was also crucial in emergencies and, especially during the war; many of them stood by their wireless tapping out their Maydays. Since merchant ships did not practice flag, semaphore and signaling by ship's lanterns, tapping the Morse code by brass key was the only communication available. In port, the ship's wireless is closed down and remains so even when shifting in inland waters. Many Sparks I have met had lots of time on their hands, since they work only a few hours a day, and are completely free in port. They never get their hands dirty, and are practically their own boss. I always maintained that if I ever had it to do over again, I'd become a radio operator.

The downside to all this buildup is that radio operators perpetrated some of the worst performances I ever witnessed aboard ship. In one particular instance, this Sparks, a notorious gas-hound as we called them (that is, one whose object in life is the avid and assiduous pursuit of the bottle), ran out of liquor about one day out of the Panama Canal en route to San Pedro. He sneaked into the crew's mess room during the watch change at midnight and systematically drank up every liquid on the condiment shelf. It must be explained that each mess room table, as well as dining table in the saloon, contains a compliment of condiments and liquids such as oil, vinegar, ketchup, and various steak sauces and mustards. He cleaned them all out and by 3:00 a.m., he was climbing the walls in his room. Since I was on watch, I asked the mate what he thought we should do.

He immediately woke the old man, and together we went to his room and tried to talk him down and quiet him, but we got nowhere. By now the 4:00 to 8:00 watch came on and so between three of us, we subdued him as the old man got the straightjacket around him and we lashed him down to his bunk. The old man insisted that we mount a watch over him until he at least calmed down, which took till the middle of the day. Though I had seen examples of the DT's in living color, this one took first prize. We were now a few days closer to San Pedro but he was still pretty sick, so we made the entire trip north with no radio contact. When we arrived, we ordered a taxi and sent him, now docile, to the hospital, and we never heard from him again. We were all of the opinion that this escapade either cured him or killed him.

I have listened to much theorizing about this type of drinking in general, and on the part of radio operators in particular. The best that the focsle psychologists can come up with is something to the effect that the loneliness on the job, combined with the "Morse code constantly buzzing in their ears," makes for an explosion when the opportunity presents itself. Be that as it may, I still think a non-drinker could handle it, and on the next time around I'd like to give it a try. One last word before we leave this subject. On the new ships being built today, few and far between, modern technology has made the radio operator both redundant and obsolete.

****

If the officers are the ruling class or the representatives thereof, then the certificated ranks are the underclass, the working drones. The lowest rank in the Deck Department is the ordinary seaman, in the Engine Room, the wiper, and in the Steward's Department, the mess boy. All these are apprentices and are there to learn the trade "from the ground up," as they like to put it. The ordinary seaman can become an Able-Bodied Seaman (AB) when he passes a test in seamanship and lifeboat handling. By the same token, the other two apprentices must do the same in their respective areas. All other ratings, such as bosn, carpenter, and electrician, were in the U.S. Steamboat Inspection Service (another small office in the Department of Commerce in those days) and, if it exists at all today, in the Coast Guard.

The AB test was very meaningful before World War II. First, it required thirty-six months of discharges. The discharge is a document showing real time spent on the trip, that is, from the day you sign on to the day you pay off, and includes point of origin and destination. Second, a short test is given in boxing the compass. The inspector usually picks out a sector say from north to south or any other two cardinal points, and you must recite the headings in sequence. It is purely a memorizing process. Third, a test is given on the contents of a lifeboat and, if enough hands are present that day, they get you to launch a boat. That's the extent of the test. All the rest such as seamanship, rope and wire splicing and the maybe dozen knots or so you will ever need to use, must be acquired through on-the-job training. In fact, one can steal a march on the knot tying by learning them in the Boy Scouts, where I originally learned them at age twelve.

In order to qualify for union membership, (my own story on this comes a bit later) an ordinary seaman must have obtained a letter of commendation from every crew with whom he sailed testifying to his willingness to learn the ropes, both literally and figuratively speaking, and ability to work with the crew. In other words: Is he a good shipmate? The reality of this idyllic world begins to recede as the sudden expansion of merchant shipping overwhelms a system that was mostly built in the past.

The thirty-six months begins to narrow down to twenty-four and then to twelve and finally to six as the manning requirements begin to multiply due to the intensification of the war. The tests involving boxing the compass disappeared since they didn't make any sense in the first place, all wheel instructions having been given in degrees rather than compass points as in the sailing ship days. As to the lifeboats, the point to the oars was to get far enough away from the ship's side so that you don't get sucked into her vortex when she goes down. Launching the boat quickly and correctly is what's important and that can only be learned on the job while in port. A sail and compass is provided in each boat to help you after you get under way. As for the rest of the work on deck, that remained more or less the same and was untestable in a formal sense— you either learned how to do it or you did not.

One more rating deserves mention, that of AB/maintenance man. When the war was getting under way and the ships were getting bigger and more complex such as C-2's, C-3's and Victories, we demanded that the manning scale be increased since in the nature of things, watch standers could not possibly do all the necessary work. Rather than increase the watches, the compromise was made to include an AB who would not be required to stand a watch but do day work exclusively, that is, from 8:00 a.m. to 5:00 p.m. Many older AB's took these jobs since it was a relief from the monotony of standing wheel and lookout watches. I too began to prefer them.

As the war proceeded and the overwhelming productive and technological ability of the American economy unfolded, the ranks of the old timers began to diminish and their places were taken by a host of newly arrived "thirty-day boy wonders" (derisively labeled by the iron men from wooden ships), who somehow or another managed to master the basic rudiments, albeit with a little friction and in many instances with reckless abandon. However, I must say that the presence of one or two "old timers" (and by then, even I achieved that dubious distinction, at the ripe old age of twenty-two) usually exerted a calming influence on the newly arrived. The test to all this was the low accident rate in comparison with the tremendous explosion of person-days worked. And the old timers, the iron men from wooden ships, those who taught me—what happened to them? Many who had licenses went up to the bridge when jobs became available; many were old enough to get good jobs ashore in various supervisory capacities and, lastly, the overwhelming majority, rather than go gently into the night, lie buried in the deep. The merchant marine, essentially a civilian industry operating in war zones, sustained an enormous casualty rate, barely exceeded by the U.S. Marines. We will speak more on this later.

This alarming death rate at the beginning of the war, which by official count reached a total of some 5600 souls and 700 ships by VJ-Day, prompted someone in the bureaucracy to start thinking seriously about life-saving methods other than kapok-filled life preservers and running for the lifeboats. Not that there is anything inherently wrong with either of them, but one should try to improve on a rather appalling statistic. When the war was about a year-and-a-half under way, an item of apparel began appearing on West Coast ships that both defied explanation and characterization. When something appears that looks and feels incongruous, a committee must have created it. This item was just such a contraption, and was immediately labeled the "zoot-suit."

To the best of my recollection, it might be described as a rubberized jump suit or diver's suit covering the entire body. It had a built-in kapok life preserver stitched to its inside and an attached hood which cinched up under the chin, as the outdoor hooded sweat shirts one commonly sees wherever the sporting crowd congregates. The bottoms were weighted down with a half-inch slab of lead attached to the soles. And attached to the front of it were a police whistle and a red light. To those readers who are still with me, please understand that I kid you not. The police whistle was for you to blow to attract attention to your whereabouts and the red light automatically was supposed to illuminate as you hit the water and were bobbing up and down in the manner of a harbor buoy— all this while running for your life out to sea, be it high noon or midnight, in calm or dirty weather. Just how the boats were to be launched while the craziness of getting into these contraptions was going on, was never revealed. We, for the most part, looked at it all with a jaundiced eye and as we read the instructions (when all else fails, read the instructions!) that certain grain of salt that the Romans speak about, grew larger and larger.

The zoot-suit soon became a conversation piece both in and out of the mess room and the butt of many jokes. However, it got damned serious when sometime in the middle of 1943, while taking the SS *Lucy Stone* (out of Kaiser Shipyard in Richmond, California) down to San Pedro and readying her for her maiden voyage two Steamboat Inspectors came aboard and asked the old man to let them test a zoot-suit. In fact, it went from damned serious to downright calamitous when nobody volunteered and we had to draw straws. And guess who got lucky?

As the crew gathered around me to both console and congratulate me on what I was about to do for the sake of science and the benefit of humanity, the skipper showed up and made some quick decisions. First, nobody would go over the side without a lifeboat in the water. Secondly, he insisted on timing the entire process with a stopwatch. He wanted a separate reading on how long it took to get into the suit as well as how long it would take to get me into the boat. However, when the Inspectors said that the only real test was to jump over the side, I absolutely refused until they relented and let me climb down a Jacobs ladder.

The outcome of the escapade was a three-ring circus, that is, if you preserved your sense of humor. It took me forever to get into the suit. Pulling it on over my work shoes, which the directions called for, became impossible, so I shed my shoes and started again. By the time I was ready, some five full minutes went by. I had to cinch the inner drawstrings of the life preserver before I could zip up the outside. After cinching the hood tight, I climbed down the ladder—the boat having been launched in the interim—and lowered myself gently into the water. Immediately my lead-weighted feet began dragging me down. (We later surmised that its function was to keep you vertical, straight up and down, as you were bobbing around in the water.) My headgear, which I cinched tightly around my neck as per instructions, to insure water-tightness, was a total fiasco. I immediately began taking on water so that a layer of water formed between the life preserver inside the suit and the suit itself, completely soaking the rest of my clothes and thereby negating the exercise. The arms were an extension of the suit and, while my fingers fit into the attached gloves all right, I couldn't grab the whistle which was attached to a piece of cod-line, which in turn was made fast to a large safety pin on the upper part of the suit.

The discerning reader will now ask, Just what were you going to do with that whistle while running for your life in the middle of the night as all hell just broke loose? Would you believe that you were supposed to blow that whistle to attract attention while bobbing up and down in the water! Finally, on the opposite side of the whistle was a four inch cylindrical shaped battery-operated red light that became activated when you hit the water, so the lifeboat could see you if it didn't hear you or visa versa. Since the lead weights were weighing me down, I refused to let go of the ladder. The lifeboat, in the meantime, began maneuvering over towards me and the two men in it took a full minute by the captain's stopwatch to haul me in, soaking wet like a drowned rat. I shed the suit in the boat since I knew I would never climb back up with it on, and finally got back on deck. The Inspectors were smart enough to say nothing and ignoring me completely, they turned to the captain and thanked him for his time and the use of the ship!

Without belaboring the moral to the story, such as do not pick the wrong straw, let us just say that the committee that invented the zoot-suit knew absolutely nothing about the sea, a position they shared with Sir Joseph Porter of HMS *Pinafore* fame. Furthermore, somebody, somewhere, made a quick buck at the expense of the seafaring man—an old, old story.

I just cannot resist another example of a ludicrous wasteful scheme, which created a stir when it happened and now lies buried in the past. It had to do with the construction of a dozen or so concrete barges for the purpose of ferrying large bulk quantities of fungibles (specific consignments of the same item such as wheat, oil, to various users.) These barges were to be towed by ocean-going tugs or ships en route to the same destination with their own cargo.

After a series of negotiations with the Maritime Commission, the ship owners, War Shipping Administration, the Steamboat Inspectors and a few more desk jockeys who demanded a piece of the action, a manning scale was devised comprising one skipper, three AB's and a cook/baker. Our union, the Sailors' Union of the Pacific (SUP) decided that the skipper's job should be given to an "old timer," that is, one of the iron men who could qualify for a " sixty-foot license." This now obsolete document covered all those who operated any boat sixty feet in length or less.

There were some old timers around the Hall at the time, but obtaining the license required a degree of literacy, since the test covered the Rules of the Road, aids to navigation in inland channels and ship handling in all sorts of weather. As it turned out, quite a number of the iron men were technically qualified (not to say over-qualified) but couldn't read or write English. After a thorough discussion up and down the Embarcadero, it was finally agreed to allow these few iron men to take the exam orally as they did and easily passed.

The problems, though, began when the towing began. In good weather, towing presents very few problems. In bad weather, it presents all sorts of problems. In addition, almost all coastwise weather can go from mildly choppy to rough, year-round. Furthermore, since time was always of the essence, towing 5000 tons of cargo just took so much longer to reach its destination. This especially wreaked havoc with Liberty ships, which at their best never made better than ten knots. Therefore, the amount of trips made by these barges was from "a few" to " not so many" depending on whom you asked.

After a few trips, what with the barge swinging wildly and helplessly in a rough sea and the towline stretched to the breaking point, taking almost forever to get there, the entire venture was closed down, some barges being shipped to various war zones to act as warehouses and the rest to the boneyard in Suisun Bay, abandoned and left to rot.

In later years I thought of this incident many times. A hare-brained scheme was run up the flagpole and instead of being shot down as any seafaring man with an average IQ would have done, it went through a dozen desks, occupied by expediters and coordinators, all signed off and foisted on the war effort. (An interesting question at the time ran something like this: What is a coordinator? Answer: One who has a desk between two expediters.) So now we know what an expediter is. The union, seeing a few more jobs opening up, jumped on the bandwagon. Such was the prosperity of the times that nobody stood in its way until the bitter end, a total waste of time and resources.

※※※※※※※※※※※

We should round out our discussion of the Deck Department with two ratings: the Bosn, the ship's carpenter known as "Chips." The bosn is the lead man. He lays out the work and supervises the crew. He is usually the most knowledgeable sailor aboard. He meets with the chief mate before the trip starts and finds out what is to be accomplished on this trip. Under the most ideal relationship, they may interface from time to time during the trip when something new comes up for whatever reason. As a rule, a good mate can see immediately whether the bosn can handle his job or not and, since he usually can, they get along by giving each other a wide berth. If on occasion a bosn cannot handle his job, it makes it miserable for everybody concerned.

How does one become a bosn? Before the period extending from 1934 to 1936, the company or the chief mate chose the bosn. After the Great Strike, when the union won control of the hiring hall, it also won control of the bosn job. The union created its own criteria, supervised by a committee, and all those who met the qualifications were given an endorsement in the form of a stamp in their membership book. The one criteria missing from the list of qualifications is strength of character. Since the bosn is at times suspended between the demands of the company (in the form of the chief mate) and the demands of the crew on guard against undue and unrealistic work expectations, it calls for a quality of diplomacy, balance and ability to withstand some pressure.

Most bosns I have sailed with could be classified from very good to excellent. It was a privilege to have been shipmates with them. But every once in a while something goes wrong. The committee misjudges in its endorsement and the wrong guy ships aboard, and a sticky mess ensues that wrecks havoc with the psyche of all hands.

One such instance took place on a long and arduous trip I made on a combination passenger-freighter, the SS *President Madison*, which was in itself a fabulous sea story. Of the many elements involved, we shipped a bosn who was technically knowledgeable on all aspects of the work required on these types of ships. However, he had a character flaw in that he was unable to take the heat as a middle man, a position the bosn sometimes finds himself in. As between some rather inordinate demands made by the mate and the countering resistance by the crew during an increasingly perilous trip, he found his way out of the dilemma by staying drunk from sunup to sundown, liquor being quite obtainable and plentiful on a ship carrying passengers. To add insult to injury, the bosn mate, a volatile denizen of the Red Hook section of Brooklyn's waterfront, was after his job. It should be explained that these bigger ships carried such ratings since work went on around the clock.

Early on in this narrative, we made mention of the fact that "destinations and ports-of-call are germane to the life of the merchant sailor, since they somehow flavor the narrative." This would be a case in point.

Somewhere close to the equatorial latitudes in the Indonesian Archipelago, there is an island called Borneo. And on its eastern coast, which is washed by the Straits of Macassar, there is a little jewel of a port called Balikpapan. On your map, you will find it some three degrees south of the Equator. One comes upon this "typical tropical paradise," as the hyperbole has it, not realizing that there is a gorgeous, pristine harbor surrounded by a lush tropical jungle. But this is only up front. Once inside, one finds hidden behind nature's bounty one of the world's important oil depots. Indonesia, then as well as now, is one of the world's important oil producers, and Balikpapan was in those days a port-of-call for many ships and tankers, the former needing bunkers and the latter needing cargo.

On December 7, 1941, after a wild chase overnight out of Manila, courtesy of the Japanese Navy, we took refuge in Balikpapan. The skipper got orders to black the ship out, a process no one on board knew anything about. The chief mate, usually a mild-mannered New England WASP, panicked and demanded that we do it all in twenty-four hours. (For those too young to remember, the word WASP is an acronym popularized in the 1950s and 1960s and stands for White Anglo Saxon Protestant.) That is to say, repaint the large midship house from white to gray; lower the boats and start up a systematic ship-to-shore run to the closest beach to fill about 250 sandbags, and return them to be hauled aboard and placed around the wheelhouse and radio shack—all of this in 105-degree heat in the shade at high noon.

The natives had already informed us that everyone gets off the streets at 11:00 a.m. and stays off until about 4:00 p.m. Work is then usually resumed until about 7:00 p.m. It is the custom of many crews sailing in these waters to strike up just such agreements with the mate since it behooves no one to work in any different manner than the natives. Our argument was that blacking out was understandable, but since we were stranded, it does not have to be done yesterday, as the mate demanded. Rather, we should do as the natives do and set up a special "tropical contract," as it was called. After the first day, we sustained two sunstroke cases and so it all boiled over into a big showdown that night. The bosn was deliberately drinking so as not to have to face the mate, and the bosn mate was playing both ends against the middle, when a number of the older men had enough and called a meeting chaired by our ship's delegate. Every union crew elects a delegate as spokesperson. The consensus was to send the delegate to speak to the mate and offer a deal to do the job under more reasonable conditions, with our firm guarantee that the job would get done before we run the anticipated blockade.

This delegate was another iron man on wooden ships who went to sea at an early age, this time from Barcelona, Spain where he was born and raised until the age of fourteen. Joe Suarez spoke an almost incomprehensible English but nevertheless made himself understood. He was built like Mr. Five by Five, as the song goes, "5-foot tall and 5-foot wide." He chaired a meeting with a no-nonsense attitude yet a totally democratic hand. After a few drinks, when the occasion allowed, he was fond of pulling out his union card from the CNT (the Spanish syndicalist union of pre-Civil War days) and show it around for everyone to see (albeit some of the printing was becoming illegible), as if he were challenging anyone to top it. At the moment, his purpose was to get some consensus on the crew's wishes but he just couldn't quiet the bosn mate who kept disrupting by trying to monopolize the discussion.

While all this was going on, one of our crew, an excitable Sicilian known as Mario, who hailed from Sacramento and was rumored to have a number of women "on the line," demanded a showdown with the bosn mate. A one-on-one encounter such as this is usually never interfered with in the code of the focsle, and both went out on deck and Mario proceeded to punch the daylights out of him, warning him that if he didn't stop trying to undermine the crew he would never make it home. (We learned later that Mario was an ex-Golden Glover during the mid-1930s, a name given to amateur fight contests to showcase future promising pugilists.) By the time the night was over, the delegate had made a deal with the chief mate: the bosn promised to quit drinking for the duration of the trip and the bosn mate shamefacedly apologized to the crew. And everyone thanked the delegate and Mario for a job well done. As it turned out, we succeeded in doing the whole job in about five days with the fifteen of us working on a negotiated tropical schedule.

Things had finally simmered down that evening and everybody turned in ready to "turn to" the next morning at 6:00 a.m. (The phrase "turn to" simply means to start work.) All I recall is that I went into a deep sleep, completely tuned out to the world, when I felt a severe jolt followed by a crashing noise and found myself lying on the deck, having been unceremoniously pitched out of my bunk. At the moment, my head was still aching but I was quite conscious. (It turned out that I had been asleep for only two hours.) I staggered out on deck and began to hear voices all around me. One distinct statement being yelled from the bridge was, "Don't pull out till we check the water line." And there in front of us was a beautiful clipper bow, gracefully curved and distinctly European.

It took us a few seconds to realize what had happened. The USS *Holland*, a submarine-tender or "mothership," as they were called, had, like us, taken refuge in the harbor, a huge lagoon surrounded by miles of clear blue water, with a full moon in the center of the sky, illuminating the entire harbor like a Christmas tree. In maneuvering around for a safe anchorage, it lost control somehow and hit us right in the starboard quarter, not ten feet away from our focsle. The clipper bow we speak of identified her immediately as a well-known prize of war taken from the German Navy as reparations after World War I and converted to her present status. The upshot of the whole late night mishap was a ten-foot gash in our side that ran to within inches of our waterline, and a lot of raw nerves.

It was obvious that we could not go to sea with this open wound. For the next twenty-four hours or so speculation was rife. The best alternative and the least they could do was to send a gang over with a welder and some sheet steel, which all the old timers insisted she had quantities of, and get the job done. Otherwise, how will we ever get this done in this part of the world? Most of the natives walk around in loincloths and barefoot. Who around here could possibly do a job like this? And on and on, ad infinitum.

The next morning, soon after sunrise, the sound of a putt-putt was heard and from a clearing on the opposite shore, a small tug pulling a barge came alongside the *Holland*. A Lincoln Arc Welder, followed by a large piece of steel, was lowered over the side onto the barge. There was a gang of six natives, loin-clothed and barefoot, aboard the barge and they proceeded over to our starboard side. We had our gangway out and down so a few of them came aboard and rigged our boom to lift up the steel and place it. By the 11:00 a.m. deadline they had it spot-welded to the ship's side. After the afternoon break they came back and finished the job. When we looked at the weld, our engineers and other mavens declared it a first class job. The boat went back to the *Holland*, returned the arc welder, and disappeared into the jungle. As they were pulling away, one of our higher-IQ crewmembers was heard to say, "In this world anyone can learn anything given half a chance." A message the Third World is trying to tell us to this day.

We conclude these job descriptions with the ship's carpenter previously referred to and known universally as "Chips." His watch on deck is from 8:00 a.m. to 5:00 p.m., and he is responsible for all woodwork aboard ship. One of his special areas of upkeep and exclusive jurisdiction is the operation of the anchor windlass, that is, that particular winch which operates the ship's anchor. Another job he has is the daily sounding of the bilges. This is that space that lies at the bottom of the ship's hold and the inside of the hull's exterior. These areas absorb the seepage and precipitation of the holds and/or any water due to a puncture in the hull that could endanger the cargo as well as the ship. Hence, a measurement is necessary twice daily at sea, which is done by lowering a marked off tape from the main deck down to the bottom of the bilges. This is a critical job and must be attended to without fail.

Just about all ship's carpenters are loners. They are the only one of their kind and usually work alone, with the exception of some rare occasion when they need help. They are mostly older men who hold valid AB tickets and obtain their rating by going before a union committee of their peers and receiving an endorsement. They are also very innovative when the occasion demands.

On the SS *President Madison*, we had a carpenter named Chris, a Latvian of about fifty or so years old. He was so independent that he never took coffee time with the crew, but rather set his own time when he pleased. By the same token, he never turned down a request from any crewmember for something he needed or wanted. We soon discovered an affinity between us. From time to time he would look me up and want to discuss what he or I was reading at the moment. Otherwise, he kept to himself and was a little too quiet.

It should be mentioned that the ship was now making its way around the world, picking up refugees from the Pacific Islands and outposts and depositing them wherever they could be accepted. In Calcutta and Bombay, we picked up about 200 women, children and some men almost all of whom turned out to be American missionaries and their families. We sneaked across the Indian Ocean into Cape Town where we were told that the Atlantic German U-boat campaign was in full swing.

The second day in Cape Town, Chris sought me out and swearing me to secrecy, agitatedly told me that he visited the skipper in his cabin earlier that morning and sounded him out on a harebrained scheme he had. He proposed to build a lifelike wooden model of a six-foot gun to be mounted on the stern to act as a deterrent to the U-boats so that they keep their distance! He further suggested that if the skipper okayed it, I could help him, since for security reasons it would have to be kept under wraps and put together on deck the last night in port. I, of course, volunteered. The old man, cognizant of the fact that we were totally unarmed, "The only gun we have aboard is a clap gun," he was quoted as having said, in desperation went along with the scheme. The term "clap gun" refers to the official street name for gonorrhea and the gun was a contraption containing a chemical-prophylactic solution that one was supposed to use after intercourse. Very few did.

That night we took some one-inch stock and started shaping them into staves by beveling them with his plane and, together, we made some brackets, and with glue and nails rounded it out into a six-inch diameter, six-foot long "gun." We then made a box-like contraption for a stand, and together that night floated it over the outboard side and brought it aboard on the stern. We set it up and painted the forward end black so as to simulate a gun barrel, covered it with a tarpaulin, allowing the end to protrude, and the next morning left Cape Town. We ran the Atlantic manning the "gun" watch on watch, with a lookout and binoculars and made it home safely. I'm sure that to this day, many still believe that Chips did fool the U-boats into keeping their distance. It is the stuff that myths are made of. But if and when a little common sense takes over from fantasy, it would not be too far-fetched to say that we probably passed any number of U-boat wolf-packs, but the skippers just couldn't see anything to be gained from bringing down a helpless ship-full of women and children.

When the authorities came aboard in New York, they invited the newspapers who laughed up a storm. They took pictures of Chris (by now not too sober) and the skipper standing by the "gun." Somebody came by with a truck and mumbling something about taking it down to the company warehouse, disappeared with it and I never heard about it again. To this day, I have no proof or pictures of this story other than the newspaper accounts wherever they are kept. But happen it did and so much for ship's carpenters.

Chapter Six
Beyond the Call of Duty

W hen we speak of sea-going janitorial work, it means something very specific and should not in any way be considered degrading or demeaning. It encompasses all the work necessary to keep the ship looking clean and well kept. This means scraping and chipping rust accumulations on any portion of the steel structure and superstructure, cleaning and slushing down with a thick black oil concoction (some recipes of which are closely guarded secrets by certain bosns) all the stays from the truck of the mast (the very top) down to the main deck (of which more later)and applying the necessary coat of paint when and where required, such as the midship house, the steel booms and smokestack.

All work aloft is accomplished while seated on a rectangular piece of wood, six inches wide by eighteen inches long, with a rope halter so as to describe a triangle, made fast to a pulley, or block and tackle as we say it, and known the world over as a bosn chair. Sailors also put together contraptions to paint the ship's side, as described at the beginning of this memoir, known as stages. They are suspended over the ship's side, again by block and tackle, and can descend all the way down to the water line. Whoever draws the assignment of cutting in the ship's name and port of registry is called "Rembrandt."

It is a source of pride to bring a ship home looking good, and that usually means a liberal application of paint, especially on the side facing the dock rather than the outboard side. Many a sailor's yarn is told about the skipper and/or mate who know before arrival exactly which side of the ship will go alongside the dock. In Pidgin English, it's called the "look-see side." The bosn is then alerted to concentrate on that particular side. Funny as this may sound, it often works, but when it doesn't, the skipper has some tall explaining to do.

The lifeblood of the ocean going freighter is the equipment on deck used for loading and discharging the cargo. Without it, the cargo cannot be carried. And carrying cargo is where the money is, and that's why freighters go to sea. The compass in the wheelhouse, the anchor on the bow and the engine in the engine room are all necessary attributes required for the operation of the ship. But without cargo and the means to handle it, the ship stays tied up at the dock or rides high in the boneyard: compass, anchor, engine and all. The boneyard is where ships are "put out to pasture." Its naval equivalent is the "mothballed fleet."

The watch on deck is responsible primarily for handling the helm (steering), standing lookout and "standing by," that is, being available for calls to the bridge if and when necessary. Not the least of these important calls to the bridge is to furnish a cup of strong coffee to the mate on watch since technically, he must not leave the bridge for his four hours. It should also be mentioned that this purveying of coffee is purely a courtesy and the mate on watch is well aware of this.

All of these tasks are shared by the watch and done in a rotational manner, one hour and twenty minutes each, adding up to the full four hours for a three-man watch, all night long. Weather permitting, no lookout or standby is required during the day, so the wheel watch is split in half, two hours each per man with the third man working on deck the full four-hour watch. Usually, the second man relieving the wheel at the two-hour break is the one who brings the cup of coffee up with him for the mate on watch.

At sea, one also sees to it that the lifeboats and contents thereof, as well as their surrounding equipment, are kept in shape and correctly

stocked. Needless to say, whatever is found amiss in the lifeboats is recti-
fied immediately in your very next port of call—sometimes.

Seafaring people are a little sensitive on the issue of lifeboats. Aside
from the quite obvious reason of needing them for a quick getaway when
all else fails, they have to be properly provisioned, stocked and built well
enough to sustain a possible prolonged stay at sea. All this requires period-
ic and careful attention. That is to say, from time to time, planned check-
outs must be made, relative to their stores and contents, usually in port,
and their running and standing gear relative to launching must be tested.
This latter is usually done at sea during lifeboat drills. Covers are
removed; the bunghole in the center of the keel is closed tight. The boats
are swung out and then returned to their cradle, thereby at least insuring
that portion of the mechanism to be in workable condition.

Unfortunately, in the bad old days of sea slavery, before the era from
1934 to 1936, the practice of caring for the lifeboats was honored more in
the breach than in the observance. Just as many an old timer told all sorts
of stories about ships going to sea without proper provisions, so it was
with their stories about lifeboats as well. Many steam schooner men, for
instance, told me stories about skippers cutting the rope falls of the
lifeboats and converting them to lumber slings for carrying lumber in and
out of the holds. The Steamboat Inspection Service in those days was
either in bed with the ship owners or maybe in some other way enjoying
his beneficent munificence.

On rare occasions, given enough time in port, when the powers-that-
be decided that launching a boat may be more important than painting
the hull, we would go through the launching procedure, row around for a
little while and return the boat to its cradle. It adds a little measure of
security; a little confidence builder, so to speak.

One day, on the SS *Hawaiian Packer*, long after VJ-Day and towards
the "twilight" of my seagoing career, while laying alongside in Honolulu

Harbor, it was decided to launch the off-shore boat and go through the whole checkout and testing routine to the very end. This ship was a state-of-the-art, C-3 type in which everything on it was electric, including an individual electric motor for each boat. When we were preparing to bring the boat back aboard, someone suggested that two of us ride up with it into its cradle. This practice of "riding the hook" was usually frowned upon but for some reason, it was suggested that this would be a perfectly safe procedure, seeing how brilliantly modern all the equipment was. As luck would have it, this job befell me and a shipmate who came from Holland who, needless to say, was known to us only as Dutchy.

Without getting too involved in technical detail, the electric winch started lifting us and we made it all the way up easily enough. It was just that when the boat was nested and firm in its cradle, the motor was supposed to automatically turn off. Well, guess what? The much-advertised state-of-the-art motor with its limit switch that was considered foolproof and the ultimate in lifeboat equipment failed to perform. The winch kept pulling and the wires holding everything gave way. The entire rig—boat, davit and all—slid back down its tracks and Dutchy and I, boat and all, went ass-over-teakettle all the way back down into Honolulu Harbor.

As I flopped around in the water, I noticed a number of my shipmates diving off the boat deck and coming after us, when simultaneously, a passing tug picked us all up and brought us over to the dock. With Dutchy though, it was a different story. At the last few seconds when I saw what was happening, I made a supreme effort to jump clear and succeeded. He could not and was crippled for life.

We will end this saga on a more personal note. As the crew gathered around us, waiting for an ambulance to take Dutchy to the hospital, they escorted me up the gangway, got me down to the focsle, undressed me and made me lay down in my bunk, covering me with a blanket. They lit me a cigarette and one of those who dove in after me, standing there dripping happened to remark off-handedly, "Yuh know, I just can't get over the fact that during this whole incident, how matter-of-fact you've been. Just as cool as a cucumber ... as if you do this every day." And as the others were standing around nodding in assent, I suddenly felt a release and my whole body began to shake. And as the shaking increased, my body began moving out of the bunk, involuntarily edging onto the focsle deck. Those attending me, quickly realizing what was happening, immediately grabbed me, forced me back and with two of them sitting down on me (all 130 pounds of me), they allowed me to continue shaking for some minutes that seemed like hours. By now the medics had Dutchy in the ambulance so all hands insisted that I go with him since they did not know what to make of me.

Within a few hours after reaching Queens Hospital, at that time the latest word in medical practice and hospital administration, I was treated for some cuts and bruises and sent back aboard. Yes, I said a few hours. The treatment given us was shoddy. Although I was relatively unscathed, Dutchy was given a painkiller shot and left on the ambulance gurney. They treated him like a leper. Had he come in waving a hundred dollar bill, I am certain they would have dropped everything and attended him.

An interesting sidelight to all this is that some days before there had been a big mess room discussion during coffee time on the whole problem of our medical coverage, quite a number of the crew being family men. Dutchy gently chided us about our fee-for-service and Marine Hospital system, counter-posing the system in Holland which sounded if anything, like a comprehensive socialized coverage. Little did he realize how close to home his remarks would become.

When I finally did get back, the focsle doctors analyzed my conduct and told me that I had what has since become known as "post shock reaction" which they called "after-effects." The body remains tense and alert while going through the incident and when the immediate danger is over, it relaxes and can afford to "let go." Hence the intense shaking after the fact. They were right, of course.

Chapter Seven
In the Focsle

What does work at sea involve, after you've stood your watch? The aforementioned seagoing janitorial work is intermingled with the repair and overhaul of the running and standing rigging and heavy equipment. The sailor on deck is responsible for seeing to it that the running and standing gear (equipment), that is, the booms, wire falls, blocks and tackle are in good working order. This also includes the requisite amount of mooring lines, both wire and manila, the latter reaching in size from eight to fourteen inches in circumference. All this must be done at sea en route to the next port. The larger and faster the ships become, the more equipment is required but the time to do it remains the same if not less. In that event, this requires the watch below to come up and do the work. This is considered overtime work and is paid for by an hourly rate previously negotiated by the union and ship owner.

When the watch on deck is over and goes below, we meet the other aspect of life at sea—life in the focsle. With the advent of steam, in most instances, the crew's quarters were placed in the after end where there was ostensibly a little more room. But the crew's quarters are still called "focsle." (Nowadays, from what is left of American merchant ships, both freighter and tanker, crews live in private rooms in the midship house and have washing machines.)

The entire after end is subdivided into rooms, each one approximately eight-by-twelve feet in dimension, and must serve as home for three men. On one side is a double bunk arrangement and across from it a single bunk. The two AB's each take the lower bunk and the upper one

49

belongs to the ordinary seaman. The rest of the wall space is taken up with three steel lockers on one side and a small washstand with hot and cold water on the other side. Usually, but not always, there is a porthole in each room.

The toilet is a common room situated in the same general area and contains a commode, shower and washboard-tub arrangement for washing clothes. A steam line and brown laundry soap is available for greasy dungarees. This arrangement is both simple and effective. A galvanized steel bucket (otherwise known ashore as a pail) containing the dirty dungarees is placed under an open steam line that hangs vertically off the main line. Some soap powder and brown laundry soap is sliced into the bucket and filled with water. The steam line is turned on and the water is boiled for fifteen to twenty minutes. The dungarees are then removed and spread out on the wooden board attached to the washtub. Using a stiff-bristle scrub brush, the dungarees are scrubbed a few minutes on each side. By the time this process is completed, the dungarees look like new. As mentioned previously, nowadays they use wash machines.

The sailor's bunk contains a kapok-filled mattress, approximating the straw-filled mattress known in the good old days as a "donkey's breakfast," which is replaced every second or third trip. Also, he receives a complete change of linen and towels, as well as soap and two boxes of wooden matches weekly.

The linen consisted of two hand towels, two bath towels, a bar of a standard perfumed soap, a set of bed sheets and a bed spread referred to as a "Matson blanket," denoting its origin in Matson Navigation Co. practice. These spreads were of a bluish-gray color, with a variegated Aztec-like design in squares and rectangles. Their significance lies in their being large enough to be doubled over and used as a curtain—stretched across the front of your bunk and suspended on a thin piece of manila line in the manner of a clothes line, fastened to both ends of your bunk posts.

Once it became a curtain, it was called a "jack-off curtain." The implication is that once you stretch it across the front of your bunk and shut out the world, you take yourself in hand and start a five-fingered hand gallop. Thinking back on it, through the years, I never heard or saw any shipmate of mine indulge in any masturbation and if they did it was somewhere else.

And speaking of kapok-filled mattresses, a celebrated story, probably apocryphal, is told on the West Coast about a certain sailor of South Slavic extraction, who took a nose-dive over the side and was lost at sea. About a day out, while the sailor was on his watch on deck, the Steward decided to change the mattresses, as was the habit then, casually taking his old one and throwing it over the side, replacing it with the new one. Amid all the shouting and commotion, the story was finally untangled. It seems that the sailor had his life savings sewed up in the mattress. Through the years as the story is told and retold, the amount of money keeps growing.

Seafaring people demand the highest standards of cleanliness and personal hygiene in and around their living quarters and eating areas. This is a must and is rigidly enforced out at sea. Those who do not get the point either through plain observation or the power of example are gently taken aside by either watch partner and told what to do. Lack of compliance is usually grounds for asking the miscreant to leave at the next American port, if not sooner.

The subject of work clothes has an interesting sidelight. Some brothers do "pier-head jumps," that is, they grab a pair of dungarees, toothbrush and razor and get aboard as the gangway is going up. In this case, they sign on in front of the master out at sea. For them, as well as the others who allow themselves a little lead-time, there is a way to supplement one's sea-going wardrobe through judicious use of the Captain's Slop Chest. This institution which became exclusively the province of the skipper's entrepreneurial talent, was nothing more than a few boxes of clothes stowed somewhere on the bridge. In short, he bought work clothes predominantly, from some ship chandlery ashore at wholesale and sold clothes to the sailors at retail. This afforded him a few extra dollars to enhance his salary while fulfilling a legitimate need of the pier-head jumpers as well as the rest of the crew. Common items sold were dungarees and work shirts, work shoes and gloves, as well as foul-weather gear such as oilskins, rubber boots and sou'wester hats. Payment for all this was duly recorded and deducted from your pay-off at trip's end.

If the focsle is the area where sailors sleep and conduct some of their routines, the mess room is where they eat and conduct more of their social life. It is probably axiomatic to say that people will be drawn to where food is, when it is available. On the average freighter there are two eating areas. One is for the certificated crew and the other is for the licensed officers. All menus are the same. This is a sore point among seafaring people. There must be no "two pot system" on any West Coast ship and to my knowledge I never encountered one, with the possible exception of the large passenger ships where the officers are expected to eat and mingle with the paying customers.

The mess room, usually attached to the galley, is where the crew eats, conducts discussions and meetings and otherwise hangs out. It is a simple setup. Usually, it is one or two long tables with two benches each. At one end is a condiment container, as previously described, holding the usual sauces, liquids and ketchups. These containers are made fast to the table against rolling and pitching at sea. So is everything else in the galley. Officers eat in a room called a saloon on white tablecloths. However, as mentioned above, the menu is the same. On occasion, when a few passengers are carried, they too eat with the officers but, again, the menu is the same.

The problem of food is a central issue aboard ship because, aside from the obvious reasons, food is also a medium of exchange. That is to say, the seafaring man considers food a part of his pay. To this day, "The Articles of Sea" (that document we signed at the beginning of this narrative), a copy of which is displayed by law on the mess room bulkhead, contains an enumerated listing and exposition of certain basic foods, again required by law, for the voyage at hand. In the days of sea slavery, these Articles were honored more in the breach than in the observance.

Not only was the seafaring man short-changed and semi-starved, the old timers also tell many harrowing tales of crooked masters colluding with nefarious stewards in selling food ashore. To illustrate the point, a famous old sea story ran something like this: The crew on this certain ship (one must now mention the name of the ship) was being short-changed daily in both food quantity and quality, not the least of which had to do with the condition of the meat. No amount of protest was to any avail. One day the crew was served some food which contained an assortment of crawling insects and they collected a sample and took it up to the skipper who upon seeing it is reputed to have said, "Well, what are you guys bellyaching about? There's your fresh meat."

By and large, food is adequate in quantity but many a tall tale has been told, not to speak of bitter personal experience, attesting to the poor quality of the fare. I would venture to say that of the few dozen ships I was on over a period of ten years of active sea going, I could single out for distinction about four or five. All the others were from adequate to lousy.

After dinner, the ship's mess room is a social hall of sorts. It becomes a general meeting room and a gambling den. Many hot discussions (and sailor's palaver is incessant) on almost any subject under the sun could be going on at any moment in the mess room. Simultaneously, there is a poker or pinochle game, and/or a checker, chess or cribbage tournament under way. Many were the times when a player had to go on watch when he had the hot hand. In those instances, if he wouldn't or couldn't leave the game, he would "hire" one of his colleagues to stand his watch for him. This was perfectly legal so long as he was of the same rating so as to cover the law.

It was also common knowledge that certain sailors plied certain passenger ships for reasons, not least including getting into the big-stake poker games. This latter activity was resented by many crewmembers, but legally couldn't be stopped. There was a certain skipper on the Hawaiian run who owned some slot machines and when the three-mile limit was passed, he broke them out. Since almost invariably he was carrying workers to and from Pearl Harbor, he made a killing.

Socializing in the mess room brought forth certain character types as well. Two well-known ones were the previously-alluded-to "sea lawyer" and the "mess room militant." The former held forth on matters judicial as they pertained to any and all matters involving life on a ship. Their counterparts may be found in almost all walks of life, the jailhouse lawyer coming to mind. The mess room militant is a type who talks tough and demands action in the mess room but soon disappears when he reaches port and it's time to do something about it.

The sea lawyer knows his rights and by logical extension knows yours as well. He discourses on any and every legal ramification of life at sea and can usually line you up with a "good lawyer" ashore if you need one. For the most part, the sea lawyer is linked with another type, the "case artist," and many times is one and the same. The case artist is one who has the unenviable facility to turn what would appear to be an innocuous shipboard accident into a major litigation ashore. Through the years, I have seen some of these characters build up a body of expertise that could only be rivaled by one who is a cross between an experienced character actor and a legal phrase-monger.

On one ship, a man came back aboard after a night carousing ashore and tripped over some gear (equipment) on deck. The resultant injury was real enough and we took him to the Marine Hospital. After the examination and x-rays showed a broken arm, they fitted him with a plaster-of-Paris cast. The next afternoon, a photographer appeared aboard and took a myriad amount of pictures that could cover any contingency. When I saw the same man again about a year later, he showed me his settlement check for some $25,000, a king's ransom in those days. The split was two-thirds/one-third, the common arrangement at the time. This is not to say that there weren't any legitimate cases. It's just that there were quite a few who stood ready to turn any and all shipboard accidents, both legitimate and staged, into payoffs.

Many of those who sustained legitimate injuries of a minor nature and lost only a minimal amount of time, had to be content with what the case artists referred to derogatorily as "nuisance value." That is to say, a compensation check—few thousand dollars at the most—was issued by the insurance adjuster.

When watches are set and the working routine is established at sea, what does the seafarer do with his time? The question has already been partially answered. In an era that knew no television, in which radios worked only for a few days at sea—and produced only near-total static at that, nobody ever went lacking for something to do. On your watch below there was lots of time and latitude for reading and writing. Some of the worst drunks I ever met were very avid readers when out to sea. And for those who didn't care much for literary pursuits, there were any number of activities involving arts and crafts, the latter including fancy canvas and rope work. Then, of course, there were those of higher aspirations. Those, for instance, who had it in mind to write the great American novel. I must say that though I met my quota for such an aspiration, I cannot remember anyone with a success story.

Finally, there were those who just slept or took sunbaths and built the body beautiful. Among these, I recall one instance where a sailor came aboard with a full complement of weights and barbells. After a full day's work, he would do a two-hour stint of weight lifting that many of us would never have believe had we not seen him in action.

The antagonisms and tensions created in the workplace ashore have their counterpart in the focsle as well. Apropos of this, one of the problems I managed to carry with me through life and hence into the focsle was what one of my more discerning shipmates once described as a "voracious appetite for reading every word passed in front of your eyes." He meant of course that I was an avid reader—in this respect somewhat akin to some of those de-toxed drunks mentioned above. This was true enough in spite of the fact that my interests were catholic and varied, such as making square-knot belts and accessories with Belfast cord or cod line, and small cabinet and woodwork.

From time to time, an organization known as the "American Merchant Marine Library Association," a typical do-gooder outfit run by the wives of skippers and ship owners, would send a wooden footlocker full of books aboard. A perusal of one of these collections, well screened and sanitized, would immediately convince a serious reader that the equivalent of the "Bobsey Twins" was pretty meager fare for even a nonreader. (To this day, educational savants are saying that one of the reasons Johnny can't read is because they feed him Dick and Jane stories, to which he can't possibly relate.)

After my first trip to sea, I realized that if I wanted to read a decent book once in awhile, I'd have to bring my own. So as time went on, my lifestyle in grabbing a ship incorporated a strange routine—shipping with a sea bag full of all the necessary personal gear, as well as a small cardboard suitcase known as a "please-don't-rain" full of books and assorted magazines.

It must be said, here and now, that in all the time I spent in the focsle I never heard a single reproach alluding to my reading habits. Though some shipmates questioned the validity of some of my material, not to speak of my taste, my wishes were always respected when I would walk off somewhere and get into my book.

The only time problems arose was when overtime was being worked, and then mostly during the war. Our union contract was very explicit on the payment of overtime for having to work on your watch below. This, it must be understood, was a normal reaction to the days of "sea slavery" when lots of overtime was unpaid. (We will see, later in this narrative, where this provision was used against us, when legislation was proposed in Congress to blanket us in under the GI Bill of Rights.)

It was the practice on many ships for the watch below to come on deck for overtime requirements, which in pretty much all instances were legitimate, although the penalty time paid for it was hardly worth it. Our union contract as negotiated and signed on November 4, 1941 (exactly one month before Pearl Harbor) called for payment of overtime at eighty-five cents per hour and one dollar and fifteen cents for handling hazardous material such as cleaning oil tanks. There was also an ambiguity. On the one hand, it was always understood that all overtime was voluntary. On the other hand, there was a strong admonition that overtime must not be turned down when "the safety of the ship at sea," was threatened.

Many men turned down overtime when they thought it unnecessary and this led to lots of heated discussions. Whereas many looked to overtime as a means of increasing take-home pay, others thought it a cheap way for the ship owner to get more work done rather than increase the manning scale. Although I was in profound agreement with the latter point of view, it was an argument that would never be settled so as a rule I cooperated and accepted the overtime when requested.

I do remember one exception. On a ship in the South Pacific, the bosn approached our watch for some overtime work and, considering it a "useless make-work" job, we turned it down. The Chief mate came running down to the focsle demanding to know why we did not want the work. His interest was painfully obvious. If we didn't work, he couldn't put in for his own overtime. With just about the whole deck gang standing around, a conversation ensued between the mate and the delegate.

To digress for a moment. Having referred to this title some pages back, it should be explained that on all union ships all three departments elect a spokesman known as the "delegate." The delegate is elected to speak on behalf of the crew to the chief mate or chief engineer on all matters pertaining to the union work rules. It doesn't take much imagination to realize why, through the years, the word "delegate" transformed into "delegoat" in the minds and hearts of the crew. It was a position least sought after, and usually the last AB who shipped was "stuckee." Giving you one guess on to whom this dubious honor fell, as I was saying, it went something like this:

Mate: Why won't you guys work? You're getting paid overtime for it. Aren't you here to make a buck?

Delegate: We've got something more important to do.

Mate: What's more important than making money? You're not doing anything, anyway.

Delegate: Oh yes we are. In my case, I have a chapter to finish in the book I'm reading.

Mate: Do you mean to tell me that it's more important to read a book than to make money?

Delegate: In this case, yes. After all, don't forget what the Good Book said: "Man doth not live by bread only."

By this time, the crew standing all around me and unable to contain themselves, broke into loud laughter. The mate shook his head and, muttering something inaudible, turned around and left. About a week later in port, I ran into him and insisted on buying him a drink. He said he still didn't understand my point of view, but accepted it. We became quite friendly after that.

On yet another occasion, I was reading Dostoevsky's *Crime and Punishment* and left it face up on my bunk when I went on watch. A few hours later, while at the wheel, the skipper walked into the wheelhouse and told me that he was down below and he happened to notice my book on the bunk and could he borrow it next. Some days later, he came into the wheelhouse again to return the book and with a quizzical expression said, "I thought this was a who-done-it. Imagine, he tells you who did it on page twenty-six and spends the rest of the book analyzing why. What kind of a book is this?" I tried to give him the five-minute version of my ten-hour lecture on the subject, after which he nodded somewhat understandingly and said, "Hmm, is that right? I suppose it could be read differently." From then on, every few days or so, he'd catch me at the wheel and engage me in all sorts of conversation on almost anything that was on his mind. I found the whole thing quite rewarding and when we paid off, he invited me to visit him at his home in Seattle. Unfortunately, I never made it and he is long gone.

Chapter Eight
Sailor Types

Much of sea-going lore is replete with references to sailing-ship men as "iron men on wooden ships" as opposed to the supposedly "iron ships and wooden men," of the present era. It should be mentioned that these types of arguments were never heard in the focsle but were rather a product of some would-be writer's imagination. However, behind this reference is usually the question, What sort of people go to sea? I was once on a Danish ship, the MV *Laura Maersk*, wherein I was the only "foreigner" aboard and my watch partner once commented to me, "In our country, when you don't want to do anything else, you go to sea." I was taken aback at hearing this, since I had assumed that coming from a maritime tradition and culture where going to sea is a much respected and honorable profession, it surely must have rated high on the scale of opportunity. I also can't help recalling somewhere in Eugene O'Neill's *Provincetown Plays* where he has a character say something to the effect that when you fail ashore you go to sea.

Both of those statements contain a great element of truth. I would venture to say that, in my seafaring days, every single type of person one would meet aboard ship would have his counterpart ashore in almost any and every walk of life. The difference would be that the seafaring man is usually running away from some failure or shame, real or imaginary, and the bottle takes over his life.

Crews in those days did carry some strange characters. If Ishmael was surprised when he met Queequeg, a book could be written about many crews that sailed American ships before World War II. However, quite a few were well read, some with college degrees. On one ship I was on, all six AB's and the bosn had licenses. When the war broke out, I later heard that one of them became Port Captain of one of the major companies on the East Coast. There are, of course, exceptions. Quite a number, albeit in the minority, smoked or used hard liquor moderately. Others reformed and quit drinking. Many remained in the calling since it was the only skill they had. Some got the opportunity to transfer their skill to another trade and so were able to make the transition back ashore.

In the focsle, regardless of your quirks and pastimes, if you made a sincere effort to learn your trade, did your job, and were a good shipmate, you were accepted. The phrase often asked is, "What sort of shipmate is he?" Broadly speaking, it boiled down to a few things such as showing respect for those who know more than you, being willing to learn, pitching in when you were needed, showing consideration for the rights of others and observing other such elements of the Golden Rule as told to me by our Port Agent way back when all this began.

On an early ship I was on, the SS *Virginian*, an old workhorse-type freighter and cattle boat of World War I vintage, owned and operated by the American-Hawaiian Steamship Company (referred compactly to by most seafaring men as "Haywire"), I had the good fortune of being watch partners with an old sailing-ship man named Johan Johannessen. He went to sea at the age of fourteen, like many others before him, making his way to the West Coast of the United States and following the steam schooner and Alaska trade (of which more, later). During a lull in both, he found himself on an offshore freighter and came on my watch.

He soon noticed, after sizing me up for the first few days, that among the many things I didn't have, a sea-bag was paramount. So he went up to the storeroom on our watch below and got some strips of canvas, and started me on "a real sea-bag." I was overjoyed, considering that until then I had been getting by with an old dilapidated "please don't rain."

Many sailors in those days carried their own palm, wax, needles and twine, the basic accoutrements required for sewing canvas. The palm is a circular hard strip of leather shaped to fit over your palm with two openings, one for your thumb and the other for the rest of your fingers, leaving them free to move. In the corner, between thumb and index finger, is a built-in piece of steel which is the mechanism used for forcing the needle through the canvas. The wax is in the form of a square bar and is used to draw the twine over it a few times to make the twine a little harder and more waterproof.

Johann was of Norwegian descent and, as he explained to me, came from a long line of seafaring people on both sides of his family. He took pride in the fact that he had been on his own, "pulling my own weight," since such a tender age. When we met, he was a man of fifty, lean and wiry, quiet and soft spoken to the point of near silence. Almost invariably, day or night, he could be seen with a pipe clenched in his teeth, sometimes lit and sometimes unlit. He later told me that he was trying to break the snuff chewing habit to which he claimed he was addicted from an early age.

I noticed that he wrote a lot of letters and mailed them in all the ports we hit, and had mail awaiting him on arrival. This was an inter-coastal run, meaning we went up and down both coasts touching many ports and transiting the Panama Canal. I later found out that he was the corresponding secretary of the "Sons of Norway" in San Francisco, a fraternal order much like any other ethnic organization. I often wondered what made such a silent, unobtrusive and painfully shy person assume a role of leadership. Somehow, he took a shine to me and it could be because I evinced an interest in his background and past.

After drilling me in the use of the needle and palm and making me practice the stitches on a piece of discarded material, he finally let me do one side of the sea bag. The bag was designed in four sections all joined together with a one-inch overlap. The stitches went down both sides of the overlap, thereby creating eight rows of stitches and making the bag look like a cylinder. Placing the bottom was the trick. The circumference had to be measured very carefully (it was the first time since I left school that I ever saw anyone apply the formula of pi times the diameter). We added an inch all around and carefully traced it out and cut it. In attaching it to the bag, every other stitch had to be "gathered in" so as to come out without a bulge. This, too, then required a double row of stitching. It was topped off with a creased fold, again with a double row of stitching, and six holes were punched in it for brass grommets to hold a cotton braid drawstring. I then made a special handle embellished with a fancy knotting called "cocks combing" which he also taught me. I carried this bag with me throughout the years, on and off ships and have it to this day, retired as it were, like a ball player's uniform. And it looks as good as the day we made it.

A year after the war broke out, I ran into Johann again. This time he was in a Chief Petty Officer's naval uniform, of all things. He told me that the Navy was looking for instructors in seamanship and lifeboat handling and offered him a good deal. He was based at Treasure Island Naval Station in San Francisco Bay where, hopefully, he lasted out the war. One thing I can say for certain: The U.S. Navy got one hell of a sailor man— an iron man from wooden ships—to teach the recruits, and I hope they appreciated Johann as much as I did.

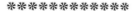

No man will be a sailor who has contrivance enough to get himself into jail; for being in a ship is being in jail with the chance of being drowned; a man in jail has more room, better food and commonly better company.

Samuel Johnson, 1709-1784

Thus spake Dr. Samuel Johnson to his friend and amanuensis James Boswell sometime in the eighteenth century, and it must have been pretty bad since the descriptions of the eighteenth century British Man-o-War and merchant men are well known.

An important and much overlooked element in the composition of the prewar American focsle was the prevalence of a rather high percentage of ex-convicts, many of them long-term who had done hard time. All these men were in a position to compare both sides of the issue. I was shipmates with a few who actually described life in Alcatraz in minute detail as only an eyewitness could. Recalling my description of an average focsle a few pages back, it should not be very hard to realize how close it comes to a description nowadays of an average jail cell as seen, for instance, on T.V. The main difference is that in the jail cell, a seat-less commode is part of the landscape whereas in the focsle the latrine is in a separate area and the commodes all have seats.

My description of the focsle has yet another important aspect. This has to do with the steel lockers, one to a person. It was a point of honor and brotherhood that no locks be used on one's locker when out at sea. In port, it was permissible to put your locker under lock and key. The prevalent attitude was best expressed in the oft-heard statement: If you can't trust your own shipmate, you might as well not go to sea. As I think back on this now, I realize not only how justified the attitude was but also that it was precisely the ex-cons who made a point of it. Their sensitivity to the issue was understandable.

There were a number of good reasons for many ex-cons finding refuge in an American focsle, not the least of which was that probation officers (whom they referred to as PO's) encouraged their charges to go to sea because in doing so they'd be out of harm's way: "Out of sight out of mind." (Another good reason, as has been previously stated, is that nobody asks you where you came from and not many really care. You tell your story voluntarily.)

It is easy to see how life in jail could be analogous to life aboard ship. In both instances, it's a confined existence for a given period of time in very cramped quarters. You don't have too much to say about your choice of shipmate/cellmate; food is prepared restaurant style and choice is minimized; and last but not least, it's a total male universe.

The rule in those days was, and I believe it is still the case, that a parolee must report to his PO at least once a month. Most of those affected by this rule had a series of preprinted post cards leaving port and date blank and just filled them out and dropped one in the mail at the required intervals. This practice was pursued, even when the parolee was holed up in an American port either unable to part from an amorous adventure or having a good run on the horses—the first a rather common experience, the second, rather dubious.

In either case, they would get a friend to take a bunch of the cards and drop them in the mail at discrete intervals. Also, many of them were heavy drinkers who got into all sorts of petty mischief while performing ashore. (All super-carousers are known as "performers.") They couldn't trust themselves with the all-important card to their PO. There was even an unwritten understanding with some of the police departments in the port cities that when they picked up one of our members for performing or minor infractions, they got him down to the union hall with the warning to get a ship and "get out of town."

Soon after the big strikes on the West Coast were over, any new member applying for membership had to prove his whereabouts during that period. In my case, for instance, I was young enough to be in school, so that was easy. But in many other cases, when you went up before a membership committee and couldn't make out a good case of your whereabouts, you couldn't get in. As for the ex-cons, the West Coast unions at one time were a refuge for some of these men, since they could easily prove where they were during the big strikes. In fact, rumor has it that they were the only ones permitted in, in those days. With the advent of the war, the floodgates were opened, though I do remember some committees challenging older men a few years into the war.

✳︎✳︎✳︎✳︎✳︎✳︎✳︎✳︎✳︎✳︎✳︎

The focsle is also host to another well-known type already alluded to—the "ex-pug" or former boxer and Golden Glover. I don't think I was ever on a ship in which there wasn't one if not more former pugilists, hence ex-pugs, as they were known. If Golden Glovers were amateurs, "ham-and-eggers" fought for just that on their way up the ladder of professionalism. Many of them never made it any higher, and from there, many of them drifted into going to sea. It goes without saying that for the most part, like ex-cons, they turned out to be fine shipmates and a credit to our union. As a matter of fact, on the San Francisco labor scene, it was known that the waterfront unions supplied the "muscle" not only for their own picket lines, but for many smaller labor unions struggling against the disadvantage of limited resources and manpower and the overwhelming police protection of scabs. In the forefront of these battles, there were many ex-pugs.

Charlie Cates was one of these. He left a small town in Middle America, cast adrift in the Great Depression in the early 1930s. He caught a boxcar and rode the rails picking up odd jobs and sleeping in hobo jungles under railroad trestles until he made it to Seattle. As an ex-Golden

Glover after his high school years, he accommodated to the many sport clubs in and around the Coast featuring, in those days, the "Friday Night Fights." To earn meal money, he became a ham-and-egger interspersed with occasional workdays on the waterfront. He had been plying the coastwise steam schooners out of Seattle and was a member of the Sailors' Union of the Pacific, an organization, in those days, long on very proud history and short on clout. In fact, at the moment it had only a few small steam schooner contracts. As mentioned before, in those days on the West Coast waterfront it was quite likely that someone in or about your purview was a Wobbly or ex-Wobbly.

Charlie and many of his friends were at one time or another touched by the IWW message and carried around with them the hope and aspiration of some sort of basic change on the waterfront, maybe a little less than the proposed New World. Their moment came in the spring of 1934, when the longshoremen struck the western waterfront and the sailors quickly joined them. The ship Charlie was on, a steam schooner, was tied up immediately next to another steam schooner on which the second mate was Harry Lundeberg, a friend from Seattle, and between the both of them, they closed down both ships. The second mate went back to Seattle and was elected to the strike committee and thence onward to eventual world fame in the shipping community.

Charlie surrounded himself with a group of like-minded friends and became the "meet and greet" committee, as he put it, for all the incoming deepwater ships in the port of San Francisco. Charlie always claimed, and many corroborated his statement, that his "committee" boarded these ships on arrival, one by one, tied them up and the rest is history. Labor historians today should take note of this important fact.

Charlie was not tall, about five feet, ten inches, weighing in at about 180 pounds. He was as solid as the Rock of Gibralter, both physically and character-wise. He was forthright, direct and had a good speech delivery.

When we met some years later, he neither smoked nor drank and told me this had been the case now for many years. He was always "in training," as he liked to put it, a carry-over from his ham-and-egger days. Most prominent about his features was a square lantern jaw, which in a tense moment tightened up and you got in his way at your peril.

One Monday evening Charlie was elected chairman of our regular weekly meeting at headquarters. This required him to sit in a large, black leather chair in the center of a raised podium so as to conduct the meeting. These Monday night meetings, it should be understood, were not only to conduct business, pass motions and "instruct" the officials as to what to do, but were also somewhat of a sideshow. Since attendance was compulsory and many of the men on the beach still had some money, there was a slight carnival air attesting to the degree of inebriation floating over the hall. For the most part, though, business proceeded as usual, and nobody "got out of line," with one exception. This one night, an apparently new member kept interrupting the proceedings and was repeatedly asked to keep order until recognized. This he chose not to do. On about Charlie's third try, he cautioned the man that he would have to ask him to leave unless he changed his ways. The obstreperous one challenged him with, "Yeah, you and who else?"

In a flash, Charlie hurdled the podium and pulling off his leather jacket, made a beeline to the third row for this guy who was built about like Charlie. As the more than 200 members in the Hall scattered and formed a circle, they began to duke it out, hot and heavy. Both got maneuvered to the entrance, and since we were on the second floor, they both went down the two long flights of stairs, flailing and punching away at each other, reminiscent of the Count of Monte Cristo dueling away down the circular staircase. Within about five minutes, Charlie walked back into the Hall, retrieved his jacket and resumed his place on the podium to the uproarious cheers of an appreciative audience who had just witnessed the equivalent of the world middleweight boxing championship.

Through the years, Charlie and I met from time to time. Quietly he got married and eventually had children. He started accumulating property and dabbling in small business ventures. He was in his seventies when he died and was rather well-to-do by my own rough calculation. These success stories are not uncommon among the generation that preceded and included World War II.

✳✳✳✳✳✳✳✳✳✳✳

If sailors work, stand watch, eat and sleep, have personal projects, read and write, surely they must talk to each other. What do they talk about? Aside from small talk, such as describing the characters they know (a "character" is one who has a special distinction that sets him apart from the ordinary in a particular aspect of conduct, be it drinking prowess, "sea-lawyering," pot smoking or sexual activity—mostly exaggerated if not a total fantasy), analyzing the conduct of officers and crew in the previous port of call is a common preoccupation. As I said, aside from all of that, seafaring people conduct normal, everyday conversations like anyone else ashore. It might be of interest to note that in spite of the fact that much of our union activity had great political significance during those years, there was a surprising dearth of such discussion at sea.

A favorite topic of conversation is a category known as "the last ship was the best one." Inevitably, comparisons are made between ships and it usually turns out that on the last ship "we did it better." Since this same conversation will be repeated on the next ship, in whatever context, the phrase loses its credibility. All the more so when the complainant is answered with another old walnut, "Different ship, different long splice," meaning you might have done it that way then, but we're doing it our way now. Both will yield the same results.

Shoreside folk get a big kick out of seafaring language. Throughout the body of this memoir, lots of focsle language is used and, wherever feasible, "translated" into everyday English. However, this is not the whole story. Seafaring people engage in "coprophelia" described by psychologists as the obsessive use of obscene language. Whenever and wherever seafaring people congregate, they would rather use an obscenity than not. Every other word, let alone sentence, is punctuated with "fuckin' this" or "fuckin' that" in and out of the focsle. All the more so when they are drinking and their guard is down. It is the easy way out, since finding a suitable word is sometimes more difficult. But it is not all obscenity. It is also a release, a venting of the spleen as it were.

It is important to keep in mind that when a sailor goes to bed, he does not "go to bed." Rather, he "turns in" or "takes a horizontal and equal strain on all parts." What's more, it will probably come as a surprise to most people that the "bunk," sometimes referred to as the "sack," which is a contraction of the term "fart sack," has now passed over into the general spoken language, albeit slightly sanitized. Finally, while on matters neological, when a seaman suspects questionable if not strange interpersonal conduct, there is "friggin' in the riggin'." And when he becomes a little testy out to sea, he is admonished, when he hits port, to go get a "good sweat over a live corpse." When seafaring people come ashore, one of the more difficult accommodations to be made is the changeover to a more acceptable, temperate language. After all, it is "our anchor to windward" and if some of the color gets lost, it's part of the price paid for becoming civilized.

Recently, as this memoir was being penned, a well-known TV anchorman, Robert MacNeil, was interviewed[2] and observed that with the advent of air travel, the influence of the sea as a rich source of metaphor appears fated to wane:

Experience of the sea used to be central to the lives of the English-speaking people, and knowledge of oceans was vital to commerce, exploration, and conquest.

He then went on to offer a partial list of metaphors owing their existence to the sea:

People who count on *their ship coming in* are pretty much all *in the same boat*. They are *taken down a peg or two* if they *don't know the ropes*. Strangers are *given a wide berth* if no one cares for the *cut of their jib*. To *lower the boom* takes *the wind out of the sails*. A gossip recounts *scuttlebutt* unless told to *pipe down*.

Not to put too fine a point on it, I've been *around the horn* myself a bit, so I can *catch someone's drift*. Especially when they *put their oar out* and start mouthing off in the mess room. Nor do I get *taken aback* when they come back from ashore, *six sheets to the wind*. In that case, I usually *clear the decks and batten down the hatches* so as to escape their snow job.

Finally, my political friends tell me that the most popular phrase in Washington these days is "It didn't happen on my watch." So it is that we too have made a contribution to the field of general semantics, not to speak of matters of the intellect.

There is one great exception that must be made between shipboard focsle conversation and shoreside job conversation and that would be the subject of venereal disease. VD is a constant worry among seafaring men. It is handled openly and in normal discourse. On any given ship, those afflicted (it is called "getting set up") are usually known to the crew but as a rule not broadcast. It is easy to see why this is so. The closeness of confinement in an entirely male civilization and the fear of possible contagion, realistic or not, almost demands an openness that working people ashore do not comprehend. Nor is anyone ostracized due to venereal infection, since working under such conditions is already onerous and painful.

Whereas time off due to illness is sometimes necessary, there is no excusable time off allowed for VD. However, the crew usually demonstrates a little solidarity with a shipmate who is set up and makes it a little easier for him in work assignments. When and if a crewmember was to be hospitalized due to VD, he was sent to the nearest local Marine Hospital to a segregated ward known as the "Rough Riders Ward." Benefits-wise, he was not permitted disability payments. Hopefully, the law has been humanized by now.

An interesting incident comes to mind illustrating certain aspects of this problem. On a ship I was on in the port of Bombay, the public health authorities came aboard to check out two cases of malaria, one of which was my own. While there, they demanded a venereal examination of all hands, known in our parlance as a "short-arm" inspection. (For the benefit of the uninitiated, the way it's done is by crooking your arm at the elbow into a ninety-degree angle and taking your penis in hand, display it to the medical officer.) From time to time, offshore sailors run into these demands and usually acquiesce. The difference this time was that it was only the unlicensed crew that they wanted and the officers were exempted in the true style of the British Raj.

But the fact of the matter was that all hands knew that the only case aboard was the Second mate, "an officer and a gentleman." The crew held a quick meeting and we took the skipper into our confidence asking him to face not only a public health issue but a civil rights issue as well. After some discussion he saw the light and got the port authority to judiciously blanket in the officers as part of the inspection. All told, the issue of VD aboard ship is a model of communal behavior.

❋❋❋❋❋❋❋❋❋❋❋

The general subject of illness at sea is simple. There is no professional medical attention available, though I must say, in all due respect to the medical profession, that some of the focsle doctors were pretty knowledgeable. The exception is if you are on a passenger ship, which if not by law, at the very least from a common sense business point of view, carries some qualified medical help. In that case, a seafaring man can get qualified medical attention while aboard a passenger ship. However, there is an important hooker here, if you will pardon the unintentional pun. He must pay for his own treatment if it is venereal in nature. But there is yet another factor involved. Ashore, a replacement can be had while you are gone since at sea the crew will double up and cover for you if you cannot work. In spite of the fact that the union agreement calls for a penalty payment when this happens, guilt feelings arise and you feel uncomfortable about "not holding up your end" as it were.

While on the SS *Cape Flattery* (of which we will speak later at greater length) my watch partner, Clarence C., and I had no idea how our bout with malaria originated. Suffice it to say that as we were leaving Calcutta in the fever heat surrounding that city, we began feeling rather ill at ease. First came the usual denial syndrome. We decided it must be the hemp burning along the Hooghly River, which gets into your eyes and nostrils.

We barely got off work the first day out, when neither of us could get up to go on watch. The mate and skipper came down to look at us and turned away with worried looks. Our temperatures suddenly shot way up and they correctly guessed it must be malaria, or something akin to it. So they started feeding us quinine and atabrine pills by the handful. As my fever rose, I remember having what could best be described as hallucinations. Visions of things and people past floated in and out of my stream of consciousness. My only real recollection was the solicitous crew keeping us wrapped up in wet bed sheets as we sweated away and they poured liquids down our throats. In what felt like a millennium of time, but was only about twenty-four to thirty-six hours, the fever broke and everyone looked at us quite relieved.

It took us both eight to ten days to feel like working on deck again, but we did return to our wheel watches a few days after our body temperature returned to normal. This skirting flirtation with death gave us all something to think about. I began to detect a more wholesome feeling both on my part towards my shipmates as well as on their part towards me. Somehow they became more responsive towards me and me to them. It could be that this close call made everyone realize how transitory life really is, surrounded by the ongoing carnage out there.

※※※※※※※※※※※

One of my few big mishaps at sea during the war was when I broke a few bones in the metatarsal arch of my right foot while working the cargo up in Alaska on the previously mentioned cockroach palace, the SS *West Celeron*. In the process of snaking out a 150-pound case of machine parts into the center of the hold, it slipped out of the grasp of my cargo hook and cut across my right arch. We were at a U.S. Army outpost called Cold Bay (and it sure was) on the Bering Sea side of the Aleutian Chain, a desolate island a thousand miles away from nowhere, with a handful of Quonset huts containing a crew operating a radar station. And one of the huts was a latrine.

My leg was swelling badly so the ship called the army and they sent a truck over. When we got to where we were going, a medical sergeant told me that there was no doctor around until tomorrow, since he flew in from somewhere else. He said it looked like a break, so in the interim he put a temporary splint on it and suggested that I stay overnight until the doctor arrived the next morning. Meanwhile, outside a storm was blowing something awful. In the northern and southern polar latitudes, sudden bursts of wind peculiar to coastal areas are known as "williwaws." This was one of them.

The sergeant told me that if I had to go to the latrine, there was a pair of crutches I could use. This was no mean feat for an inexperienced crutch handler, so to speak, trimming myself against the wind and inching along on a wooden plank walkway. (There were no such things as sidewalks.) Once inside the latrine, it wasn't much different. There were no doors, so the wind just blew right through. Getting yourself seated on the pot was a formidable task. The pot was a long plank running the length of the barrack with cutout seats every few feet to fit the dimensions of the average male behind. Somehow I negotiated it all and got back to "sickbay," where there were six bunks, five of them occupied, the sixth one readied for me. A fellow next to me, a baker, had a stove blow up on him and he looked awful. He was waiting; all pumped full of morphine, to be flown out the next morning. Another GI had frostbite on all his toes and they were turning black. They flew him out too.

The night I spent there, in sickbay, turned out to be quite entertaining. Along about 8:00, after dinner, the wind had died down considerably and the pot-bellied stove was glowing away in the center of the room, when I suddenly heard a thumping sound of wood on wood, becoming more distinct as it got closer to the door. Within a few moments the door flew open, and there stood a short, squat and powerful looking older man, holding a gallon jug of some white-colored liquid and a peg leg stump on one leg a la Captain Ahab. With an ever-so-pronounced Scandinavian accent, after everyone greeted him with a hardy "Hi Chris," he answered, "I understand you have a sailor man here tonight." With a perfunctory "yeah," all eyes suddenly were riveted on his jug.

He approached my bunk and we shook hands. He told me he was the only human inhabitant of the island when the U.S. Army arrived, and furthermore, he hoped it "will get back to that when this mess is all over."

His wife and two married daughters lived in Seattle and he saw them once a year or so. The army had made him sign an agreement that he could live there but must abide by army regulations, one of which was no home brew to the troops. He signed the agreement, but opined that nothing prevented anyone else, such as a visitor, from offering a round.

As all eyes focused on me, I immediately invited all hands to imbibe. Before we could uncork the bottle, the hut was full of GIs all saying hello to Chris and me as if we were long-lost buddies. Chris explained that he was "dismasted" in a whaling ship accident some twenty years before, hence his peg leg. He said he had a special shoe that he wore when he visited "the lower forty-eight" to see his family. He bought some staples with his monthly social security check from the supply ship that came around once or twice a month and for the rest of his food he lived off the land and the sea.

As all this was going on, the bottle kept going from hand to hand. Since the contents of the bottle can best be described by a popular waterfront phrase of the day as "potent panther piss" (whose counterpart in the world of indigestible solid food was "sour owl shit"), it didn't take long for the party to get real lively. Soon enough the empty bottle got back to Chris who kept up a steady drum beat of sea stories from his whaling ship days, in both the Northern and Southern Hemispheres. There must have been a ration of beer available, since a few dozen cans of beer suddenly materialized, so Chris hoisted a few of those while I barely managed to nurse one along.

Before long somebody produced a pair of dice and a heavy crapshoot started up in the far corner. I quickly realized that money was of no consequence here. For instance, I was told about one GI who sold a useless radio to another GI for two hundred dollars. This was a part of the world in almost continuous communications blackout; only official military channels were open. The crap game reflected the phenomenon. I lay there watching one guy making seven passes in a row for one-thousand dollars each and then crapping out; he just went right on playing as if nothing happened.

All told, other than a few short engagements in fisticuffs, it was a fairly well-behaved evening. By about midnight, everybody started leaving and Chris bade me good by. As I drifted off to sleep, I couldn't help but reflect on the loneliness of the outpost and the lives spent this way. The loneliness was the enforced price paid for the war effort but weren't there things to do other than drinking and gambling? As for Chris, he seemed to have gotten the best of both possible worlds.

The next morning the doctor arrived and substantiated the sergeant's original diagnosis. Within an hour or so, they had a plaster of Paris cast on me up to my knee. Much to my surprise, as the doctor and sergeant were putting on the cast, it was revealed to me that the doctor was a veterinarian, attached to the Medical Corps, and was an expert in handling horses. He came from Minneapolis and was an avid weekend sailor as well as a walking encyclopedia on the New England clipper ships. When we got back to Seattle and I reported to the Marine Hospital, they looked at my cast and laughed. They told me it was a good job but really unnecessary, since a taped up ankle and foot would have done the job. As for me, it didn't make much difference, since I would have had to stay off of it, one way or another. Furthermore, without an x-ray machine handy, I thought it was a good diagnosis by two very experienced people.

The presence of the cast precluded my doing any work. The crew further decided that I couldn't possibly live down in the focsle, which was in the after end below the poop deck. So, for my own safety and their peace of mind, they made me move up to the radio shack on the boat deck so I could have immediate access to the lifeboats if necessary. An active Japanese U-boat campaign was raging in the Gulf of Alaska at the moment.

As luck would have it, I did get a chance to appease my guilt feelings about lying around and reading great literature while everyone else was working. I decided to do something about the poor food we were ingesting. I became an expert fisherman and so was able to make a contribution to the crew's welfare as well as bill of fare. I mentioned previously that the ship was a "starvation bucket" and the cook was a "stew bum." After a while the steward relieved the cook and took over his chores. And I felt proud of my newfound piscatorial talents. The term stew bum originated with the American hobo and is one of many that passed into maritime lexicon. It was originally defined as an "elderly tramp wasted by rotgut." In seafaring parlance it somehow became a rotten cook.[3]

✳✳✳✳✳✳✳✳✳✳✳

Before I leave the discussion of character types such as sea-lawyers and focsle doctors, would-be professionals brought about by dire necessity, I must say a word about focsle psychologists. In spite of the fact that, as I have been saying, nobody questions your past so long as you do your job and are a good shipmate, seafaring men are constantly "figuring things out"—which is another way of saying that the "psychologising" goes on endlessly. There must be some real inner need for this, since each new crew is a new environment and although the precious little elbowroom you have is respected, adjustments must be made accordingly. All this leads to all sorts of thoughts on human motivation and conduct.

Whatever focsle you are in, you are always forced to take account of and observe your watch partner's activities and habits as well as everyone else's. Also, the conduct of ship's officers towards each other and towards the crew is carefully observed and all sorts of interpretations are offered.

A perfect example of this, but carried to an extreme, is the Hollywood version of the aforementioned Eugene O'Neill's *Provincetown Plays* that became transmogrified into *The Long Voyage Home*. In the picture, the crew begins to suspect a character called "Duke" as a foreign agent. They build up a story on him, which later is shown to be totally false. True or false, sailors do this sort of thing in the process of getting to know each other. Many, having been stung so badly in life, build up defenses hard to overcome.

And while we are on the subject of Hollywood, it's worth digressing for a moment to consider how our leading ambassador of culture handles the seafaring venture. And as you might have guessed, it's strictly phony. In an effort to glamorize and set everything against a human-interest plot, the story becomes totally unrecognizable from the original play. The original plays were written about World War I, but this turned out to be about World War II. (Luckily O'Neill was given screen credits or we'd never know the connection.)

For example, an air attack takes place and the ship takes a direct hit on one of its hatches and catches fire. The character called "Swede" (played by a young John Wayne with a simulated accent) grabs a fire hose and drapes it over one shoulder and with the other hand grabs a long-handled fire axe and swinging it with that one hand chops a hole in the hatch, while lowering the fire hose through it to extinguish the flame.

This, I submit, is a total impossibility for any of us mortals and that goes for Superman-to-be John Wayne. Try swinging a long-handled fire axe with one hand. Then try bearing down hard enough to penetrate the hatch cover. There are usually three layers of thick canvas tarpaulin and the old wooden hatch boards carried on these types of freighters were three-inch thick oak planking. And as for the fire hose, all I can say is that during our regular fire and boat drills out to sea, when the bridge called the engine room for "water on deck," it took all the strength I could muster, not to mention "all hands and the cook" to barely hang on to the full hose under full force. How Swede ever maneuvered that hose over his left shoulder with one hand and forced it down into the newly chopped hole with the other hand, I'll never understand.

To end this thing on a positive note, the picture was a good yarn and brilliantly played by an all-star cast such as Thomas Mitchell, John Wayne, John Hodiak, and the brothers Barry Fitzgerald and Art Shields of the Irish Abbey Players. Catch it on the tube as a rerun.

Chapter Nine
Mickey Finn and the "B" Girls

A number of incidents have now taken place in the life of this narrative in which physical violence or the threat thereof has been used to settle issues between people, on both a personal and institutional level. Unfortunately, violence is a way of life on the waterfronts of the world as well as in the society at large. It is in the very nature of things that this has become so, and the perceptive reader will have picked up some clues by now as to its whys and wherefores. Whatever the manner, when the seafarer puts out to sea, a new element comes into his life. It is the psychological dimension of enforced proximity, as well as enforced loneliness. It was mentioned earlier that the seafarer feels imprisoned. He is thrown together with about forty other males, and there is no escape. Rules of conduct do apply and considerations of space are respected. But as one day gives way to another and a full month goes by, as nerves become fine-tuned and personal quirks and idiosyncrasies take on a sharper image, the safety valve sometimes pops in the form of violent confrontation. At times, the explosion takes place at sea but most times ashore, when under some liquid stimulation incidents are recalled and embellished. For the most part, these encounters are consummated quickly and forgotten. It is an integral part of life at sea.

Most people who have read about the sea know about sea slavery, albeit in an intellectual sense. They have probably read some Melville, Conrad and Jack London about shanghaiing and the Barbary Coast. All of this came about because the seafaring man had no power. A world of sheer brutality kept him working and living the way the ship owner wanted it. In those days, "The Articles of Sea," mentioned somewhere at the beginning of this narrative, was a meaningless document. It was totally unenforceable out at sea, as well as in a foreign port. By the time the sailor got back to his homeport, if he had any money left from his meager wages, he was in no position to hire a lawyer or, worse yet, argue with corrupted union officials and gangsters hired to do the ship owner's bidding. The deplorable living conditions of rotten food, bad accommodations, and no overtime pay for endless hours of work, has been documented by many eyewitness testimonials.

In January 1848, gold was discovered at Sutter's Mill in California on the American River some sixty miles east of where the city of Sacramento now stands. Legend has it that entire crews deserted their ships in the mad dash to the alleged gold fields, which reputedly were turning out millionaires daily. In order to control these crews and see to it that ships were crewed up when required, a system of boarding houses, crimps and runners came into being whereby the owners of boarding houses with liquor bars attached kept their hold over seamen by developing usurious bills for lodging, food, liquor and provisions through a system of advances which kept the seafaring man in never-ending eternal debt.[4]

In order to come ashore, a system of small boats, called Whitehall boats (actually large skiffs) went out to greet the incoming ships. They carried the pilots and company representatives to the vessels. But by far, their best customers were the runners who usually worked for crimps who in turn supplied the local boarding houses with customers and skippers with crews. The crimps, it should be said, were middlemen who cemented the whole relationship, charging on both ends of the deal. He usually employed the runner. Working on a per capita basis, their job was to bring the seaman to the boarding house, as well as return him to any ship that needed a crew. Once ashore, either with or without money in his pocket and with the proper female and liquid stimulation, he was soon parted from any and all his earnings in record time. The seaman then went into debt to the boarding house keeper and was soon supplied as another crewmember, for a price, to any crimp or runner that was assigned the task of filling a crew. In many instances, it was the ship he had just left.

It was also mentioned earlier that seafaring people are in many respects those who failed ashore. So, those who do fail ashore tend to drift down to where seafaring people live and socialize. This world, the world of the waterfront, was an unseemly world of low-level mercantile shops, some flophouses and lower status hotels and gin mills rather than fancy watering holes. However, they were not slums. In this environment, violence is more likely to be out in the open rather than contained. Many saloon keepers, with the help of low-life type women known as "B" girls behaving no better than piranhas, have been wont to part a sailor from his total trip's wages, all within the space of a night's carousing. This type of situation breeds a legacy of hate and vengeance.

A "B" girl, it should be explained (in no way to be confused with a cocktail waitress or a woman making an honest living in the oldest profession) is a woman who works around a bar, who makes some money by plying "live ones" to buy them drinks. (A sailor is "live" when he has some money on him, usually immediately after a trip's payoff.) These drinks bought for the "B" girls, are often diluted and watered down by cooperating, crooked bartenders who nevertheless charge the full price. Pretty soon, as is the pattern, the sailor gets drunker and drunker as she remains sober and the sailor wakes up sooner or later parted from his money. To all intents and purposes, he was "rolled." That is to say, he was physically stripped of his money while he was unable to defend himself. Another well-known way of rolling a sailor was to "Mickey Finn" him. This old piece of American slang means that a narcotic or purgative is added to a drink and the unsuspecting sailor is made temporarily helpless. This is cardinal sin on the waterfront, and still happens on occasion, but nowhere near as often as in years past. In my time, most seafaring men would hope that the "B" girls would finally come up in the world and make an honest living as a prostitute.

Through the years much legislation protecting seamen's rights was placed on the books, but the act of legislation and actual enforcement are two different things. There are numerous incidents and examples of illegal practices continued long after legislation was on the books. A perusal of the files of the *Coast Seamen's Journal* will easily bear this out. As a matter of fact, there would be no reason to have unions and representation if all this great legislation were enforced, especially in their time. But it took much longer for these bad times to pass.

In 1895 the Maguire Act abolished the desertion law (imprisonment for leaving a ship) in the coast-wide trade and outlawed the crimps' right to obtain an allotment from the seaman's wages from the captain. In 1898 the White Act abolished the desertion law for seamen on offshore ships in U.S. ports. It also abolished beatings and corporal punishment by officers. In 1915, the LaFollette Act, among other things, extended complete freedom from the desertion law to U.S. ships in foreign ports and to foreign vessels in American ports. It took years for all this legislation to really become meaningful.

This brings us to a slight digression so as to better understand the psychology of the times and some of the politics involved in the labor union organization as they were reflected in the focsle of a West Coast contracted ship.

Chapter Ten
Brotherhood of the Sea

I have spoken somewhere above of the seafaring man's division of time into two eras: before and after the years 1934 to 1936. The era before 1934 is remembered as the era of sea slavery and the one after 1936 is the union era.

The Sailors' Union of the Pacific has a logo. It consists of a picture of the Earth with the words "Brotherhood of the Sea" emblazoned around it. In its center in large white initials is S.U.P., and under it in smaller printing is the message, "ORG. 1885." Most maritime historians place the date as March 6, 1885. In fact, they say the union was organized as the Coast Seamen's Union on that date on a lumber-pile on the Folsom Street wharf in San Francisco, California.

The original membership was composed of sailors plying the coastwise or steam-schooner trade. This trade was distinctive in that these small vessels sailed in and out of small ports up and down the coast, picking up lumber and rolls of newsprint up north and coming south to San Francisco and what is now Los Angeles, picking up general cargo for the return trip to the northern ports. Since the earliest coastal trade required putting into ports where there were no longshoremen available, the sailors together with whatever casual local labor was at hand became the longshoremen. When steady gangs developed, the acquisition of one hatch by the sailors became a tradition and was written into the union contracts; this became especially necessary during the jurisdictional warfare between the sailors and longshoremen in the 1930s and 1940s.

Most of these sailors were of Scandinavian background and nationality. They knew each other and this practically insured a built-in solidarity.

A few years later, the Steamship Sailors' Protective Union was formed to cover the offshore or deep-water men and by 1891 both organizations merged but retained the name of the Sailors' Union of the Pacific.

Although names, places and dates are buried in the archives only to be resuscitated long afterwards, luckily, we now know who were the prime movers in this series of events. In what was one of the most unlikely combinations of characters one would ever expect to encounter, a self-educated lawyer and utopian socialist, Burnette Gregor Haskell, and a part-time sailor/longshoreman (who some historians claim to have been an itinerant barber), a wandering Polish Jew named Sigizmund Danielewicz, came together at this moment in history and were there with the answers. Both these men were members of an organization called the International Workingmens Association, which later became known as the First International as organized by Karl Marx and his followers in September 1864. History records that soon after they pointed the way, they either dropped out of sight or went on to bigger and better things.

In January 1887, a new secretary was elected, a Norwegian born, Viking-like sailing ship sailor, thirty-three-year-old Anders (which became Andrew) Furuseth, who had been going to sea since the age of nineteen. From that time on until the outbreak of the 1934 and 1936 strikes, the personality of Andrew Furuseth was intertwined intimately with the Sailors' Union. He presided over the union, or what was left of it, with infinite patience through the darkest years, when the membership roll was down to a mere handful. His attitude and outlook could probably best be described by his oft-repeated famous one-liner, "Tomorrow is also a day." This, after a while, became translated into, "Tomorrow is another day."

His lifestyle was ascetic and frugal. Many times there was hardly enough money in the treasury to pay him. His stock-in-trade and modus operandi was to try to influence legislation, and he became a fixture around the nation's capital. The passage of the LaFollette Act of 1915 is credited to him as well as a famous statement attributed to him, whose origin has been lost in antiquity and ostensibly made to a Congressional committee but nevertheless is quoted constantly:

You can put me in jail, but you cannot give me narrower quarters than as a seaman I have always had. You cannot give me coarser food than I have always eaten. You cannot make me lonelier than I have always been.

In 1892, Furuseth managed to get some other small unions together and formed a National Seamens' Union. In 1896, it became the International Seamens' Union, the blanket umbrella organization which stayed alive until 1937 when it all but passed into oblivion, a totally corrupted organization, top-heavy with parasitic bureaucrats and gangsters who knocked themselves out doing the ship owners' bidding every which way they could.

Although the Sailors' Union accepted Furuseth as its patron saint, the end of the story is not nice. He consistently resisted any and every form of direct action and militancy at a time when this was the only course of action. He opposed both big strikes and even advocated the Sailors' Union's expulsion from the International Seamen's Union. He died in January 1938, at the age of eighty-four, a disappointed and broken man— a perfect example of what happens to certain leaders whom history passes by. However, and it bears repetition, he was the union's secretary for approximately fifty years and is honored so to this day. A beautifully sculptured bust of him now stands in front of the Sailors' Union Hall on Harrison Street in San Francisco.

The persevering reader will remember my new-found friend Duffy, who when he initiated me on my first ship, mentioned that he was a "Wobbly." That is to say, he was a member of the Industrial Workers of the World or IWW and carried a membership book in the Marine Transport Workers Union Local 510 (or as the parlance of the times had it, "MTW Five and Dime"). The IWW preached a philosophy of industrial unionism, that is, the organization of everyone and anyone in the workplace into "one big union" segregated only by industry, hence an industrial union. This was in contradistinction to the American Federation of Labor (AFL) which organized strictly along craft lines regardless of workplace, hence separate unions for carpenters, plumbers and electricians sometimes all in the same workplace.

The "one big union" would be the sum of all industrial unions brought together in the shape of a wagon wheel, called Father Haggerty's wheel, in honor of the Jesuit priest who first thought of it. Each union represented by a spoke of the wheel would send a delegate to the hub of the wheel called the "General Council," which together by the declaration of a General Strike would institute "The Commonwealth of Toil," a rather nebulous, utopian, cooperative-socialist scheme to run society. Many seafaring men were touched by this philosophy since its implementation was via "Direct Action" tactics and the strike weapon. This philosophy showed them the way and when the propitious moment came along in 1934, men like Duffy were there to seize the day. It was the Wobblies who educated an entire generation in rank and file unionism.

A second active organization on the American waterfront during the same time frame was the Marine Workers Industrial Union (MWIU), which purported to organize all maritime workers also, but with an altogether different political agenda in that it was created by the Communist International and thence applied to the American scene by its agent, the Communist Party, U.S.A., sometime in the late 1920s early 1930s. Suffice it to say that it met with a singular lack of success. By the mid-1930s, with the first glimmerings of a revived industry and economy, the Committee for Industrial Organization (CIO) was organized by John L. Lewis with the United Mineworkers Union as its base. When the winds of maritime organization blew east after the 1934 to 1936 strikes on the West Coast, remnants of the small and by now disbanded MWIU organized the National Maritime Union (NMU) and received a charter from the CIO early in 1937. Simultaneously, the International Longshoremen's and Warehousemen's Union (ILWU) on the West Coast, whose Secretary was Harry Bridges, received a similar CIO charter for its jurisdiction.

The picture is rounded out by the Socialist Workers Party (SWP), a much smaller sect adhering to the principles of Leon Trotsky who lost out to Joseph Stalin in the power struggle in the Soviet Union and the Communist International. In 1936 they started colonizing in the Sailors' Union and assisted its new Wobbly-inspired leadership in consolidating its victory and defending it from being taken over by the Communist Party. This process was helped along by the SUP joining the AFL.

From then on and until long after World War II there was a constant and never-ending underground as well as above ground guerilla war between both organizations, the Sailors' Union and its AFL affiliates on one side and the NMU/ILWU and its CIO affiliates on the other. Through the years, all economic issues handled by both organizations were colored by a non-visible but nevertheless ever-present political antagonism that to this day is probably still unknown to many of its respective members.

In fact the waterfront General Strike of 1946, which was fought ostensibly to break the stranglehold of the War Labor Board in its wage-setting policy, was nothing of the sort. Rather, at the moment an organization called the Committee for Maritime Unity (CMU), created by the CIO unions and totally dominated by the Communist Party, was attempting once again to capture control of the western waterfront. And once again they were thwarted in the attempt. It should come as no surprise that today, after the original cast of characters have long drifted from the scene, many to their final resting places, and with the almost total decimation of a once thriving industry and culture, that the remnants of these once proud and competing organizations, albeit still adhering to their autonomy, are united under the umbrella of the AFL-CIO.

Whatever good or bad one reads into the situation today, both unions are a mere shadow of their former selves. The NMU has been in and out of federal courts in recent years on charges of nepotism, racketeering, embezzlement of hundreds of thousands of dollars of union funds and other related charges. It grieves us deeply that this once proud organization of 75,000 members in all certificated categories is now down to 3,000 and in shambles. And the SUP, although untainted to this day with any financial scandals, is struggling to keep its head above water both financially and contractually. A once proud organization of 10,000 men is now down to 1,000 with not much change in sight.

In the spring of 1934, the world turned around for the seafaring man. It can truly be said that he had nothing to lose but his chains. "Direct Action" or "Job Action" as he got to call it, was the order of the day. And when it was all over, the seafaring man became empowered. After the 1934 strike (May 9 to July 30), the seafaring unions went back to work without a written contract. It took the three-and-a-half month 1936 strike (midnight, October 30, 1936 to February 4, 1937) to finally win one. In the interim, a series of job actions were executed on many individual ships by their crews to "make believers out of the ship owners."

The buildup of hatred and violence dictated the seafaring man's conduct, both during and after 1934. Violence became the modus operandi in settling differences. His anger was now focused against his former union officials, the ship owners and their private army of gangsters as well as the official armed might of the state, such as brutalized police departments and National Guard divisions and the politicians who controlled them. For honorable mention, lest we forget, the establishment newspapers and radio of the day (like today, those who insure the psychological preparation and molding of public opinion) were almost unanimous in their condemnation of the strikers and never missed an opportunity to either put an anti-union spin on every story or publish blatant prevarications at every opportunity.

Any and every problem affecting the direct welfare of the crew, be it working conditions, watch standing, behavior of officers or food and lodgings became subject to direct negotiations on the spot with the skipper or company representatives as all work ceased. It was also called "hanging the hook," which means that the cargo hook that traveled in and out of the hatch came to a halt. In this way, the accumulation of small victories was a major step in forcing the ship owner to acquiesce to our demands and finally sign an exclusive bargaining contract after the 1936 strike, incorporating all of these gains.

When the smoke had cleared away, the very essence of this new empowerment was the direct and exclusive control of the hiring hall by the union, codified in a signed agreement and enforceable by law. This is not to imply that we achieved Nirvana after 1936, but it does say that a working mechanism was set up whereby the seafaring man and other allied tradesmen found a way not only to make their wishes known, but to enforce them using the strike weapon as well as a court of law. And the element that bound this whole relationship together was the union control of the hiring hall. It would not be an exaggeration to say that for the first time in labor-management relations in the United States, if not in the world, the West Coast sea-going unions were the first to obtain not only sole exclusive bargaining, but also sole control of their hiring hall.

Simply put, this means that from here on out any placement or replacement of seagoing certificated personnel must come from the union hiring hall, not from the ship owners' personnel office or the dock. Barring any anomalous or esoteric situation in some little-known provinces or anywhere else off the beaten path that labor scholars may know about, nothing like this ever happened on so massive a scale. In addition, in the forefront of this victory, which was finally secured in 1936, was the Sailors' Union of the Pacific.

It would be instructive to pause for a moment and reflect on how the hiring hall worked. Simply put, to paraphrase the Apostle Matthew, the first will be last and the last will be first. When one is ready to register for work, he goes directly to the union hall and takes out a shipping card, dated and numbered that day. The card is good for a stipulated amount of days, depending on the ability to get a job. In our time, it was ninety days. (As of this writing, it is about to be extended to one year.) That means that any member, after officially registering for work, can get out in ninety days. The new "registree" now goes to the bottom of the list and will go out last. As jobs appear on the Dispatch Board, the dispatcher calls them out and those who want the job will throw their cards in. The oldest date gets the job since he has been on the beach the longest, and he therefore goes out first.

The member now has three days to decide whether he wants the job. If he does, he stays there, but if he doesn't, he goes back to the hall within the three-day period and retrieves his original card. He is then allowed just two more choices and if he loses out, he must take out a new card and go to the bottom of the list. By anybody's reckoning, this has to be the most humane working rule ever devised. These rules and this system apply to all jobs both at sea and ashore (there are some) in all ports where the union has jurisdiction.

Another important subject is the handling of seniority. In most unions, seniority, strictly defined, means the oldest member in point of time served gets first choice at all jobs. This would have led to a situation whereby the older members would have gotten all the work and the newer ones what was left over, if any. One of the first acts of the membership after setting up its hiring hall was to abolish this system and institute the leveling process as stated in Matthew. It was argued that all members regardless of age or time served suffer the indignity of unemployment equally. A full book in the union makes every member equal in terms of employment.

I cannot leave the subject of union empowerment without speaking of the "Fink Book." When the Merchant Marine Act of 1936 (of which more later) became law, one of its sponsors, Senator Royal S. Copeland (D-NY) had the dubious distinction of introducing, as part of a giant omnibus bill, a thing called a "Continuous Discharge Book."[5] Simply put, all seamen were to be issued an identification book with the relevant vital statistics, mug shot and identifying fingerprint. The rest of the book was to be made up of blank pages to be filled in by each master or chief engineer attesting to his conduct (sobriety?), seamanship and work habits over the course of the trip. These categories were graded from Excellent all the way to Unacceptable. Taken to its ultimate conclusion, the seaman was to be saddled with an internal passport system, wherein he could in no way escape his past and would dog him forever if he in any way displeased his officers, such as, for instance, by being a pro-union advocate.

This system was a carryover from some seedy practices of the past, for the most part from the end of World War I and the defeat of the 1921 Strike. At that time the U.S. Shipping Board was the regulating body and it issued a thing called a "Blue Book" which in its day was immediately labeled a "Fink Book." When it was re-legislated in 1936, the Sailors' Union, not only cognizant of the past but also facing the living reality of the Soviet Union, Fascist Italy and Hitler's Germany, all of whom incorporated such a system in its everyday life and times, categorically rejected the entire concept and refused to have any commerce with it. It also had to overcome the insipid waffling of the East Coast unions whose political program was to support the Roosevelt Administration, and had consequently become a source of embarrassment to them. Eventually, the entire idea was dropped and the "Z" numbers as explained earlier were used. Had it not been for the fierce independent stance taken by the Sailors' Union at the time, life would have been different. Saddled with a Fink Book, our empowerment would have been meaningless.

Union empowerment came in many ways, not only on the job but outside the workplace as well. One morning, and this as late as 1941, while on the beach in San Francisco, one of our old-time members came up to the Hall and complained to a group of us that he was rolled the previous night at a local well -known gin mill within shouting distance of the union hall, whose owner-operator was a character known to us all as "Portuguee Jack." This time we decided to do something about it.

We walked into the front office with the story and asked our Secretary to look into it. After hearing the man out, he picked up the phone and demanded the owner to come over to the hall immediately, which he did. With the rest of us constituting ourselves as an impromptu drumhead court martial, we demanded that he come up with the money and make a fair restitution. When a decent interval passed in which he weaseled around and wailed loud and long about "not wanting to get in trouble with the union," he left and returned with a mutually agreed upon sum. This story passed around like wildfire and things remained relatively clean for a good long while. Can you imagine what would have happened had the member gone to the authorities with his story? Or just let it pass as most seafarers are wont to do, too ashamed to have it aired in public?

There were also some that combined a great knack for moneymaking with the empowerment and did quite well for themselves. A good example of what I mean was an old friend and shipmate, Andy Anderson, who was bosn on the SS *Young America* for some of the time I was on her. Andy was one of a thousand of his name (or so it seemed) in the Sailors' Union at the time. Like the rest of them, he came here on a sailing ship and went on the beach in San Francisco sometime before World War I. It didn't take him long to discover the steam schooners and he plied them throughout the twenty years between the wars—a hard life.

In 1919, when Prohibition set in, Andy discovered that he could buy liquor in certain ports and resell it to longshoremen and other dockworkers in other ports. This supplement to his income soon exceeded his wages on the steam schooners. By the time Prohibition was repealed in 1933, he had a nest egg of no mean proportion.

Through the years, I've met people who find this portion of the story hard to believe. As a matter of fact, bootlegging was quite common, as common as drug running and pushing is today. A certain shady character I knew once stole the key to the liquor locker from the Steward on a passenger ship while in port, ran uptown and had it duplicated and helped himself to the inventory from time to time, undercutting the Steward's prices while out to sea. By the time the Steward woke up and changed locks, the shady one had made a small fortune.

Andy in the meantime had met Helga, a Swedish compatriot who worked as a domestic in one of San Francisco's major hotels. She soon became acquainted with one of San Francisco's leading families, who enticed her away from the hotel and over to their mansion, to become their cook and housekeeper. They became so enamored of her culinary prowess and working ability that they set her up with an account in their brokerage firm, she depositing most of her weekly paychecks into it. When Andy and Helga got married, soon after the 1936 strike, he stayed on the steam schooners, but now earning decent money. They combined their resources, and by the time we met just before the war broke out, they were millionaires—from a workingman's point of view, that is. They owned their own home, had a car and lived well.

During World War II, Andy, already in his fifties, was a top rigger in one of the local shipyards, but would make a trip from time to time "just to keep my hand in," he would say. As soon as the war was over, still childless, they upgraded themselves and moved to a bigger house. From time to time we would meet and have a drink in one of our favorite bars.

One day, a few years after the war, they both came up to visit and Helga was quite agitated. It seemed that Andy had decided to buy a better car. So for three weeks in a row, he went out and bought a car, one each week, turning the previous one back and upgrading himself until he finally settled on the best Cadillac on the market. She further said that Andy always used to tell her that they were saving money "so as to be ready for a rainy day. Now he's going out and throwing it all away."

While she was telling us all this, she was on the verge of tears. I stole a glance over at Andy and he was smiling. When she wound down, he said, "That's right, that's just exactly what I said. Now Helga, look outside. What do you see?" And as she looked up, it was raining outside, whereupon Andy broke out into laughter. Poor Helga sat there totally nonplussed and at a loss for words at the silly joke. Finally, she plaintively asked, "Yes, but how much longer do I have to work?" "You don't have to work at all any more. I told you to quit long ago. You should go out and buy a new dress. Just like I went out and bought a new car," he answered.

I eventually broke into the conversation by trying to reinforce Andy's point that they did not need to count pennies anymore, and what was more, they would soon qualify for Social Security. And furthermore, at that very moment, the Sailors' Union was negotiating a welfare package that would encompass a retirement plan for which Andy will surely qualify. This would bring them even more money ($150 per month) just staying home, and "how about a visit to the old country"? I piped up. "It might be just the thing at this time in your lives."

After some casual conversation, Helga seemed to calm down and as they got up to leave, Andy said, "Well Helga, what do you say. How about a trip to Sweden?" To this she casually answered, "We'll see."

Some months later, Andy showed up again. Yes, that very next day Helga said "yes" and off they went. They both found all sorts of family still around and they wined and dined each other for weeks on end. They toured the entire Scandinavia and they didn't worry about money for an instant. Furthermore, they planned to return the next year, maybe to stay. They both lived into their eighties and I hope they spent it all. They deserved it. This too is empowerment.

Just about every sailor I ever met, in or out of the focsle, was forever scheming about retiring some day either to some small business in some small town or getting a little "stump ranch" somewhere in the boondocks. The term "stump ranch," as far as I could make out, had to do with clearing a small piece of land of its stumps after the trees are cut down so as to build a house. I must say that I was privy to many soliloquies on this subject reminiscent of the Lennie and George discussions in John Steinbeck's *Of Mice and Men*.

The whole idea behind this dreaming was that you should never have to go back to sea. But the fact of the matter was that we all had a love-hate relationship with ships and the sea. Many were the seafaring men I knew who harbored the hope of someday "finding a little stump ranch to build a house on" as well as "making another trip just for old times sake." Sailors often joked about this. One old walnut used to be: "When I retire I'm going to put a set of oars on my shoulder and march inland. The first place I reach where someone asks me what that thing is I'm carrying, that's where I stop and settle down. It's only then that I know I'm far enough away." And another old walnut favored by many others was: "When I retire I intend to invest my money in Lots and Houses, lots of booze and whore houses."

The subject of pensions alluded to above has had a happy ending and is yet another feather in the cap of the Sailors' Union. Somewhere about the time that I quit the sea, a welfare plan including a retirement pension was negotiated with the operators. First and foremost, an entire group of old timers past the age of sixty-five were automatically blanketed in, with few questions asked. This was necessary because, for the most part, although they were known to have been going to sea for years, it was only in recent years that they were able to start saving their discharges. Until then, they either lost them all or threw them away, never for a moment even dreaming that they would be able to retire on a pension.

To accommodate those who had little proof of their time at sea, a brilliant scheme was devised to help them remember. A well-known old-timer, my old friend Tom Hookey (of whom I will speak more later), was placed in the front office to interview all those who qualified and he was given the power of decision. After a short interview with the prospective retiree in which he helped them draw up a list of all their sea time by ship and approximate date, he would usually say "yes" and send them upstairs to the newly created pension office. This simple expedient was acceptable to the ship owners. Using the immediate post-World War I period as a marker, by the early 1950s at least thirty years intervened. Anyone who lasted that long and survived the war deserved that pension.

The advent of union empowerment made a difference. It helped many seafaring people become "respectable." The increase in living standards, the betterment of working conditions and the broadening of opportunity brought on by the war, lifted many borderline derelicts into the main-stream of life. In fact, not a few of them returned to the old country and from what I understand, "lived like kings," as one of them put it to me.

When the discussion over pensions took place, many old timers began to realize that there was a slight possibility— an outside chance—that this might happen. I would be remiss if I did not report in the body of this memoir, the latest thinking on the subject back then. During discussion with the ship owners, the question was asked:

"Just what is the difference between the various welfare plans from a conservative, a liberal and radical point of view?"

And the answer given was:

The conservative wants full coverage from the cradle to the grave.

The liberal wants full coverage from the womb to the tomb.

The radical wants full coverage from erection to resurrection.

Chapter Eleven
A Job Action

In the autumn of 1940, some months after I had passed my twenty-second birthday, and soon after the first military draft law was passed by Congress, the ship I was on put into San Pedro, California and I, together with two others—the only ones eligible out of a crew of forty—went ashore and registered. On thinking back about this in recent years, it still amazes me that all hands from the skipper on down agreed to the statement made by one of the old timers that contrary to what the powers-that-be said about its temporary nature, the draft would be permanent until the war (which was then a year-and-a-half away) was over. Approximately eighteen months later, I received a card from my draft board classifying me into a category that "froze" me into going to sea for the duration. Their only requirement was to keep them informed of every ship I was on, which was the practice used by all seafaring men of my age group. I followed the rule conscientiously.

One year after I had registered for the draft, I had accumulated a sufficient amount of time to qualify for my Able-Bodied Seaman's Certificate as well as full membership in the Sailors' Union. The former I passed easily, but the latter, a more involved process, took a little more effort. Each and every crew whom I had sailed with, would have had to write a letter stating the time I had served and evaluating my character and seamanship. And each and every letter was to be signed by the crew.

The letters more or less followed a standard pattern in that they answered the very points made by our Port Agent to me as he handed me my assignment slip, in what seemed so very long ago. I well recalled his admonition: "Listen to the AB's; pitch in when there's work to do; show that you're willing to learn and don't talk too much." And as it turned out, all the letters answered these very points as if put in question form.

All these letters together with my spanking new Able-Bodied Seaman's Certificate were to be presented to the port agent, who would convene a committee to check out the letters, ask some questions ("Where were you in 1934 and 1936?") and inform you to appear at the very next Monday night port membership meeting for induction.

On the appointed Monday night, I appeared at our Port Meeting in San Francisco at 59 Clay Street, an old but solid structure the second floor of which the union occupied. Sailors' Union meetings, as our Secretary mentioned, were also sideshows worth coming to. Anybody who has something to say is entitled to the microphone as long as he's on the subject. And when the verbal persuasion runs its course, fistfights take over, as alluded to earlier on in this memoir.

The last item on the agenda is the induction of new members. There were five of us that night. The ritual of induction was said to date back to the early beginnings of 1885, and its core, the induction pledge, reputedly written by Burnette Gregor Haskell, our very founding father.

Like many other crafts, the Sailors' Union stressed pride of craft, ("Doing a seamanlike job at all times") brotherhood and solidarity. The contrast was all the more startling when one realizes that this was in an era that saw the birth and build-up of mass industrial unionism.

As the membership was asked solemnly to rise, our secretary, Harry Lundeberg, the third of his kind since 1885, delivered a speech extolling the virtues of the organization and all its positive accomplishments and achievements to date. He spoke of the sole control of the union hiring hall with no ship owner and government interference; of how our wages and conditions had improved far beyond the dreams of the men who struck in 1934 and 1936, many of whom were standing there that night in that very hall and had sacrificed much to make this possible; of how all contracts signed must be ratified by the membership; and even of not tolerating political programs as other unions do, (a sly swipe at the opposition National Maritime Union and its Communist Party influence); we still monitor all Congressional activity through our Washington office, and much more. "We are not the biggest union in the world, but we're certainly one of the best," he said, finally finishing with, "We do the best we can with the tools we've got"—statements we were to hear repeatedly through the years, and which took on the significance of a mantra. When he finally came to the end, he asked us to raise our right hands and repeat a few lines that I have always remembered and can still paraphrase somewhat as follows:

I pledge my honor as a man that I will be faithful to this union and that I will always work for its interests. That I will look upon every member as my brother. That I will not work for less than union wages. I promise that I will never reveal the proceedings of the union to its injury or to those not entitled to know them. And if I break this promise I ask every brother to treat me as unworthy of friendship or acquaintance. So help me God.

Not since I learned the Pledge of Allegiance in the first grade, did I make such a commitment! As my new book was handed to me, Number 2241, with the secretary's signature on the title page, I felt a surge of pride in that I was accepted into a band of brothers and was not so alone in the world. Furthermore, I had a voice and a vote on the same level with shipmates twice and three times my age; the iron men from wooden ships. And although I still wasn't going to talk too much, I would now start talking a little more.

A story that comes down through the years, probably apocryphal, has it that when Andrew Furuseth directed this very ceremony, he would ask the new inductee, "How do you take down a royal yard?" Chances are that the inductee was a sailing ship man and knew the answer. When our secretary handed me my book, he looked me straight in the eye and to this day I'm sure it was because I was the youngest looking in the group, and said, "Do you know the difference between a Liverpool and a logger-eye splice?" As luck would have it, I did, having learned it from an old-timer shipmate and practiced it just some weeks before. I answered him by describing both splices. While many young seafaring men would be at a loss to know it, since it was such a rare requirement, many an old-time AB confessed to me that they too would have had to think twice about either one of them, if asked to do so.

The story does not end there. Standing behind me was one of our officials, Rangvald (which usually came out as Ringbolt) Johansen, whom I later got to know quite well, and as I answered the question, he quickly said, "And how about you Harry, do you remember the difference?" Which of course led to an uproarious laugh by the group encircling us. The rest of that memorable evening was spent in a gin mill, listening to the old timers sailing around the Horn as they vied in snowing each other under. And it was all made possible by the presence of a live one, that is, me, having just paid off a ship.

❋❋❋❋❋❋❋❋❋❋❋

Another cardinal principle in the belief system of my friend Duffy and his fellow Wobblies was embodied in a phrase often repeated when union matters came up: "Beware of the leader; the one who leads you out of the forest will lead you back in."[6] One can easily see how such sentiments could dovetail readily into the mood and outlook of an already rebellious person in perpetual challenge to authority. In spite of the fact that some sort of organizational form is necessary in operating any institution, I was nevertheless struck by the earthy wisdom of this concept. To this day, the problem remains: How do we keep our leaders honest and responsive to us?

The subject of leaders and leadership on the West Coast comes down to what has been referred to by the pundits of the day as the battle between the two Harry's—that is between Harry Bridges of the Longshoremen's Union and Harry Lundeberg of the Sailors' Union. In the beginning they were well acquainted with each other and although not personally friendly at least respectful of one another. As the struggle between the AFL and the CIO progressed, with the further political complication of the sub rosa battle between the Communist Party and the other politicos on the waterfront, they became bitter enemies and the personalities of the two men began to symbolize all the issues.

The maritime historians have handled many of the objective issues and we would be wandering too far afield to rehash all the problems of the times, but the fact of the matter is that looking back at it all at this late date, Harry Bridges and the Longshoremen, in a manner of speaking, won the public relations battle; known these days as P.R.

Not that we weren't respected. We certainly were. Many uptown unions could trace their success to the Sailors' Union providing them moral and material aid, that is, the money and muscle required for successful unionism. I can personally point to a number of incidents, which includes the all-powerful Teamsters Union, wherein they needed our resources, goon squad and all, to win their beef. A "goon squad" is a usually small group of members, quite adept at engagements in fisticuffs, who can help a picket line mix it up with scabs and keep them out of the workplace. It is a perfectly legitimate countervailing force to the Police Department and/or the National Guard organizations, as well as private security armies who are employed to break strikes. And when we speak of a "beef" we do not mean the hindquarter of a head of cattle but rather to a grievance that has escalated to a sharp disagreement.

The reason for this P.R. victory by Bridges and the Longshoremen's Union is not too hard to come by, when one looks at the political forces on the San Francisco waterfront as well as uptown at the time. Although San Francisco was headquarters to both unions, the CIO unions were in the overwhelming majority, membership-wise. They were also the ones doing most of the new organizing among working people whom the AFL completely neglected, looked down on and disdained.

It was also enormously enhanced by the large Communist Party membership both on the waterfront and uptown, in many walks of life, who considered the AFL with its building and metal trades councils as moribund and conservative and spoke authoritatively and loudly on many progressive issues. Not the least of these issues was the Spanish Civil War (July 1936 to March 1939) that seized the consciousness of many working people and intellectuals and in which many seafaring people were involved. All this was proliferated through many front organizations and influential sympathizers among the professional groups. The Sailors' Union had no such P.R.

The P.R. story has one more aspect that added a significant amount of sympathy to the Bridges presence and this has to do with the Federal Government's persecution and prosecution of him on the issue of membership in the Communist Party. The government alleged that he committed perjury in his application for citizenship in denying membership in the Communist Party. This was the time of the McCarthy era in our post-war history, which as time goes by, becomes increasingly shameful in retrospect. After three separate trials, they never were able to put the case away and Bridges was never deported. In fact his citizenship remained and there were rumors in later years that he was voting Republican! The amount of publicity and sympathy he got was incalculable.

The personality of Lundeberg fit very well into the waterfront world. He was absolutely indefatigable and fearless in his pursuit of the cause of the Sailors' Union, working day and night, almost never taking a vacation, until it did him in at an early age. It is a well-known fact that he personally led every major battle, up front, of the Sailors' Union all through the years. His courage was legendary. Once, when a certain official committed a real dereliction of conduct, I happened to be standing near a group discussing its consequences with him. He raised his voice demonstratively for everybody to hear and said, "I know the toughest guys on this or any coast and if that guy comes after me, he may not be able to tell the tale after I get through with him." This, in view of the fact that the individual in question was a pretty tough one himself, a former heavyweight boxer with known Mafioso connections.

He was a fiery speaker, explosively volatile when he was crossed and could not bend an inch. His talk was strictly salty and he could cuss a blue streak. His sense of humor was minimal but some of his language was worth the price of admission. A lot of people I knew who were real close to him seldom heard him crack a joke, although once in a while he'd get off one of his standard one-liners that made things more interesting. A few well-known ones were, "It looks good on pencil," when referring to a ship owner's proposal that sounded good but was suspect. Or "Quit blowing smoke up my keester," whenever one of his toadies used too much hyperbole on him. Or, when a ship owner negotiator refused to commit to an agreement, he would complain, "He wouldn't say yes, no, or kiss my ass." And when he denounced any U.S. Navy or Maritime Commission brass, "He looks like an Admiral in the Bolivian Navy." (The latter, of course was an inside joke, referring to over-uniformed types since Bolivia is land-locked and has no Navy.) In denouncing a poor proposition, "You sound like a man overboard," or, better yet, when you were completely off base, "Your cock is hanging out a mile." And for any one who tried to curry favor with the ship owners or, perish the thought sold out to them, it was, "He's nothing but a meat-swinger," an oblique reference to oral copulation. A diamond in the rough, he was a true iron man from wooden ships, representing the original backbone core of the Sailors' Union membership. Although he was always "strictly business," his saving grace was that, like Harry Bridges, he loved betting on the horses and was generous to a fault in helping old friends and former shipmates.

A perfect example of his explosiveness was a famous incident that was reported in the *West Coast Sailors* concerning the well-known San Francisco newspaper columnist, Herb Caen, in which Caen stated an opinion on the contemplated move of two East Coast passenger ships to the West Coast, quoting some anonymous waterfront pundits as to the politics behind the move. What followed was a vicious and malicious anti-Semitic diatribe on a very low personal level against the hapless columnist, that no self-respecting newspaper would ever dare publish, completely obfuscating the issue instead of a sober objective appraisal of the situation from the Union's viewpoint. Since the diatribe was printed in the *West Coast Sailors*,[7] it became not only part of the public domain and hence never forgotten, but also incorrectly stamped us as common bigots.

This criticism should in no way be taken as characterizing Lundeberg as a common anti-Semite because he wasn't. It just shows, given his explosive nature, to what extent he would go to keep his position which he equated with the best interests of the Sailors' Union at all times. It must also be said that when he died, our New York port agent, Morris Weisberger, who was one of his long-time friends and associates and happened to be Jewish, became Secretary and held the office for some twenty years until his retirement.

The point is, that we were not in a personality or popularity contest, neither then nor now. It was just a matter of two different styles expressing two diametrically different viewpoints. We entrusted our leadership to them and on balance, looking back at it, it probably could have ended up much worse had some of the other unsavory types hanging around the union hall at the time, seized control of the Treasury. The Longshoremen accepted a containerization and mechanization concept which bought out most of the old timers and the industry became constricted over time, while the Sailors' Union went into decline because of the perceived national interest—perceived, that is, by the ship owners and their political operatives.

The matter of "direct action" or as we called it, "job action" was another one of those cardinal principles that my friend Duffy and his colleagues stressed as the sine qua non of good and effective unionism. The rationale for this action is that we must confront the ship owner's representative, be it the Captain, Chief Engineer or Steward (and many times all three) directly, at the "point of production," (another of Duffy's favorite phrases and simply meaning the workplace). This confrontation usually meant anything from a complete work stoppage ("hanging the hook" as previously described), to a "conscientious withdrawal of efficiency" or any other form of persuasion deemed necessary by the "rank and file" (the very workers themselves on the job).

Examples of job actions abounded in the waterfront lore of the pre-war period. Even within the confines of a signed agreement, job actions were constant. The incident of the cockroaches on the SS *West Celeron* related earlier on, would be one such example. That had to do with living conditions. Another example took place on the SS *Elk Hills*, the T-2 tanker I spoke of earlier. It had to do with disciplining officers. It should be borne in mind that these incidents took place during wartime when even a mention of strikes was outlawed and long after the era of our great liberation.

One evening after dinner, during one of those freewheeling mess room discussions, I heard a stentorian voice declaiming, "Well, my problem is that my father forgot to marry my mother and all I can remember is that my mother died and I wound up in this orphanage."

The voice was the voice of Seabiscuit. Again, a sailor who liked the horses picks up a sobriquet that stereotypes him. (These names were rather common on the waterfronts of the world at the time. Other examples come to mind, such as "Suitcase Larson" and "the Danish Consul.") His real name was John Francis Nolan, a name he almost never used and which very few of his shipmates even knew existed. As we became friends, I never used his nickname again. It began to dawn on me that, as a mature man, he carried this underlying lack of self-worth, using the supposed shame of an accident of birth to shield himself from striving to feel equal to his peers.

"And at the orphanage, I met Father Houlihan, and that saved my life," he told me the next day when I spoke to him again.

"How was that?" I asked.

"Well, this was when I was about five years old and as I look back, I couldn't have felt more alone. I had no family or at least no one who said I belonged to them. Father Houlihan was director of the orphanage in Philadelphia at the time, and he took me aside and said, "Now John, don't talk that way. You're a member of a great family and somebody knows you're there. If you put your faith in Jesus Christ, come to church on Sundays, go to confession every week and receive absolution, then there will be someone by your side all through life. Our Mother Church welcomes all her children as equals before God. There is no distinction because of birth.""

"So how long did you continue going to church?" I asked.

"Not very long," he answered. "I started out pretty good, but I soon got more interested in playing baseball. And pretty soon that's all I did. Some people came along and took me out of there. They had me working all the time; they just couldn't find enough jobs for me to do. But as soon as I turned sixteen, I ran away from them and got a job on a tugboat on the Schuykill River and pretty soon I got on the big ships and came to the Coast."

"Looking back at it now, do you think you did the right thing?" I asked.

"I never look at it that way," he answered. "It was the only way out for me at the time. I was already getting a record on the police blotter and it would have gotten worse. And I'll tell you another thing, and I don't spread this around see? Whenever I come in from a trip or get lucky on a horse, I take ten percent off the top and send it to Father Houlihan."

On the *Elk Hills* we had a problem with the Chief mate who hailed from Galveston, Texas. He was constantly parading around on deck during working hours, offering opinions and second-guessing the bosn. One of the cardinal tenets of our working arrangement was that officers stay on the bridge and speak to the bosn when and if necessary. Mates coming down on deck and interfering with the work process was unacceptable. At the beginning of each trip, the Chief mate confers with the bosn and tells him what he expects done this trip; the pressing problems of the moment or those that can wait. If a change of course (plan, that is) is required during the trip, he sends word down to confer with the bosn.

On a certain lovely morning, in the tropical latitudes, the chief mate from Galveston was scurrying around on deck, watching us at work and offering little bits of non-requested advice, when he approached John Francis, who was busy putting another coat of paint on the midship house. This particular task does not require a high degree of scientific knowledge. Suffice it to say that sooner or later, one develops the simple technique of applying paint to whatever object at whatever rate of speed.

John Francis was standing there wielding the brush and applying a coat of paint in a vertical, that is, up and down manner, when Mr. Galveston decided to question his methodology. As I recall it, the conversation went something like this:

Galveston: Why do you guys paint up and down that way?

J.F.: Well, that's because when the paint dries and hardens, and we start taking seas, or during a rainstorm, the water runs down the vertical tracks made by the paint. Also, it looks better.

Galveston: Yes, but what makes you think that if you painted horizontally or any which way, it wouldn't go on any better and accomplish the same thing?

J.F.: Well you got me there. I really don't know. Maybe you can show me how that would work?

Galveston: Okay. Let me show you what I mean.

And as Galveston extended his gloveless hand, John Francis, holding the handle of the dripping brush, thrust the dripping bristle end at him, whereupon Galveston instinctively grabbed it. Realizing instantly what he had done, he let out a blue streak of cussing, slammed the brush to the deck, and his bare hand now dripping with paint, quickly disappeared from the deck. Needless to say, we never saw him again down on deck while out to sea. This is how we educated the officers with first class job actions.

An important tenet in our modus operandi, as mentioned above, was the strict line of demarcation we kept with the ships officers, not the least of which was that they keep off the deck when the crew is working. By the time I came on the scene in 1940, most officers and crews kept their distance from one another. Most chief mates were educated enough to keep off the deck during working hours. Those like Mr. Galveston, who hailed from the Gulf coast, were a little ignorant of the West Coast style. When I came aboard my first ship, the MV *Willmoto*, I watched the older men closely and constantly, taking my cue from them as I was told to do. To a man, they never called the mates by name and I was immediately made aware of a deep sub rosa hostility, an over-arching antagonism and distrust of any and all company and governmental representatives. After all, many of them finked (scabbed) during the big strikes.

As the war progressed and many men out of the focsle went up on the bridge, this began to change and thaw out. These same men exchanged their union books for a book in the Masters, mates and Pilots Association, an affiliate in the AFL. This open-ended mobility between the focsle and the bridge helped considerably in changing some basic attitudes, bringing some of the old hostilities if not to an end then at the least to manageable proportions.

Chapter Twelve

Gas Fires and Oil Spills

I f freighters carry dry cargo, then tankers carry liquid cargo. On the West Coast there was very little tanker traffic, limited mostly to short coastwise runs. During the war, there were some larger ones built such as the previously mentioned T-2's, in fact some 430 of them, as well as thirty T-1's, a junior edition, both used for the most part to service the Navy and its installations in the various theaters of the war. The T-2's are dwarfed by today's supertankers.

Of the liquid cargo that tankers carry, eighty percent of it is crude oil. There is no real cargo working equipment to keep up since the holds are now tanks. From afar, a tanker looks like a model of cleanliness and simplicity. To the naked eye, long catwalks stretch fore and aft but hidden under them is a labyrinthine mass of coiled pipes. It has been estimated, for instance, that there are sixteen miles of pipe throughout a T-2. Part of the work at sea consists of their upkeep.

Tankers rarely come alongside a dock. They are for the most part anchored or tied up to a barge offshore. Hoses are fished out of the ocean and hooked up to valve-operated pipes aboard, which in turn are connected to the ship's tanks. When and if tankers come to a dock, the refineries that accept the oil for processing are, for the most part, on the outermost edges of bays and harbors thereby requiring long distances for transportation of both crew and material.

In the nature of things, tankers load and discharge in record time. In many instances they turn around in twenty-four hours, and that is so even for the supertankers today. What all this means to the crew is that they just about never get ashore, and if they do, they can't stay away too long. Many a tanker stiff, when going ashore, is admonished to "double park in front of the cat-house and keep the motor running," since the ship's departure whistle will be sounding real soon. (A "stiff" is an old Wobbly expression for a workingman.)

Early in life, the ship owners realized that they would have to do a little extra to keep a crew on a tanker. For tanker stiffs this resulted in just a little better living conditions, maybe a cut above a freighter. Consequently, tankers traditionally have better quarters, larger focsles and recreational areas, as well as better food. The only two tankers I was ever on were also the best feeding offshore ships I was ever on. (The discerning reader will notice the qualifying adjective, offshore. That's because the steam-schooners and Alaska run were even better, but they were coastwise.) They also carry a perpetual odor of gas and oil, which gives one a cheap "high" if you inhale too deeply. And lastly, they're very dangerous even in peacetime.

Tankers are not only dangerous polluters but incendiary bombs as well. Some ten years or so after World War II, a decommissioned tanker was removed from the boneyard and taken to the outfitting dock of a nearby shipyard. While work was getting under way, the hatch and tank tops were removed and the empty tanks exposed to the air. A welder near one of the tanks, in preparation for burning off some steel plates, lit up his torch and the area was instantly engulfed in a fireball and explosion that was heard for miles around. The death toll was very low because of the few people in the vicinity.

The cause was immediately explainable to any old-time tanker stiff. The hold was never "gas free." That is to say, for all the years that the ship was laid up empty, the gas pockets from her last load that formed in the corners of the tank were never quite eliminated and there they remained, an accident waiting to happen. Most authorities agree that it is not the oil itself that burns or explodes but rather the gas given off by it.

There is much evidence to support this claim.[8] In October 1970, there was a collision off the Isle of Wight between the 77,000-ton *Pacific Glory* and the *Allegro* wherein the *Pacific Glory's* engine room was torn by explosions and ravaged by fire, which destroyed her superstructure and spread across the surrounding sea. Her cargo of Nigerian crude, however, was kept totally intact and she was towed to her destination in Europe and discharged.

Hydrocarbon gas has a very low flashpoint and burns or explodes at temperatures as low as minus-forty degrees fahrenheit. The gas lies in the tanks after the oil has been discharged and so it is that when tankers are emptied, traveling in ballast, that they are most dangerous.

Tankers have been known to explode without warning and disappear without a trace. A certain eighteen-day day period starting December 15, 1969, was witness to an extraordinary series of explosions that alarmed the seafaring world, but the knowledge of which was deftly contained by the establishmentarian press and kept from spreading too far and too wide. The following events took place:

The 206,000-ton Shell Oil Co. *Marpessa* sank off Senegal on her maiden voyage, killing two men. Her sister ship, the *Mactra* exploded off Mozambique Channel, also killing two men. The 220,000-ton Norwegian *King Haakon VII* exploded off Liberia. The latter two were salvaged and subsequently rebuilt. There were striking similarities to the three explosions. All three tankers were new ships, all were about the same size, all were in ballast and all were cleaning tanks at the time of the explosion. Whatever the reason—and nothing definitive has ever been decided—it was the economics of shipping applying an "economy of scale" formula that dictated the monstrous sizes of the ships. Safety was the last of considerations. All these tankers are too deep and wide for the Suez Canal. It has been estimated that it costs half as much to transport Persian Gulf oil to Europe via the Cape of Good Hope than by smaller ships via the Suez Canal, which is 6000 miles shorter.

Tankers carrying fuel, be it oil or gasoline, have been sailing the seas in ever increasing numbers since the end of World War II. The T-2 which I sailed on during the war, the largest in its day, is now dwarfed by ships three times its size. In the 1960s, the SS *Universe Iran* was the largest ship in the world. A comparison of its dimensions with the SS *Elk Hills* and the SS *Ardshiel* that Noel Mostert sailed would be instructive (see Table 1, p. 120).

The carrying capacity of the *Universe Iran* translates into 2.3 million barrels of oil, which further translates into some 96 million gallons. Some ten years later a 500,000-tonner was launched. Since the T-2 cost $2.8 million per copy, in the absence of officially published figures, only a quantum leap of the imagination can come close to the cost of a super tanker.

Today as yesterday, oil is the major source of fuel for most ocean-going vessels. That, coupled with the fact that the vast expansion of world energy consumption, of which oil is a primary source, has led to the tremendous increase in transport by sea. Among other things, the consequence of this exponential rise has resulted in a dramatic worldwide rise in maritime pollution. Some authorities have it that all ships are constantly leaking some oil, but tankers especially, due to their cargo are an ecological disaster when they have an accident. And as we can see, there have been just too many accidents.

On the SS *Elk Hills* we used a system called Butterworthing. This is a steam-cleaning machine and process named after its British inventor, whereby hot water at almost live steam consistency is poured down and circulated in the tank, cleaning the bulkheads of residue and sludge. It is this material that is dumped at sea while under way. We also hung up large canvas wind sails that led down the ventilators to get as much fresh air as possible into the empty tanks before reloading.

Numerous observers have testified to the pollution of large areas of the oceans. Thor Hyderdahl on his Ra expeditions, Sir Francis Chichester's testimony after his solo circumnavigation of the world and many scientists collecting samples all talk about floating clumps of oil, patches or slicks of oil film, tar-thick sticky globs and other non-appetizing descriptions. All this, granted, is anecdotal, as the academics would have it, but it doesn't make it any the less scary.

In 1975 the National Academy of Sciences issued a report[9] well known to scholars of the subject (but pigeon-holed by the Ford Administration), which came up with a startling conclusion. In one year, 1973, some 6.7 million metric tons of oil entered the world's oceans. Since seventy percent of our planet's surface is covered by oceans, and any school kid today knows that oceans provide homes for many thousands of plant and animal communities which in turn provide the necessary food chain for the diverse species that inhabit it as well as the land and help regulate the climate to boot, it is downright incomprehensible why humankind is killing the goose that lays the golden egg.

Limiting ourselves to oil spills at sea, the following is a sample rundown to illustrate the "tip of the iceberg" (see Table 2, p. 120).[10]

The image of ships splitting apart and breaking up under pounding seas makes for media events: dramatic, spectacular and devastating. It is the way we are immediately conditioned to think about the subject. All this comes about through structural failures, groundings and collisions, explosions and breakdowns, fires and rammings. Fires and mechanical breakdowns can occur almost anywhere. Collisions, rammings and groundings are caused by navigational errors as in the case of the SS *Exxon Valdez* within living memory. On or about the last week of March 1989, she ran aground in Prince William Sound off the coast of Alaska and deposited an estimated eleven million gallons of crude oil into its pristine waters. For the most part, these accidents invariably occur close to

shore and their consequences to the continental shelf and sediments are devastating, especially to the fishing industry.

Many American shipping companies, maybe all of them, keep corporate offices in such exotic places as Panama, Liberia and the Bahamas. In this way, they fly the flag of these countries and are not much subject to the insurance and safety requirements of the U.S. Coast Guard, where the old Steamboat Inspection is now lodged. Nor do they have to pay the wages or fringe benefits required under a union contract. These foreign-flagged ships are referred to as "flags of convenience" or "runaway flag ships."

Structural failures are closely linked with the age of the vessel. Smaller and older vessels, as well as almost all the supertankers afloat, are registered to flag-of-convenience countries and have, by far, the worst accident record. The flag-of-convenience vessels, of lower standards and older age, must be drastically upgraded in order for any positive change to occur. Attention must be paid to structural and equipment standards and traffic management of coastal waters if pollution is to be controlled. Incredible as it may sound, this is only the beginning of the problem.

When we cleaned the tanks on the SS *Elk Hills*, the oily water and residue was pumped directly into the sea. That was the practice of the times. All ships, when their fuel tanks are emptied, are filled with seawater. This aids stability, or "trim," when the ship is under way. In all other vessels, be it dry cargo, passenger or man-of-war, lubricating, hydraulic and fuel oil leak from the machinery and pipes and flow into the bilges on the ship's bottom. This oil and water mix must periodically be pumped out in order to prevent flooding and/or fire. In all these instances, the ocean is the final repository of the polluted mix, except that in these instances the ship is now closer to shore; let's say one day before arrival, weather permitting. All of this has deleterious effects on the fragile coastal environment and ecology.

Oil from ships is but a portion of the total. Just as important is pollution from coastal refineries, municipal wastes, urban and river run-off and offshore production, all of which are most harmful in that they too are discharged in a concentrated form into the shallow and ecologically sensitive coastal areas. Suffice it to say, lest we get too far afield, until some political will is exerted by the maritime interests and coastal nations to curb the mesmerizing effect of oil on the western world as well as the developing nations, the future looks bleak.

Table 1: Comparison, Oil Tanker Dimensions and Capacities

	SS *Elk Hills*	SS *Ardshiel*	SS *Univiran*
Overall length (feet)	523	1063	1133
Extreme breadth (feet)	68	158	170 (est.)
Carrying Capacity (tons)	16,500	206,000	327,000

Table 2: Oil Tanker Spills, 1967-1989

Ship	Date	Gallons Spilled	Cause Given
Torrey Canyon	3/18/67	35 million	Grounding
World Glory	6/13/68	13 million	Hull Failure
Sea Star	12/19/72	34 million	Collision
Argo Merchant	12/15/76	8 million	Grounding
Amoco Cadiz	3/16/78	66 million	Grounding
Atlantic Empress & *Aegean Captain*	7/19/79	88 million	Collision
Burmah Agate	11/1/79	11 million	Collision
Castillo de Beliver	8/ 6/83	73 million	Fire
Exxon Valdez	3/24/89	11 million	Grounding

Chapter Thirteen
The Neptune Party

Passenger ships and troop transports were the bane of my existence. Other than the SS *President Madison* that weaves its way throughout this document, I tried to avoid them with singular un-success. Before the war, there was a lively, well-scheduled series of passenger runs to Hawaii, South and Central America, the Orient and a few round-the-worlders. There were also a smaller series of ships on regular runs up and down the coast, such as the SS *H. F. Alexander* and the *Ruth Alexander* as well as commute runs between San Francisco and Los Angeles on a pair called the SS *Harvard* and the SS *Yale.* Those were the Prohibition days of the early 1930s, so, as soon as they got out past the three-mile limit, out came the liquor. The old timers referred to them as floating whorehouses.

There also were the American President Lines going around the world and to and from the Orient, as well as the Matson Line and its four white ships on the Hawaiian and Australia-New Zealand run. Passenger ships (not to be confused with combination cargo-passenger ships) are exactly what they say they are. Their purpose in life is to carry, coddle, pamper and cater to the whims of, and make money from passengers. Any cargo involved in their operation had to do strictly with stores and baggage, which for the most part, were handled through side ports.

There was no special breed of seafaring man who sailed passenger ships. In fact, some of the best sailors on the West Coast plied these runs. It was rather a matter of personal predilection. Many of them were heavy gamblers; others just loved Hawaii and the Orient. Some of them were married there. Also a few of my friends on those runs used opium from time to time and were only able to obtain it and use it undisturbed in the Orient.

Passenger ships also contained some jobs not found on freighters such as quartermaster and watchman. The former refers to manning the ship's helm or wheel. He stands a full four-hour watch at the wheel, relieved only midway through the watch for thirty minutes, usually by an AB. The watchman works nights only and patrols the entire ship, passenger stations and all and punches his time clock at each station at prescribed intervals. In certain instances, there is an understanding to allow older members to have these jobs; in fact, the watchman's job was limited to those sixty years of age or over or with a physical disability. There was at least one older sailor who lost an arm in a shipboard accident and he was given special dispensation by the membership to ship as watchman.

We have all heard lots of stories about romances at sea. There were some men around the union hall known as "Don Juans," who supposedly got their reputations on these particular runs. Since lots of sailor's stories fall into the category of "sea stories," which escalate in embellishment in direct ratio to their repetition, I would venture to take them with a rather large grain of salt. It is a matter of known fact that passengers and crew are kept at a long arm's length. If at any time, work is required to be done in the passengers' rooms, a ship's officer (usually a member of the purser's staff) must accompany the crewmember. Since there are very heavy penalties involved in the apprehension and conviction of a trespasser, rendezvous are few and far between. What goes on in and among the passengers themselves is another story.

This whole subject is now somewhat moot since, as of this writing, there are almost no passenger ships with a West Coast port of registry. That means that there is no passenger trade running under the American flag out of any West Coast port. There are quite a few passenger runs to

Alaska and Mexico and points south, but they are all under foreign flags. The laws covering Cabotage (coastwise trade) do not permit foreign-flag ships to trade between American ports.

✳✳✳✳✳✳✳✳✳✳✳

When World War II came upon us, all passenger ships available as well as many large freighters were converted into troop transports. Throughout the war years, I tried to avoid troop transports like the plague. On those few unlucky occasions that I could not avoid it most of the crew and I had a pretty miserable time of it. On a transport, not unlike a passenger ship but a little more so, the crew is relegated to second-class citizenship. The "little more so" has to do with the fact that the branch of the service being transported, in the nature of things, sets up its own internal rules and procedures, many times out of all context with the requirements of the ship at sea.

Any and almost every GI who had to go overseas during the War got there by transport. Today, it's different; you usually get there by air. But then, some of the most fancy passenger ships were converted to transports, which in turn became the nucleus of a large variety of converted freighters, and together they managed to solve the logistics of getting all hands overseas. One of the war's first big tragedies in the fall of 1942 was the loss of what was the most fancy, if not the newest, first-class passenger ship on the West Coast, the SS *President Coolidge*. At the entrance to the harbor of Espiritu Santo in the New Hebrides, she struck two American mines. Amazingly, of the some 5,400 souls aboard, only four GIs and one merchant seaman, a fireman in the engine room, were lost.

When the passenger ships were converted, time permitting, they were stripped of their finery which was in turn stored in company warehouses. But this wasn't always feasible. In many instances, only the furniture and possibly some expensive Oriental rugs were salvaged. The fancy mahogany railings and banisters remained, eventually falling victim to a display of the whittler's art. By the time the last GIs were repatriated, these highly varnished exotic woods were a mass of carvings identifying the initials and point of origin of the artists, in their attempt to bestow immortality on themselves. For the most part, the urban moron and rural idiot from Brooklyn and Texas respectively didn't show very good judgment.

Life aboard the transports was ugly for the GIs as well as the crew. The crew, that basic unit required for the operation of the ship, was augmented by a gun crew proportionate in size to the ship's capacity and function. This crowded us even more. For the most part, as stated previously, the GIs came aboard with their own field kitchen and stores and policed themselves. The merchant crew tried to be as unobtrusive as possible, but this didn't always work. In many instances we saw the conditions which we gained over a period of years of struggle erode away while young shave-tail officers, fresh out of Officers Candidate School, would grab the former staterooms and commandeer the poop deck (that is, the after deck which traditionally belonged to the crew) for their own purposes. In at least one instance, they took some of our stores away and our complaints fell on deaf ears. All this must be understood against the fact that although we were civilians, we were under military authority.

The MV *Laura Maersk,* mentioned earlier, was an interesting case-in-point in that she was a foreign ship belonging to the A. P. Moeller Line out of Copenhagen. When Hitler invaded Western Europe, rather than risk capture, the Allied powers ordered all their ships to put into the closest American port. They were then turned over to American companies to operate for the duration.

Their crews, for the most part members of various transport unions in Europe, were immediately given books and membership in the Sailors' Union as well as in the other West Coast unions. So far so good.

But the crews were not given citizenship, not that they wanted it, since they all intended to return home at war's end. It's just that they felt inhibited from expecting the same rights and privileges as their American counterparts. And in that mode, they accepted lots of unnecessary abuse. As of the moment, I was the only "foreigner" aboard, in that I was the only American citizen. As time went on, however, the crew started changing and when I last heard about her after VE-Day, only a few from the original crew were left. In fact, quite a few of them got married here.

Within a few hours after I boarded, we set out for San Diego where we picked up about two thousand marines, mostly fresh out of boot camp. They were led by a grizzled, dirty-talking Colonel and eventually deposited in Wellington, New Zealand, the logic of which escapes me to this day. We were no sooner outward bound to the South Pacific, when the Colonel came up to the bridge and started telling the skipper all about everything he wanted. If this ever happened to an American skipper, I have no doubt that the old man would order him off the bridge. In this case, it didn't happen. The skipper, a most decent type, feeling vulnerable under a "foreign" flag, couldn't get rid of him. It seemed that the Colonel wanted daily reports about positions, covered distance, and anticipated weather—none of it his business and furthermore, in the language of the times, a breach of security. In order to appease him, the skipper got the Third mate to send him extracts from the ship's log. I remember feeling terrible about the whole incident.

The second day out to sea we experienced a situation that all seafaring people dread most: one of our diesel engines caught fire. The skipper immediately sounded the General Alarm, which should have warned the Colonel to get all his troops out of our way so we could stretch our hoses as necessary. But this was too much for the old bird. He immediately started assigning all his junior lieutenants to line up details to start "helping" us. As luck would have it, since they didn't know what to do, they allowed us to man the hoses.

The engine room was midship and in order to prevent the steel decks and plates of the midship house from buckling due to the intense heat, we started pouring water on them to try and keep them cool when our attention was diverted to lots of scuffling on the boat deck above us. As it turned out, the Colonel had ordered a contingent to stand by the boats and to launch them if necessary. Launching a boat, though not an overwhelming science, does require some knowledge, especially in a choppy sea. Later, we all asked ourselves what would have happened if they tried and lost them, a distinct possibility. The final outcome was that the engineer on watch cut the engine out and so the oil stopped feeding the fire, and fire extinguishers did the rest.

In describing an out-of-control type situation, seafaring men inherited an expression from the peacetime Navy: "Like a Marine at fire and boat drill." Apparently, on the pre-war battlewagons, the U.S. Marine complement, the policemen of the Navy, usually didn't know where their fire and lifeboat stations were, nor what to do when they got there. Consequently they ran around all over the place, helter-skelter, trying to fit in. This was a near-perfect example.

On all transports, crews automatically try to keep their distance from the "passengers." However, in walking back and forth to and from the bridge or lookout on the focsle-head, or handling the ship's gear in the normal course of the working day, it is almost inevitable that some contact is made; a word or two is exchanged about how things are going, about the work being done. It wasn't very long before we began picking up some information (G-2 they used to call it) that things weren't quite so lovey-dovey between the Colonel and his officer caste, and the troops down in the holds. In fact, there was lots of grumbling and discontent.

One day, on deck back aft during a lull in the work, one of the GIs snuck back and started questioning us about the Equator crossing ceremony, known as a "Neptune Party." Without belaboring the point, on occasion, there were such things to put on a show for the passengers, but on freighters in those days, these rituals were never observed. I, for one, by that time had crossed the Equator about a dozen times but never participated in a Neptune Party, though the old timers told me lots of stories. We told this guy what we knew and forgot about it when much to our surprise, a few days later and about a day before we got to the Equator, word got around that a big Neptune Party was scheduled for the next day at high noon.

What happens to a large group of men in forced confinement for from ten to twelve days, sea-sick for about half of the time, nearly all of them having just survived boot camp as only the Marines can do it, away from home for the first time, and harboring a grudge against a half-crazed Colonel who won't leave them alone? As I say, when given an opportunity for retaliation, what with a slow-burning fuse of built-up resentment, something had to give and something did. There are many ways to settle old scores.

At the appointed time, two lines were formed on both sides of the deck, fore and aft. From out of nowhere, there materialized a huge pile of wooden staves, about two feet long and four inches wide, one end shaped into a handhold. (Chips later told us that the committee stayed up all night in the shop getting this done.) The object was that if you wanted to be "baptized" a true "old salt" and receive a certificate from the Colonel attesting thereto, you have to run the gauntlet. The GIs went first and it wasn't so bad. Buddies beat each other's rumps, as they exchanged positions, the beaters becoming the "beatees." Then came the officers' turn to go through and that was just what they were all waiting for. The results were gruesome and quite a few wound up in sickbay looking like "The Spirit of '76." What started out as a playful extra-curricular activity, to eat up some time hanging heavy on everyone's hands, ended as a near massacre. Luckily, the Colonel put an end to it as soon as everyone got their licks in, for as we later found out, they had a full program arranged for the rest of the day.

Through the years, as I reflected back on this scene, I realized that all this was going on at about the same time all of Europe was in flames; Hitler was perpetrating his Final Solution and the Japanese were committing atrocities against civilians. The type of brutality was different but the underlying inhumanity was the same.

✳✳✳✳✳✳✳✳✳✳✳

Transports were also used in repatriation. After VJ-Day, there was a concerted movement on the part of the GIs to get home real fast. It seems there was a short period after the war where the powers-that-be in Washington were dragging their feet. Scholars allude to the fact that there was a school of thought that wanted an American show of force to remain in the Pacific against a possible threat from the Russians, as well as a possible counter against the Chinese Communist moves on the mainland. This probably must be the least investigated area in our post war history and to this day, there is hardly any research and/or scholarship devoted to this important problem. Whatever it was, the "natives were getting a little restless," and large protests started up in Manila, as well as various bases and islands, when things were moving too slowly in getting the GIs back.

When things finally were settled, and the repatriation started up in earnest, I caught the SS *Sea Cardinal*, a C-4 type freighter converted to a troopship. The "C" designation referred to a cargo ship and the number to its size in terms of tonnage capacity. The C-4 was the largest built during the war, bigger ones coming much later. We took the ship over empty and brought back a few thousand GIs from Manila. The trip going over was uneventful and routine but coming back, we were treated to a lesson in pure waste.

Many around the world have commented to me that the American serviceman was probably the best-dressed soldier who ever lived. Those who had occasion to either wear or just feel the quality of the material in either work or dress uniform, clothing and shoes, will testify to the veracity of that claim. As for merchant seamen, they buy regular work clothes ashore and it's no better or worse than what money ordinarily buys. But GI clothes, regardless of color and however drab, are of superior quality. Most seafaring men in those days prized a good Navy blue pea coat for standing a cold lookout. We also prized a good pair of work shoes, like those issued by the Army. During the war, it was only by accident that a merchant seaman could obtain GI clothes.

The "repatriation syndrome" was exactly 180 degrees opposite of the "you're in the Army now" syndrome. In the latter state you were under military discipline and did what you were ordered to do, albeit grudgingly. In the former state, the tide had turned. All the way back, there was a bare minimum amount of orders given for anything. The officers and men gave each other wide berths. Going about our business, the crew, as usual, kept to ourselves. From time to time, however, we noticed an interesting thing. The soldiers were tossing clothes over the side. As days passed, the amount of clothes disappearing increased to the point that a big party was declared in which a huge mountain of clothes was built up on deck, and the next day, everyone piled in and vied with each other as to who could confine the most clothes to the deep. It was like an orgy; they couldn't get enough of it. Some of our Stewards Department crew, who lived in San Francisco's Chinatown and had the proper connections, tried rather valiantly to salvage what they could for their various shoreside enterprises, but to no avail. The stuff kept being jettisoned.

When we got the word to them that we consider some of this stuff valuable, they were quite nonplussed. They soon began allowing us to do some "rag-picking" and we managed to extract some good working gear, which in my case lasted me way into my new life ashore some years later.

When this whole escapade was over, the focsle psychologists concluded that the clothes were symbolic of their stint in the Army and the act of destroying the clothes was symbolic of not only what they thought of the whole thing but acted as a purgative to get it out of their system.

On a social level, this phenomenon is probably the mirror-opposite of human greed. In one instance you accumulate more and more of what you didn't need and in the other you waste and destroy what you got for free. All this is in sharp contrast to a world lying prostrate as a consequence of human insanity.

The tragedy of waste extends itself from peacetime to wartime, all the more so since all warfare is conducted in an atmosphere of human and material waste and expendability. A favorite story which made the rounds in the South Pacific had it that a diver was sent down to spot a recently dropped Sherman tank (they weighed sixty tons) so as to ascertain if it was salvageable. When he came back up he asked, "Which one?" War is hell and war is waste.

Among many other things, I also participated in most of the New Guinea campaign, from a landing on Morobe, a short overnight run up from Brisbane, Australia, to the invasion of Finschhafen (now called Jajapura in West Irian) and Hollandia. All this took about a year, and in my case, it was two trips of approximately six months each. In both instances, we took a brand new C-2 out of Moore Shipyard in Oakland, California, the SS *Flying Yankee* and the previously mentioned SS *Young America*. (Sailing ship buffs will immediately recognize both names as famous clipper ships of the nineteenth-century China trade.)

We did the same thing on both ships in maintenance and mission. When a ship is taken out on her maiden voyage, the coat of paint applied in the shipyard is "paper-thin." A second coat should be and was applied immediately. In addition, in their haste to ready the ship for use, ship-yards usually do the minimum in preparing the running and standing gear. This must also be attended to in the course of the maiden voyage.

In both instances, we transported U.S. Navy CB's (Construction Battalions). These troops were unique in that their mission was not so much to fight but rather to build. In the two groups that we transported, there was enough talent in each of them to build anything from a chicken coop to a skyscraper. Just about every one of them was a tradesman and almost all of them were members of one or another AFL craft union. Their average age was thirty rather than twenty among the fighting men. They were invariably married men and many of them had children. In talking to them, one immediately elicited a more critical view of things as well as intelligent comments about the war, their officers, and just about anything else worth talking about.

In the nature of things, there wasn't much enemy action to worry about, since they came ashore only when an area was secure or being mopped up. Usually, the first thing they did was lay down an air strip in record time. Then they would start building quarters from the material carried in by the cargo planes, and then roads, and so on. In one instance after a certain landing, for some reason or another the word came down to start building officers' quarters first. This immediately angered them and they practically declared a strike, until the base commander rescinded the order.

The United States was the "arsenal of democracy" and that meant that America was responsible for almost all of the production of material and ordinance it took to fight the war. Anyone spending any time at all in the South Pacific, island hopping from New Guinea on up, must have been struck by the enormous amount of material waste that went on. At one point, I saw an open field of over one hundred brand-new jeeps, never touched and rotting in the equatorial sun. The natives, somewhat akin to Rudyard Kipling's "fuzzy-wuzzies," stripped the side and rear-view mirrors and walked around admiring themselves. They also stripped the seat cushions and placed them on their heads to balance the loads they carried. As the troops made their way up, all kinds of material became expendable. The story told above was apropos of many other things, not just Sherman tanks.

Once, when picking up our anchor so as to get under way, the windlass began to audibly strain as if a weight was holding it back. We kept clear of the bow as link after link of anchor chain came up through the hawse pipe, ever so slowly, and as it began to break out of the water, we suddenly realized what happened. An enormous contraption, still half crated, was impaled, as it were, on the fluke of the anchor. It was identified immediately as an entire spare airplane engine. We tried every which way to shake it off but it hung on tenaciously. So one of the CB's volunteered to swing over the side on a bosn chair and burn it off with his torch.

So what happened to all that good stuff that remained behind, bought by our Victory bonds and taxes? Focsle historians, depending mostly on eyewitness accounts (anecdotal evidence again) have put together the following scenario: as soon as VJ-Day was declared, a swarm of merchants and businessmen with connections to the Chinese Kuomintang Party and Nationalist government, swept through the South Pacific and bought up everything they could, a few cents on the dollar. They then turned around, collected the stuff on leased Liberty ships and sold it to the Chinese Nationalist government so as to fight the Communists (Mao Zedong and the Chinese Red Army,) expedited, to be sure, by American foreign policy and monetary "grants" to help in the effort. The Chinese communists immediately captured the material from the demoralized Kuomintang troops and used it to go on to victory in October 1949.

※※※※※※※※※※※

The concept of repatriation applies to the crew as well as the passengers. An important work rule in our union agreement had to do with repatriation. When a ship is joined on one coast and abandoned on another by the company, for whatever reason, transportation back to point-of-origin is mandatory. Before this agreement was made, the ship owners were in the habit of stranding the seaman wherever they pleased, whatever the reason. We put a stop to this when the Lend-Lease days started in 1940. Ship deliveries to the allied powers became common. Many West Coast ships were brought around to the East Coast and given over to foreign crews, thereby stranding the seaman on the beach in a place not of his choosing. In those days, there was no other way to get back except by train. Inter-coastal ships were practically non-existent, thereby foreclosing the chance to get a ship back, and flying was unheard of.

Such a situation occurred to me in the first year of the war, when we had to surrender a ship to the U.S. Navy in Baltimore, Maryland and were given transportation money back to the West Coast, at the time a flat fee of $125. With the system of priorities then in place, I managed to get out as far as Chicago. Getting from there to San Francisco was another matter. The train terminal was a seething mass of humanity, day and night. Thousands of soldiers and civilians poured in and out, all with pressing priorities. I remember speaking to people who were stuck in the terminal for a number of days.

Buying a ticket was also a problem, in spite of the fact that you had the money. Volunteers, usually elderly men and women, were organized to sit in depots and all civilian ticket requests were directed to them before you got to the ticket window. It was the volunteer's job to talk you out of the trip. Large signs appeared all around the station asking, "Is this trip necessary?" usually combined with the sneering remark by the volunteers, "You're old enough to be in the service, so why aren't you in uniform?" Most of these people unwittingly chose a nasty job for which to volunteer and soon disappeared when they realized that the legacy they left was lots of ill will after many stormy arguments.

As luck would have it, my wait was only twelve hours and I managed to get a train for the coast. Strangely there were no seat assignments, only car numbers, and I soon found out why. This was a troop train, with two thousand "dogfaces" and two civilians, an elderly lady in her sixties who played a mean harmonica, and me. It should be explained that merchant seamen have nicknames for all the other services, and I'm sure all the others have their share of nicknames too. In peacetime, a soldier was called a "dogface," a Navy sailor was called a "strawberry" and a marine was a "gyrene."

The image of a soldier in the eyes of a seafaring man was conditioned by his peacetime presence in the Panama Canal Zone as well as in Schofield Barracks and on Hotel Street in Honolulu. (For further reference into this matter, James Jones' *From Here To Eternity* would be an excellent start; the book as well as the film.) With the rapid expansion of all the services after Pearl Harbor, these appellations didn't hold water, since the services now contained a preponderance of draftees who were there to put in their time and go back to where they came from at war's end. Suffice it to say that what with two-thousand men, all with shaved heads, all dressed exactly alike, and all looking down in the mouth, they all seemed like dogfaces.

When we boarded the train we were in for a series of surprises, the first of which was that we would be sitting up all the way, on hard seats. The second was that the cars, vintage 1890, were illuminated by lamps designed for gas, and when converted to electricity, they kept the original fixtures which made the lighting miserable. The third problem was that there wasn't any dining car but there was a snack bar in every third or fourth car. By the end of the first night out, there weren't any snacks left. To compensate, the train stopped every four hours or so somewhere at a station, whereby some two thousand or so souls piled out, raided whatever supplies were available at the depot, ran around looking for liquor, and barely made it back.

The elderly lady, who was called Grandma, led the troops in song at various intervals during the day and halfway through the night. If you were tired enough you could sleep a little but not much. Her sole perk was the enjoyment of a personal toilet that the troops granted her. The troops were for the most part unruly. There were big card games all over and combined with the drinking, fights broke out at regular intervals, which ended after a few punches were traded.

After the first two days, I noticed another problem. As food was being consumed and beverage bottles emptied, the wrappers and empty bottles were beginning to pile up. In making one's way to and from the can, it became apparent that somebody had better start some KP. I spoke to a couple of sergeants (the ruling class) and they weren't too anxious to start new projects. The conductor and porter, if there were any, had long disappeared. So, in desperation, I took off on a trip through the cars, looking for a broom closet or anybody authoritative enough to help. As luck would have it, when I got to the last car, I found the conductor involved in a hot poker game. After explaining my problem, he took me to the corner of the car and miraculously produced a number of brooms, dustpans and some empty burlap sacks.

When I made my triumphant appearance back to the car, Grandma immediately put down her harmonica and began rolling up her sleeves. Together, we started from our seats and methodically began sweeping up all the debris into piles to eventually fill up the burlap sacks. It didn't take very long before the point was well taken and the soldiers jumped in and relieved us both of our jobs. They emptied the sacks at the very next stop and continued the operation all the way to the coast.

The best that we can say about this small incident in my life, is that it was an experiment in human relations that had a positive outcome. I have no illusions that this is a recipe for settling all human conflict, but in a state of semi-anarchy and with no communication going on, I took it upon myself to show, by power of example, that things can get done, albeit in a very small setting. True, both Grandma and I were prepared to do the whole job ourselves; but I, for one, banked on the fact that it would become contagious, and so it did.

✳✳✳✳✳✳✳✳✳✳✳

The subject of uniforms used to come up quite frequently during the war. Without going into an in-depth philosophical discussion, every organized society has to do with uniforms, especially in wartime. During the war, the tenor of the times was such that all young men from the ages of eighteen to somewhere in their mid-thirties should be in some sort of uniform. However, as a merchant mariner you were a civilian, and consequently did not rate a uniform. In peacetime, passenger ships demanded that the officers wear uniforms, essentially for the titillation of the cash customers. During the war there were no passenger ships, except for those that carried troops and/or civilian employees to and from Pearl Harbor and some Pacific islands. Merchant mariners, who felt uncomfortable in mufti, would invent a uniform and some of them were dillies, or, as they say it today, "weird." One thing was certain; they never showed up at the union hall wearing it more than once.

However, having said all of that, West Coast seafaring men did have a "uniform" of sorts. That is to say, a certain amount of articles of clothing, worn together and consistent in appearance and form, was adopted during peacetime on the West Coast among merchant sailors. It consisted of a gray hickory shirt, black Frisco jeans, black shoes, white socks, and a white cap known as a "Lunchbox Stetson." Unofficial to be sure, this uniform became a "trade mark" of West Coast seafaring men. Its origin is probably shrouded in antiquity, and I must say that when I inquired of many old timers as to its origin, "It was here when I got here," was the usual answer. As for the term "Lunchbox Stetson," it was a takeoff on our Secretary's name and his ethnic identity. Since America is the land of ethnic racism par excellence, it was always my belief that the "box" part of the name referred to "box-head," a common reference to Scandinavians. A favorite piece of ethnic derogation heard at the time was, "How much does the barber charge you per corner for a haircut?"

At first, some of the younger members felt a little lost without some sort of uniform. Those who came out of the Great Lakes Training Station and such places were already equipped with blue sailor uniforms, a la U.S. Navy. Almost all of them shed these uniforms after their first trip on merchant ships. They got the idea fast. The uniform was packed away for visits back home, if and when possible.

But the uniform, like the tattoo, makes a statement. It marks you as a member of an exclusive group. As my friend, Eric Hoffer, used to say about organizations, "It's there for keeping others out" rather than inviting them in. Some old-time East Coast friends of mine commented on the fact that West Coast sailors are more clannish and insular than East Coast sailors, who are more accepting, less clannish and more "brotherly." If that is true, then maybe there was a good reason why West Coast men adopted a "uniform," whereas this was not so on the East Coast and Gulf.

Whatever the reason, we're going to have to let the anthropologists argue it out. As for me, I'll always cherish the day I was able to walk into Joe Harris's famous clothing emporium on the San Francisco Embarcadero the first time I came ashore there, having drawn some money against my account, and purchased my very own first "uniform," complete from Lunchbox Stetson down to black shoes and white sox. After he allowed me to use one of his dressing stalls to try everything on, I walked out of there on Cloud Nine, a transformed person, a member of an exclusive fraternity, identified outwardly as a West Coast man, and inwardly as one who is playing a certain unique role on the stage of history, no less. For the sake of historical accuracy, I should add that a white shirt was substituted for the hickory one on Labor Day parades.

❋❋❋❋❋❋❋❋❋❋❋❋

Many people who think my past lurid, ask me whether I have any nice tattoos to show. Though I, myself, to the great disappointment of some of them, do not carry any, they would be highly embarrassed if they saw some of the more vivid ones I've seen adorning certain parts of the anatomy of some former shipmates. People, since time out of mind and to this very day, have had drawn on them pictures and various designs for whatever tribal reason. It could be that an element of this is present in our psyche. Like outward raiment, as mentioned above, it too makes a statement. I have been shipmates with many men tattooed with such statements. Interpreting them is hopeless; in fact, doing so would require an in-depth psychoanalysis for whatever it's worth. Limiting these observations to my own experience, I nominate a good shipmate and fine sailorman, one Twin-Screw Morgan for first prize.

Twin-Screw and I were watch partners on the aforementioned cockroach palace, the SS *West Celeron*. A recitation of his art gallery should give a museum curator pause to wonder. On his chest was a fully rigged bark under full sail. In the crook of each elbow and behind each knee was a door hinge approximately two-to-three inches in length. Various swords, daggers and snakes adorned his upper and lower arms with the words "mother" and "love" interspersed. On his feet above his toes was a rooster standing on one leg with the inscription, "I never crow;" and on the other leg a pig saying, "I never squeal." And as a piece de resistance, a three-pronged ship's propeller blade totally covered each buttock of his behind. Hence the appellation, "Twin-screw," referring to a type of ship that has two propellers, known in seafaring parlance as "screws."

A prize sea story of my day has it that a certain character had a bumblebee tattooed on the topside of his penis and when it became activated, it assumed the proportions of a bird of prey. These stories are heard constantly and vary only as to their original insect and resultant animal. One could logically argue that the artist deserves the plaudits. In fact, conversations in the focsle occasionally turned to comparing notes and trading information on tattoo artists in their respective ports.

After we got acquainted, I ventured to ask Twin-Screw about the artwork. His answer was, "I must have been needle punchy," implying a deep-felt desire to be stuck with needles. He further explained to me that he was a former "Asiatic," which means he was in the pre-war U.S. Navy's Asiatic Fleet "and went crazy with the rest of them." This was the Navy that came to an end at Pearl Harbor on December 7, 1941. After listening to my fair share of stories over the years, I came to the conclusion that almost all of my tattooed shipmates invariably, on second thought and after some calm reflection out at sea, reconsidered the wisdom of their pictorial displays and would think twice if they had to do it over again.

After his discharge in the mid-1930s, he became a circus and carnival roustabout and began helping the elephant trainers. He worked as an elephant trainer in some of the major circuses touring the country. In fact, there happened to be one in Seattle when we got there and he asked me to come with him to visit backstage and possibly see some old cronies. And sure enough, about half of the people there knew him. That day, I met my share of sideshow performers and carnival types.

Recalling one of our conversations, I asked him about elephants. "How do you guys make them do those tricks?" His answer startled me with its simplicity. "We beat the shit out of them." He gave me to understand that this was standard procedure if you want trained circus elephants. After a while, he drifted to Hollywood and got work on the sets. Soon he began handling all the heavy rigging and moving jobs at MGM. This makes sense in that this type of rigging is almost synonymous with ship's rigging. I dwell at length on this biography since it begins to show yet another of the type of people who gravitated towards deepwater merchant shipping. It was the war that finally brought him back to sea.

Chapter Fourteen
Wartime Accommodations

When World War II broke out, the new order of things created a difficult transition for the older seafaring man. A civilian industry operating under a signed labor contract with an employer and enforceable in a court of law was now placed under military discipline where labor contracts and courts of law did not apply. For example, no alleged violations of the contract were to be settled other than when you returned to homeport. By then, interest was lost and the offense was repeated on the next trip. For another thing, no mention of destination was permitted on the dispatcher's hiring board. Those of draft age were automatically frozen into the industry for the duration, and, as mentioned earlier, though we could use "job action" against the operators in the ever-present war that went on between us, we were not permitted the strike weapon.

An overall New Deal type agency, the War Shipping Administration (WSA), was imposed on the industry. It was made up of professional bureaucrats, former admirals and ship owner representatives charged with the franchise of seeing to it that the waterborne commerce and backup to the military, which is the first and foremost function of a Merchant Marine, should run smoothly and efficiently.

The sudden expansion of facilities, ships and manpower, especially the latter, forced the older members into making choices whether to put up with the new situation or just try to find something ashore in the sudden availability of related jobs. Interestingly enough, for the most part those few who had families chose to go ashore into shipyard work and those who didn't, stayed aboard.

Of all the colossal irritations and major calamities the war brought forth, the most pressing and immediate was the advent of guns and gun crews superimposed on a way and style of life that was hard to accommodate. The ships available did not increase in size but the guns were necessary for defense. The crews' quarters never expanded but the addition of twenty to thirty more hands was at the expense of an already crowded and confined situation. The WSA, in its turn, created an auxiliary bureau called "Recruitment and Manning Organization" (RMO), which proceeded to mount a national campaign to get kids off the farm and onto merchant ships. While this national recruitment campaign was going on, the U.S. Navy decided to start shipping special crews aboard merchant ships whose sole purpose was to man the guns. All sorts of ideas were put forth at the time to train the merchant seamen to qualify as gunners but to no avail. The admirals were not about to lose a new bureaucracy.

The qualitative change this made must be appreciated in light of the fact that whereas before I and maybe one other were the only raw first trippers on the first few ships I was on, this time over half the crew were first trippers, and it was extremely difficult teaching so many things on sailing day. The very handling of the booms and equipment was hazardous for the experienced hand under normal sailing-day conditions. Now, with so many raw recruits fresh off the farm or out of school, it became extremely dangerous. It was stated somewhere in this narrative that the accident rate in the workplace during the war was very low. It is to the credit of these RMO recruits that in the main, they responded intelligently to our teaching efforts.

But the business of the gun crews was another matter entirely. This group was regular U.S. Navy enlistees who were assigned to man the guns on merchant ships. They were approximately twenty to thirty young kids fresh off the farm with a thirty-day boy wonder Jr. Lieutenant as their officer. (This phenomenon refers to the instant commissioning of draft-age college students or recent graduates, who are put through a quickie course such as gunnery and consider them-selves overnight self-styled experts.) In all due respect to their knowledge of guns and gunnery, and not to detract in any way from their record of service in and out of convoy including many acts of heroism under fire, the end result left a residue of bad taste and feelings. For the fact of the matter was that out to sea, they, for the most part, displayed an innate propensity to mount guard on the mess room refrigerator. Also, it must be remembered that the living area on any ship does not expand in direct proportion to the quantity of bodies added to the crew. In fact they must be crowded into the already existing space.

Out to sea, there was very little for them to do but be confused and get in the crew's way. On General Quarters, as part of our fire and boat drill, all hands turned out anyway to help in manning and operating the guns, such as passing the ammunition. When the war was over, however, the entire problem disappeared. All these young kids went back to the farm, and I venture to hope that something had rubbed off on them and if so, they never were the same again.

❊❊❊❊❊❊❊❊❊❊❊

Fatalism seemed to be a most prevalent philosophy of life, if one could call it that, among seafaring people in that their basic idea about death was expressed in the succinct little formula, "When your time is up you're going to go, regardless of what you do." It could very well be argued that with a feeling like that, one can throw lots of caution to the winds and can afford to be reckless. The seafaring man looks at the world as a place where he is "rigged to lose," a favorite phrase often heard. When he comes ashore he must run an obstacle course of an array of sharks all out to part him from his hard-earned money. First in his pantheon of ratfinks are the "B" girls (defined earlier on) then the prostitutes, and following close behind, certain bartenders. As part of our lexicon, the phrase, "as cold as a whore's heart," was often heard. As for the bartenders, the best description often heard was: "Every two-bit piece he gets, he tosses up in the air. If it sticks to the ceiling, it goes to the house; if it comes down, it goes into his pocket." Then come the shoreside merchants and certain rooming house keepers. In the latter category, some rooming house keepers turned out to be the best of friends (but not many.) They would stake us for whatever it took until we could get out. Finally would come the former shipmate, now down on his luck and looking for a "piece-off." This means that he wants a few dollars from a "live one" to get by, now that he's broke, and will do the same for the "live one" when the worm turns. Since most seafarers understand that they could very well be on the receiving end next time around, they readily acquiesce.

In the category of women, all were divided into two types: "Nice" women and "bags." A nice woman was usually your mother, sister or pretty much any female family member back home. It could also include your rooming-house, housekeeper and a few others whom sailors deal with. A "bag" is any female the seafarer comes in contact with in and around a waterfront bar or related joints, not to speak of bordellos.

All this by way of the fact that soon after Pearl Harbor Day the powers-that-be came to the conclusion, under union pressure, that seafaring men should be granted life insurance just like the members of the armed forces. The first such policies were for $5,000, but with the alarming losses at the beginning of the war, it was quickly raised to $10,000. As mentioned earlier in this memoir, the merchant marine rate of loss during the war was staggering (more about this later).

As this began to take effect, a strange situation was uncovered in that some of the old timers who had no known living relative were naming certain beneficiaries who, upon investigation by the insurance companies, turned out to have been better known under such pseudonyms as "Muscatel Annie" and "Embarcadero Kate," to name just two. It was also discovered that some of our members were using our Secretary as beneficiary as well as the Sailors' Union itself. The Sailors' Union got to worry about this and soon an idea was advanced to form a "School of Seamanship," the seed money for which would be any money collected naming it as beneficiary. The result was the Andrew Furuseth School of Seamanship, named after our first Secretary.

The brilliance of this move answered a number of questions. Those kids off the farm, recruited by the RMO, were now funneled around through the school whereby they got some instruction in launching and manning a lifeboat, as well as some idea of what the deck gear is like. Along the way, they were taken aside and told about the union so that when they returned from their first trip, they would be asked to pay some dues and assessments, which would in turn eventually give them membership. The school served the further purpose of bringing some very knowledgeable older members into the process, since they acted as instructors. Other methods were soon found for enhancing funding for the school and it lasted through the Vietnam era. I understand there is one still functioning back east. This is an example of how side effects and fringe benefits can ensue from a widely unrelated cause.

Chapter Fifteen
Liberty Ships and Steam Schooners

A mong the many bragged-about heroes of the war, the Liberty ship seems to have captured much space and ink and churned out lots of hyperbole. Called "ugly duckling" and "floating bathtub," the Liberty ship was a product of standardized design, each one a replicated copy of the original with the possible exception that one might vary a few tons in gross tonnage from the other. It was based on an old British tramp-ship, worked over for the Maritime Commission by the old-time New York naval architect firm of Gibbs and Cox. Admiral Emory Land, a member of the Commission (of which more later) was reputed to have shown the basic design to President Roosevelt who commented, "She isn't much to look at, though, is she? A real ugly duckling."[11]

It was this simplicity of design that in no small way made these ships easy to mass-produce. The first of their kind, the SS *Patrick Henry*, was launched on September 27, 1941 at the Bethlehem-Fairfield shipyard at Baltimore, Maryland, and became operational exactly twenty-three days after Pearl Harbor. The organizational genius of Henry J. Kaiser, a well-known builder/contractor of the time, who had the Boulder Dam on his list of credits, was put to work to build a shipyard whose sole purpose was to turn out this basic bread-and-butter cargo hauler. This he did in Richmond, California, across the Bay from San Francisco. A standard joke of the times was a cartoon in the *New Yorker* magazine showing Kaiser standing on a launching platform with the usual ship owner's wife carrying a large bouquet of flowers in one hand, a bottle of champagne in the other, and saying, "But Mr. Kaiser, there is no ship here," and he answering, "That's okay, Madam, start swinging and it will be there."

Once Kaiser told some reporters that he was now launching a ship a day. When they challenged his statement, he invited them out to one of the three shipyards in Richmond and told them he would launch a ship in one day, from 8:00 a.m. to 5:00 p.m. And he did just that. What he didn't tell them was that he massed all the largest cranes at one dock and used them for the day to accomplish the job. Even so, it was formidable, if a bit flamboyant.

I used the phrase "bread-and-butter cargo hauler." It was shaped like a huge bathtub, and was certified to carry any kind of cargo up to some seven thousand tons. Having said this and recalling our discussion earlier on about Plimsoll marks, their usual load was somewhere around ten thousand tons. It could make every bit of ten knots and its engines almost never failed. One good reason for this was its tried and tested, old fashioned, three-cylinder, up-and-down reciprocating engine, fed by two oil-burning boilers, producing 2,500 horsepower. Most marine engineers will tell you that the reciprocating engine has some remarkable attributes, such as ease of availability, simplicity of operation and ability to obtain spare parts almost anywhere in the world.

These were the first large-scale, fully welded rather than riveted, such ships ever produced. In ship construction, all internal frames and bulkheads were riveted as well as the outer skin or plates, which were riveted in double rows both laterally and longitudinally. The innovation introduced by Liberty ship construction was that all outer plates were welded with the inner remaining riveted. There must be one exception made in that 384 Liberties on special order for some European Allies were outer-riveted. Yes, there were some flaws in the welding, but other than one or two mishaps, they always came through. All told, some 5,000 ships were built between 1942 and 1945 and approximately 2,750 of them were

Liberties built in eighteen different shipyards from coast to coast. The observation has been made that other than minor design features they were not much different than their predecessors of World War I, the Hog Islanders, all built in one shipyard. All of which recapitulates the old walnut that all wars are fought with the weapons of the previous one. However, since the function of the merchant marine in wartime is to supply the armed forces with men and material, then the Liberty ship did the job. A comparison of their essential dimensions with the Hog Islander and later-day Victory ships would be useful:

	Hog Islander	Liberty	Victory
Overall length (feet)	390	441	455
Extreme breadth (feet)	54	57	62
Molded depth[12] (feet)	28	37	38
Gross tonnage[13]	5,000	7,176	7,600
Number built	122	2,750	597
Cost per ship (millions)	$1.9	$1.7	$2.5

There are some interesting facts about the Hog Islanders that should also be mentioned.[14] The U.S. Government built the shipyard at a cost of $65 million and sold it to the city of Philadelphia after World War I for $3 million. All told, it was in use for three-and-one-half years. Then the federal government, having built 122 ships at an approximate cost of $1.9 million per ship, sold off the fleet that had remained mostly intact, in some instances for as little as $35,000.

Today, things are different. For one thing, ships and trips are faster. Turnarounds are quicker than they ever were. Also, ships are much larger. As of this writing, the largest American freighter is the MV *President Truman* at 903 feet in length and with a 129-foot beam, thereby making her too large to transit the Panama Canal. It also has a 42-foot draft requiring that most harbors of the world must effect special dredging operations to allow her to dock. Another example is the MV *Marchen Maersk,* some 965 feet long and probably the largest freighter in the world. Its interior is air-conditioned and it has a swimming pool on its top deck. It is a fully automated ship and carries a crew of fifteen. (You will recall my first ship, an old rustbucket, half the size and carrying a crew of forty.) Last but not least, many married couples as well as some single women are now sailing together in various capacities and ratings. All this is for the better and tends to take the edge off. The same problem of learning to give each other some space remains, except that now it requires mutual respect between the sexes.

One other instance is worth noting. My old union newspaper, *West Coast Sailors,* arrived today and the following item appears in the President's Report. It reports that the Matson Navigation Company,

... has a ship on the drawing board that they could start building in an American yard later this year. This diesel ship with a 21-man crew would be 785 ft. long. ... It would have two houses, one forward for the mates and one aft for the Engineers and unlicensed crew. Each seaman would have his or her own room, 20 ft. by 12 ft., with big windows. Beds would be fore and aft, 80 inches by 44 inches. The ship would have all the modern conveniences.

Never in my wildest imagination would I have hoped to see anything like this. But the irony of it all should not be lost when we realize how few jobs are left.

❋❋❋❋❋❋❋❋❋❋❋

Shipping on a deepwater ship takes place under different circumstances. Many seafaring men follow certain runs. Some will ship only to the Orient and others will sail only coastwise. Some known as "fair weather sailors" never go past Hawaii or Central America. While the great majority of the membership sailed offshore, a small percentage of contracts covered runs like the Alaska trade out of Seattle and the Catalina Island run out of San Pedro. Both these runs were specialized, seasonal and highly remunerative. And as these particular runs developed, so did a certain group of seafaring men become associated with them in these ports. This in turn led to a "homefront" group who settled down in their respective areas, married, raised families, built homes and joined the American dream.

Socially desirable as this may seem, it led to large political problems. Suffice it to say, rather than get too far afield from these memoirs, the leadership of our union consolidated itself into power by the judicious use of these shoreside/home-front groups. They became not only clannish but were always available as the backbone for strategic votes when necessary.

It is rather difficult to pinpoint exact dates when changes began taking place. Like everything else, it was a process. My own particular recollection is that soon after the war got under way, sometime toward the end of 1942, our secretary stood up at a regular Monday night meeting in San Francisco, and in what started out as a rambling discourse about the new order of things, began voicing a litany of complaints, such as a lack of old timers in the hall to help in job actions when and if necessary to enforce the Agreement, the overwhelming and sudden influx of "new kids off the farm who didn't know their ass from a hole in the ground" or thirty-day boy wonders "who didn't know a backstay from a mainstay."

The upshot of it all was the punch-line, a point of view not heard before and expressed in his usual rather concise matter-of-fact manner:

"Some are willing but not able and some are able but not willing," to serve on the various committees, to be available to jump aboard non-union ships quickly so as to get them under contract, to work behind the counter and collect dues, and to help the dispatcher when it gets real hectic. In short, what with all these problems mounting up and multiplying, he asked for extraordinary powers to take over and delegate authority to those whom he saw fit, when and if necessary. Needless to say, he got his way with a quick motion and second from the floor and an even quicker voice vote; all very legal according to Roberts Rules of Order. And so it came about that our secretary, in all due respect, could do anything he pleased and had no one to answer to. This, regardless of how fine a Constitution we had, and how democratic we thought we were, is the way things became.

Also, there was a thing called "stand-by work" where shoreside companies who serviced merchant ships in port hired crews from the Hall for so many days in order to bring a ship up to sailing-day requirements. These, too, developed a tendency to make their livelihood from this work and consequently take root ashore in the same manner as those on the specialized runs. This type of work was known as "stand-by work," that is, you pick up a few days' work while waiting for your shipping card to mature or join a permanent gang, if the opportunity presents itself. This permanent gang became part of the "home front."

One of the best of the specialized runs, year round rather than seasonal, was the coastwise steam schooner trade mentioned earlier. Sailors working steam schooners made more money than their offshore counterparts and attracted those who liked this type of work. After a time, they became settled into a way of life that brought them home more often. This then is how a settled shoreside sailor developed.

In the days when sail was harnessing wind power as the common means of locomotion at sea, immediate decisions and actions were required relating to sudden changes in wind and current. It was entirely both possible and probable to be called out, all hands that is, any time of the day or night, either to take in or let out more sail. In many instances, there was no other power other than hand power to do the job. The application of human labor power to the end of a line became known as "Norwegian steam."

As time went on and real steam replaced sail, the old habits persisted. The phrase was used a lot on prewar ships, in a semi-kidding, semi-derogatory manner to signify all those who would rather pull on a line than take it to a winch, and does not apply exclusively to any one people. When Americans started plying the coastwise steam schooners, they met their foreign-born counterparts and predecessors. The American native-born insisted on using machinery to haul with rather than brute strength. It took a little getting used to but they finally won out.

In the beginning, most steam schooner crews were almost entirely made up of foreign born, mostly sailing-ship men of the various Scandinavian nationalities. Little by little, the native born started sailing them and by the war's end, most of the prewar old timers disappeared. There wasn't much navigation required either, since almost all the skippers, also Scandinavian, took bearings on well-known landmarks "through the wheelhouse door," as it was said, and they never missed a landfall. Furthermore, neither I nor any steady or casual steam schooner man I ever met saw a skipper or mate use a sextant or take a sight while out to sea! In fact, I had an old skipper tell me that the last he saw of his sextant was his grandson playing with it on the living room floor on his last visit home.

When sailors came to their homeports, they were able to arrange time off and equitably divide the work. Watches were rotated at specific intervals and just bare maintenance was carried out. But the work in port was hard. Whether loading or discharging lumber, each load was made up, one length at a time, that is, handling each board individually. You worked your hatch around the clock, discharging and reloading, whereas the longshoremen switched gangs every eight hours. Most sailors worked on them for a certain given amount of time and then quit for a rest.

It was the same on the Alaska salmon run, where the season started around May 1 and ended before Columbus Day. This date was mandatory, for, as the natives used to say, "If you're not out of Kotzebue Sound (above Nome) by Columbus Day, you might as well get yourself a squaw and shack up for the winter." The port becomes icebound and remains so until the following spring. Another way of putting it also heard:

Visitor: What do you people do up here all year?

Native: In the summer time we fish and make love; in the wintertime it's too cold to fish.

The Alaska run was almost similar to the steam schooner run except that it took place in Alaska during the salmon season. The focsle maritime historians record the fact that many of the sailors alternated between both. After September/October, the Alaska stiffs would start shipping on the steam schooners. Before the hiring hall, some favorites always managed to get back on the schooners almost immediately without losing a day's pay. Of course, a cask of salmon bellies passed to the mate helped considerably.

Immediately after the war, I had the good fortune to make the salmon season on a steam schooner, the MV *Square Knot,* out of Seattle. We carried general cargo up and loaded case salmon in all the outlying ports called "dog ports." These latter were nothing but improvised docks to which you attached yourself for a few hours and took whatever they had. As room became available, you filled up the space with case loads of canned salmon "nine high and a binder," which is to say that you stowed the cases nine high in two columns and placed a tenth case straddling the two. The tenth one was the "binder," and there was just enough space to cram it in.

You made your way up the Inland Passage, a breathtakingly beautiful trip. (If you're going to do it on the fancy passenger ships plying the trade, do it in the early spring or early autumn.) Eventually, you head out the Gulf of Alaska to Unimak Pass, an eternally fog-bound opening in the Aleutian Island chain, and thence Northeast to Bristol Bay, at that time one of the world's great salmon fishing grounds. You drop your anchor, the packing company barges come alongside, and the same process repeats itself. When the ship is loaded, you double back and visit some of the other dog ports on Kodiak Island and the Kanai Peninsula, doing the same thing, and thence back to Seattle.

The technology of the salmon industry is a subject unto itself. An entire packing plant is brought ashore in Bristol Bay and assembled in the form of an assembly line. It takes the fish in at the beginning of the line, and at the end a case of labeled canned salmon emerges. It was known in those days as the "Iron Chink," a derogatory term used to refer to the mostly Oriental men working the line. In my time it was mostly Filipino workers. The fishermen work in shifts of forty-eight hours out and twenty-four in. They fish in an open boat in some pretty miserable weather, and there is a quota to be made. If they come in short, that is to say, their hatch is not full, the company has the right to order them out again. If they come in with too much, that is, overloaded, they run the risk of going under. Back in pre-union days, the dock to which the fishermen brought their catch was controlled by a man with a "clicker" (a small meter held in the palm of the hand which clicked off the fish as they were unloaded from the fish hatch onto the dock gurneys). If for some reason your hatch was short or the clicker didn't record too well, technically they could make the fisherman go out again. It has been said that the clicker job, much sought after, went to the highest bidder and the recipient was able to build a mansion on the Puget Sound after one season.

In the mid 1940s, Italian fishermen out of Genoa were contracted out for the Bristol Bay season. They flew directly to Seattle and thence to Bristol Bay, worked all summer on a permit and flew back home after the last day of the season. Theirs was the miserable side of the job. Many a morning, we got up and found one or two small boats hovering around our stern, trying to untangle their nets, hopelessly enmeshed around our rudderpost.

Our end of the work was involved in loading and discharging the ship, and so we had to follow the catch. That meant that everything had to be done at once. It was a heavy, labor-intensive operation. Upon arrival at our first port, watches were broken and a rotational, round-the-clock system kicked in—twelve hours on and six hours off. Since all hands are required to tie up, some stay up and continue working so as to finish their twelve hours. But some of the ports have only a small amount to load, say a few hours of work, so if you're on watch, you remain awake and work it, and if not, you go below and get called back to cast off again after those few hours. You then proceed to the next dog port a few hours away and it starts all over again. Now, some one else catches a few winks. Eventually you get to Bristol Bay and you stay put on a regular twelve-and-six cycle until you're loaded, or they run out of salmon. In that case, you may go around to Kodiak Island to top off the load. In this way, regardless of how the watches fall, you can put in a lot of twenty-four-, forty-eight-, and I know of some seventy-two-hour stretches, relieved only by a few cat naps, or if you're real lucky, some six-hour breaks.

A can of salmon on your supermarket shelf weighs about one pound and there were twenty-four to a case. There were forty-eight cases to a pallet board, sixteen per layer and three layers high. This means that three of you in one corner of the hold must not walk, but run with a twenty-four

155

pound weight from ten to twenty feet and stow them nine high and a binder as explained above. In the interim, while you're stowing your load, the hook goes back to the dock or barge and it picks up a load for the other side of the hold where the other watch is waiting. In other words, the hook is in continuous movement in and out of the hold and stops only if there is an accident or they run out of salmon or the hatch is full.

In thinking back on all this, there was no saving grace to this type of schedule, except that you could make a lot of money in a short period of time. We should also add that the food was constant, and top quality around the clock. Each coffee break every two hours, as I recall, was a meal in itself; all sorts of coffee cake, rolls and sandwiches. Each meal, and there was one every four hours, offered t-bone and sirloin steaks. I don't quite know how it happened, but some shipmates actually gained weight on this run. On balance, the fundamental memory we take away with us is that steam-schooner work, whether coastwise or on the Alaska run, was damned hard work for everyone: monotonous, boring and back-breaking.

Before I leave this subject, I would feel remiss if I didn't enter an encomium for the pilots who navigated through the inland waters. They joined the ship in Seattle and left before heading out the Gulf, taking us through the rather narrow and labyrinthine passages. In one instance, at night in thick fog, the pilot came over to me at the wheel and said, "You know, we must be awfully close because I smell skunk. Move over three degrees." Sure enough, within seconds, with the wheelhouse door open, I caught a small whiff of it. That too is part of navigation.

Chapter Sixteen
A Study in Darkness

In art I pack no highbrow stuff;
I know what I like and that's enough.
W. W. Woollcott, 1877-1949

He knows all about art but he doesn't know what he likes.
James Thurber, 1894-1961

When the war was under way for about a year or so and I was waiting for a ship in San Francisco, my old aforementioned shipmate and well-known old timer, Tom Hookey, who was doing some work in the front office, called me aside one day and asked me if I knew anything about art. It seemed that a certain habitue of North Beach (the Bohemian and Italian ethnic quarter of San Francisco at the time) who claimed to be an artist as well as a former sailing ship man, wanted to know whether the Sailors' Union was interested in a mural depicting the seafaring man and the war effort. And as the scuttlebutt would have it, he further understood that there was some money around that had been bequeathed to the "Andrew Furuseth School of Seamanship" from whence ostensibly his fee would derive. Tom asked me to come into the Secretary's office and meet the artist, ask some questions and add to the interview. The artist, whose name I have since forgotten, specified that he would paint mostly ships in action battling the elements as well as enemy gunfire. He envisaged a series of five murals to be mounted in our San Francisco dispatch hall and, as I recall, to be delivered in one year.

After some discussion, he invited us up to his studio to look at some preliminary sketches. The committee had now expanded to five and the Secretary's parting shot was that if we knowledgeable ones thought it was okay, then he'd recommend it to the membership. This committee of five, made up of Tom, myself and three other would-be-connoisseurs, all issuing the usual disclaimer, "I don't know much about art but I know what I like," together, appeared at the appointed time the next afternoon at his studio. As to the identity of the other three, I have luckily forgotten their names but I do remember that one was a "Sunday painter," like Eisenhower and Churchill, and the other two, I later discovered, were both color-blind.

In response to our knock, the door opened and there in front of us was a breathtakingly good looking blonde, dressed in a somewhat abbreviated ensemble modeled exactly after the pin-up heroine of World War II, Betty Grable, whose countenance and body adorned every red-blooded GIs locker the world over. She ushered us into a living room and there was the artist standing in front of what could only be described as an improvised bar with all the necessary accoutrements. And along the wall were the preliminary sketches for our perusal. I have to say that we all got a pretty good look at the preliminary pencil sketches and they looked more like on a par with Anton Otto Fisher (in those days the illustrator of the famous Glencannon stories of the *Saturday Evening Post),* than Winslow Homer.

And as the drinks kept coming and the conversation swung all around the world on and off sailing ships (Tom was a sailing ship man) and as the flashy blonde with the classy chassis, as they used to say it, saw to it that no glass ever stayed empty, the sketches became more and more vivid and our imaginations took flight. We all realized that this would be a great work of art, both authentic and aesthetic, and so we informed our secretary. The work was commissioned and the artist retained. The one-year promised delivery became two, and after a whole series of dunning phone calls, the murals were ready for unveiling.

Another thing seafaring men like is that when important things break, they are out to sea. However, in this case, I very much wanted to see the final result. So, approximately three months after the great unveiling, I returned from a trip and the very next day I ran up to the Hall to view the long-promised work of art. And there on the wall were the five murals as promised, but all I saw was a study in darkness with some things that looked like ships scattered around. The only illumination on the canvas was bits of silver colored objects that turned out to be tracer bullets. Some of the ships portrayed were in various stages of sinking with flashes of fire emanating from what could be considered blazing machine guns. (All American merchant ships were armed with anti-aircraft machine guns.) Some years later the pictures were moved to our new building and a special arrangement was created to throw more light on the subject, but to no avail. They remained almost totally obscure.

In the annals of psychology, there is a phenomenon called "retroactive rejection," which might be described somewhat as follows: An item or idea rides a wave of popularity or seeming acceptance but doesn't work out. It is then almost impossible to find anyone who says they were ever for it. In fact, all those who were for it now claim they were always against it. Even old Tom, when I looked him up in the front office, told me, "I never voted for anything like that." Since then, I have been told this happens to all great patrons of the arts. And before we leave the subject of art, it must be mentioned that some of the finest ship models ever carved were by sailors, and two of them adorn the entrance to our union hall, ensconced in specially built glass cases. May they last forever and outlive time itself.

Criticism is easy; art is difficult.

Philippe Nericault, 1680-1754

Chapter Seventeen
The Jungle Run

In recent years, historians have been looking into the question of the "day which will live in infamy," as F. D. R. euphemistically termed December 7, 1941. Was this an unprovoked attack? Who started it and why? Though it is not in the province of this narrative to deal with such matters, the fact is that many seafarers have their own theories on the subject, especially those who were actively sailing those waters at the time.

On or about the first week of October 1941, I shipped out of San Francisco on the previously mentioned SS *President Madison* in what was purported to be a short ninety-day round trip on the "Jungle Run," that is to say, China, Indochina and Burma via Honolulu and Manila. Our first stop was Honolulu and after a two-day layover, we headed out for Manila. Approximately five days into the run, and while relieving the quartermaster at the wheel at 2:00 a.m., the captain came into the wheel-house in his bathrobe, an altogether unexpected occurrence, and asked the mate on watch to change course and head back to Honolulu! After a quick few minutes' conference in the chart room, they gave me the new course and we turned the ship around. By breakfast time that morning the first pools were organized on the question of just what time the war would break out.

After a few days in Honolulu, where rumors flew around like mad and the whole town was talking about the turn-around, we set out again, this time on a more southerly course, to the Fiji Islands. (It should be noted that when we returned to Honolulu, I picked up a copy of the local newspaper on both days of our stay and there wasn't a single word mentioned about it on either day.)

When we finally got to Manila, I ran into two old shipmates on the beach who were doing so well, that they positively refused to believe that there was any danger. This feeling of security on their part was reinforced to a great extent by the fact that they were "shacking up" with a pair of island girls who were guaranteed to stand by their men so long as the money held out. These two men wound up as prisoners of the Japanese for the duration and returned after the war, shadows of their former selves. Both died shortly after repatriation. I look back on it now, realizing that the curative powers of elapsed time tend to cover up and soothe the guilt of the survivor. I kept thinking that had I applied a little more pressure in entreating them to stow away, a thing I could have easily accomplished, they would both be alive today, given the natural life span.

It is important to mention one more happenstance while on the "guilt of the survivor" subject. It was about Thanksgiving Day 1941 when we made it to Shanghai where we discovered that the sister ship of the *President Madison*, the *President Harrrison*, was there too. Since many members of both crews were well acquainted with each other, it was like homecoming week. On the day before December 7, when we both left Shanghai, our orders read to proceed to Balikpapan Borneo and their orders read, as we later discovered, to proceed North to Tientsin (a little closer to Japanese waters) to pick up the State Department legation and its marine guard. When we got back to the states, we were informed that the ship and crew were captured that next morning and interned for the duration, just as we were making it into Balikpapan. It was quite a few weeks after VJ-Day when they were repatriated and we were able to see them again. And as of this writing, pretty much all of those I knew are all gone. I can't help thinking to this day: What if the orders were reversed? I'm sure I would have survived, but I am also sure life would never have been the same. None of those I knew ever got over their time in captivity, and furthermore, that experience shortened their lives. Again, it's the luck of the draw.

Shanghai, then as now, was a thriving, vibrant metropolis with its extremes of wealth and poverty and its International Settlement, a private colonialist enclave where the British and French enjoyed rights of extraterritoriality. On the other side of the city, known as the Hong Kou side, there was, among other things, a detention camp for German-Jewish refugees, operated by the Japanese.

Jake Brose was one of those characters rarely found in the sea-going trades, an old country Russian Jew, who was brought to the United States as a baby and grew up on the lower East Side of New York City. Soon after World War I, escaping a miserable childhood, he ran away to sea and kept on going for the rest of his life. He died a few years ago in his early seventies. On the *President Madison,* he held the singular job of ship's painter; that is to say, he was responsible for the interior decoration of all passenger staterooms. But we all deal in many lives, some secretive and some open. Jake appointed himself a committee of one—and whoever wanted could join him—in establishing an unofficial underground railroad to spring as many of the refugees as possible from the camp on the Hong Kou side.

The Hong Kou side belonged to the Japanese as a result of the ongoing invasion of China that started in 1937. In the hiatus of time between then and the capture of the whole city soon after Pearl Harbor Day, the Japanese Army imposed their will on the native Chinese residents. It was easy to get into the area. You crossed a bridge and entered. However, stationed at the head of the bridge, at full and rigid attention, was a Japanese sentry, approximately five feet tall, armed with a rifle topped by a bayonet both of which together reached to about three feet over his head (or so it seemed). As each Chinese national approached the bridge, they were forced to stop, face the sentry, remove their hat and bow low from the waist. The sentry then nodded them on. It was a commonplace to see a Chinese septuagenarian doing obeisance to an eighteen-year-old Japanese soldier. All Europeans, that is, white people, were exempted from this ritual and waved forward. As we watched this little exercise, it wasn't too far-fetched to conclude that this was a symbolic kowtow, the real thing being the kneeling down and touching your forehead to the ground. Since this was impractical, the bowing—the deliberate imposition of an act of humiliation by the conqueror on the conquered—was substituted.

A French steamship company, operating out of Genoa, Italy, hauled German-Jewish refugees out of Central Europe around to Shanghai. They were stowed in the 'tween decks, not quite down in the bottom of the hold, but not in the midship house either. By the time of arrival, all their money and possessions were gone—with the possible exception of some Leica cameras—considering the fact that they had to bribe their way through Europe and the Nazi authorities, let alone purchase tickets for the voyage.

The Japanese opened up the camp, and anyone who could be vouched for by someone on the outside was free to leave and take up residence anywhere in Shanghai. Since many of the myriad bars and nightclubs could use "hostesses," this afforded many of the younger women an opportunity to get out. Eventually they brought their families out, who in turn even bought out some of the nightclubs. American tourists and sailors supplied the financial wherewithal for this operation.

Jake's role was equally simple. He helped supply some of the money and, through his "Chinese connections," set up a system to help smooth the way out. It was some years later that I learned, as I more or less surmised, that the "Chinese connections" were part of the opium smuggling underground of Shanghai, sometimes referred to as the "Green Gang." Jake liked opium and used it whenever he could get some. Looking back on it all, I seem to feel that he was drawn to the Orient and round-the-world run not only by his love of the people and things oriental, but also for its proximity to a pipeful of opium.

One day, Jake invited me to dinner with some people he had brought out the year before. We showed up promptly at 6:00 p.m., the family awaiting us. It was a rather well-appointed home with the usual amount of Chinese help at your beck and call from the moment you entered until you left. This family consisted of three people. The man of the house was a physician and his wife, according to Jake, was a "former opera singer." They had a daughter named Kitty, aged about twenty, rather undistin-guished looking and a bit on the plump side. We sat around and chatted amiably, enjoying a sumptuous Chinese dinner catered by the surround-ing help and, I venture to say, prepared by them as well.

The conversation ran to Western literature and art and other such lofty subjects. It didn't take me long to realize that the doctor and I were doing most of the talking, if not all of it, while Jake couldn't take his eyes off Kitty. Apparently, I was not only on display to this family but they were also on display to me. The evening was almost ruined when the mother decided to give us an example of her vocal ability with a rendition of Musetta's Waltz from *La Boheme*. It was awful.

When we left there and got a rickshaw back to the Bund, Jake decided to let me in on the problem. It seems that he got the family out of the camp because he took a shine to Kitty. The fact that she was half his age was of no consequence. However, she was "just dying to get to America." He offered to marry her so as to accomplish this almost impossible task and then "call for her family." Her parents, in the meantime, were anxious to know what these people Jake worked and associated with were like, hence the invitation of Exhibit A to dinner. The trip back to the ship was rather long since we had to traverse most of Shanghai and then take a boat out to the anchorage, all told about two hours. He talked almost all the way about his feelings on settling down and having a family. He said he liked Kitty and thought she'd make a good wife.

This was a family emanating from the upper areas of Viennese-Jewish society who spent their entire financial resources escaping Hitler and coming out alive in this part of the world; they were traumatically scarred and worried. They usually presume to speak in terms of high culture and look disdainfully at "Ost Juden," a derogatory term commonly used by German and Austrian Jews to refer to their East-European co-religionists, Jews who come from Russia and Poland, people of Jake's background. It seemed to me that though Jake's sentiments were of the noblest in trying to get them out of their trapped existence (a thought they voiced constantly) they would think long and hard before they would give away their only daughter, the apple of their eye, unless she really loved him. I somehow tried to convey these thoughts to him on the way back to our anchorage, but I got the distinct impression that he wasn't listening.

About ten days later, December 7, 1941, found us barely scampering into the Dutch East Indies after a high speed chase by the Japanese Navy, as mentioned earlier in this tale, thereby making moot the subject of Kitty for the next four years. Approximately a year after VJ-Day, I ran into Jake up at the union hall. This was the first we had seen of each other since we returned in early 1942 from that trip. Eventually, I ventured to ask about Kitty. Yes, he immediately grabbed a ship after VJ-Day and found her. She accepted the marriage proposal and came out within a few months. When she got to the airport, he asked her if she would give the marriage a chance now that they got this far. She said she'd think about it. The next day an aunt showed up from Chicago and took Kitty out for a walk. Jake never saw her again. About a week later the divorce papers were served. On Jake that is.

✲✲✲✲✲✲✲✲✲✲✲

As alluded to above, when we first came to Shanghai in the Autumn of 1941, there was no sign of any portended change in anyone's way of life from the International Settlement to the rest of the city with its myriad amount of street people, beggars, rickshaw pullers, prostitutes (from ten years old and up), waterfront workers and coolie laborers by the thousands, all with a life expectancy of thirty-five to forty years of age.

Before World War II, the very experience of a ship going up the Huangpu River, which joins the Yangtze where Shanghai is located, is in sharp contrast to the almost antiseptic treatment this same ship would receive about ten years later in say March 1950, about six months after Liberation, as the Chinese Communists called their victory in October 1949. The smell of victory was still in the air and it was about a month before the outbreak of the Korean War.

Before Pearl Harbor the world was different, especially in the Orient. Most seafaring men will remember the trip up the Huangpu River at its confluence with the East China Sea. Dozens of sampans and assorted craft would crowd around and jostle for position under the "slop chute" by the galley. Using long bamboo poles with butterfly nets attached to them, they would beg for whatever food was being thrown away that day. In fact, a popular ditty of the day, sung to the tune of "Let Me Call You Sweetheart," went somewhat like this:

> Meet me at the slop-chute on the old Huangpu,
> Bring along your dip-net, there'll be room for two.
> Dollar Line potatoes and American Mail Line stew,
> Meet me at the slop-chute on the old Huangpu.

Soon the pilot boat arrived with the Immigration and Customs authorities, known universally in those days and parts as "Ali Baba and the Forty Thieves," and a certain established ritual was executed which had been that way since time out of mind. The skipper had a few cases of good quality Scotch sitting in the middle of his cabin deck. All members of the crew had their lockers open, which included, among other things, the usual stash of sea-store cigarettes. In those days we got a carton of cigarettes for fifty cents, that is, tax-free. Every member of the crew, smokers as well as non-smokers, had about ten cartons or so on hand for both smoking and bartering purposes. It was the established custom, as part of this ritual, that Ali Baba got the Scotch and the forty thieves took no more than two cartons apiece out of each locker. After they were through "checking out the manifest and crew list," they adjourned to the galley and steward's storeroom and loaded up on just about everything that wasn't nailed down. Each thief came aboard with an empty gunny sack, and when the lot of them disembarked at the anchorage up river, their backs were weighted down and bent with a full gunny sack.

The scene now changes and it is six months after Liberation, approximately ten years later, and I am on the SS *Pacific Bear*. At the confluence of the river and the sea, there are no sampans. We come up to the pilot boat station and drop the Jacobs ladder awaiting the entourage of thieves. But it's different from the very beginning. The pilot boat comes alongside and the pilot starts up the Jacobs ladder. However, this time he is Chinese and not English. (Could it be that he was once rowing the boat?) Then a half dozen men follow him up, all in blue Mao suits and peaked visored caps with a red star in its center. One of the six, whom we take to be the officer in charge, has a Mauser strapped to his side. We later learned how to differentiate. It was called the four pockets-two pockets system. Officers had four pockets on their jackets, whereas the ranks had two.

He stopped in front of the chief mate and addressed him in impeccable English, saying, "Please show me a copy of your cargo manifest and crew list." No, he was not interested "in going up to the captain's cabin" nor were they interested "in looking into the crew's lockers." There was stunned silence all around while the asked-for documents were brought forth. The officer scanned the crew list, and he randomly asked the mate to identify and point out some names. He then turned to the cargo manifest and studied it for a few minutes. He asked some questions about our itinerary. The mate ventured to ask again if they wouldn't like to step up to the skipper's cabin and look at our lockers, to which the answer was still, "No, that won't be necessary." On signal, a few of the retinue detached themselves and took a turn around the deck, fore and aft. Satisfied that all was in order, he gave the signal to the men to disembark and down they went to the boat that had been waiting patiently alongside. The last one to leave was the officer and as he swung onto the Jacobs ladder wishing us "Good luck," one of the sailors on watch leaned over and ventured to ask, "Hey fella, where did you learn such good English?" The officer hesitated, looked up and said, "University of Washington, class of '38." And one more point. The Chinese pilot was every bit as competent as his previous English counterpart in taking us up river to our anchorage near the Bund. As I said, without Liberation, he'd still be rowing the pilot boat.

Cynics will argue that this couldn't last too long before the old pre-Liberation routine reasserts itself. Maybe they're correct. The recent spate of reports on corruption in industry and business must be looked at from a perspective of forty years of changes that have come about by trial and error. One thing for sure, it set one hell of a good example for the troops.

Political philosophers speak about a thing they call "revolutionary Puritanism." It seems to say that all revolutionaries, especially those from national liberation movements, like to wrap themselves in an aura of holier-than-thou purists, who wouldn't ever dream of attempting such immoral conduct as being on the take. Rather, their pose as ethically super-human sooner or later breaks down under the pressures of everyday life. This may be so, but the fact of the matter is, that at many junctures in history, when intense social change is in progress, the upwelling *has* brought about such conduct, demonstrating the participant's desire to introduce a better model for living, using him or herself as an example, wrapped in the mantle of the eternal verities. Since the previous regime was so corrupt, the contrast, however long it lasts, is startling.

Chapter Eighteen
A Complement of Misfits

Corruption in its many guises makes itself evident to the seafaring man just about everywhere he goes from day one of his career. Surely we realize that this is not a novel aspect of human behavior since one gets a head start with it at home. It's just that when encountered outside our shores it becomes another human link between people, as if to say, "Hmm, they're just like us, aren't they?"

The SS *Cape Flattery* was one of the very first of her type known as a C-l. Its cargo capacity wasn't very much different from a Liberty ship but its engines were a little more sophisticated in that they could work up speeds to fifteeen knots. For freighters this would be considered "getting up there." In the course of our peregrinations around San Francisco Bay, we put into Howard Terminal in Oakland and took on a few thousand tons of coal free-loaded into the hold, that is, dumped in bulk rather than in one-hundred pound sacks. This was most perplexing, since most of our cargo looked like the usual South Pacific stuff, and coal got us all thinking Alaska. Strangely enough, when we got out past the Golden Gate we headed into the South Channel, indicating a South Pacific destination. And imagine our further surprise when the skipper opened his orders and our first stop was Samoa.

Samoa in those days was off the beaten path, and in spite of Margaret Mead's popularizations, there weren't very many Westerners around. So imagine our further surprise when on arrival we were informed that the coal in the lower holds would be discharged there, and furthermore, the only available labor was a typically segregated battalion of black GIs, while we the crew would have to drive winches. The winches are the machinery on deck that operate the cargo mechanisms, which in turn load and discharge the cargo. In this case, huge canvas nets would be stretched out in the holds and the GIs would shovel the coal into the nets. The nets would then be discharged into big U.S. Army dump trucks and hauled away, I know not where.

To this day, I find myself every now and then referring back in memory to that incident, and find it more and more perplexing. A few thousand tons of coal are delivered to a South Pacific paradise, as the hype would have it, and handled by Black GIs, since the natives would have no part of it. One rumor at the time had it that this was part of a road-paving project into the interior. If that was so, then it was one heck of a dumb and expensive way to get a road paved.

Every once in a while, you get on a ship that contains some sort of maverick or other type of misfit. This is so, notwithstanding that we start out with an entire complement of misfits. It's just that in the world of the misfits there are degrees, and there would occasionally be one who threw a monkey wrench into the gears of progress. Such a one was our second mate, a native of Mississippi, an incessant chatterbox and a gas-hound who couldn't hold his liquor, who made himself twice as obnoxious that day by hovering over the all-black longshore crew and yelling meaningless instructions down into the hold.

When the operation was under way a short while and we were all beginning to get the technique down pat, the hold began to resemble a dust storm, and so we broke out the fire hoses and they sprinkled things down at various intervals, while spelling each other off. We, on deck, found ourselves doing the same since we too were full of coal dust.

At some point during the proceedings, the second mate had some objections to what was going on, ordered the fire hose treatment stopped and went down into the hold to show them exactly how it had to be done. The sergeant in charge of the operation, seeing what was happening, went right down after him and, as all production came to a screeching halt, they both squared off in the center of the hatch in a pushing and shoving match, punctuated with threats and counter-threats. As the dust began to settle, and both faces were within a centimeter of each other, the sergeant had the last word somewhat as follows: "And furthermore, Mr. Mate, we is all the same color down here." As all hands laughed uproariously, the yahoo made his way out of the hold, his face and hands covered with coal dust.

People bring their pettiness, meanness and bitterness with them wherever they go. They also bring their brotherhood, togetherness and human decency as well. Hopefully, we salvage something positive out of these situations. We were treated to a raw piece of racial animosity on one side and an attempt to salvage a measure of dignity on the other.

As we dragged our way around the world, VE-Day (May 8, 1945) was declared, and so we were ordered through the Suez Canal—a ditch carved out of the desert where, in many instances, two ships cannot pass each other without one of them crowding over to the bank and waiting until the other got by. As we were slowly making our way through the ditch, the desert stretching out in both directions for miles on end, a camel caravan was slowly inching its way forward while a squadron of military planes was maneuvering overhead. Three distinct technologies of transportation, animals, ships and airplanes, representing three different stages in human development, were in existence and competing side by side.

We no sooner stepped off the gangway in Port Said when we were "adopted" by a character who called himself "Buffalo Bill." In those days, travelers in what we call the Third World today would tell you about being "adopted." It is yet another mechanism used by the poor in their struggle for survival against never-ending, grinding poverty. A local street person approaches you and offers to act as your "guide." Usually, money is not discussed but left to the discretion of the visitor. Whether accepted formally or not, he "guides" you to just about anywhere and in most cases makes "suggestions" as to where the best of anything and everything may be obtained. The proprietor of the establishment, be he shopkeeper, cafe owner or bordello operator, then cuts him in for a percentage of the price of the transaction, which incorporates the cost of the guide's services, like it or not.

In comparing notes with other travelers, I have never met anyone who successfully shook off a "guide" once "adopted." People have only to realize that the "guide" is usually hovering in the background giving the proprietor the "high sign" denoting his presence. As for the name, "Buffalo Bill," this again was just one more way the local people make themselves subservient to the conqueror. Although Bill spoke a flawless English, he was Egyptian by national origin and had a name. Instinctively, he knew that he would get much further ahead by comicalizing his persona and making it easier for the white man.

Seafaring men in those days, when coming ashore in a new port where no one in the crew had been before, tended to orient themselves from a strategic gin mill. That is to say, they seek out a saloon where they think they can either get all the straight dope as to what the town is all about, or meet the proper people to help them get acquainted. It is therefore not unusual for the crew to go uptown together before they start separating, going their respective ways. It so happened that Port Said was new to everyone. No one aboard had ever been there. Buffalo Bill was therefore in his element.

He somehow or other got us all into a bar a little ways up from the waterfront and, before we knew it, we were being waited on by a rotund, bullet-headed little guy sporting a big "I gottcha" grin and wanting to know what he could do for the honored Americans. He told us he came from Alexandria, was of Greek extraction and his name, needless to say, was Nick. An interesting fact about the "mysterious East" is that no matter where you live, native born or not, you almost invariably identify yourself by your patrilineage. Though Nick's family could have been living in Egypt for a thousand years, he would still refer to himself as Greek.

As we took over a number of tables all pushed together for the occasion, probably a dozen of us all told, we blankly searched each other's faces as to what to order in this part of the world. After all, you wouldn't want to miss a good bet if a native drink is available. As expected, Nick came to our rescue, and suggested maybe we'd like to try some choice Scotch that he had been especially saving for such honored customers (translation: those who have American dollars to spend). Seeing no reason to vote against it, all hands shook their heads and Nick disappeared behind a curtain emerging after a decent interval with a pinched bottle of Haig and Haig, probably the most expensive Scotch to be had, if not the best, according to the cognoscenti.

Back in San Francisco, my wife Ann and I had a friend, Norman Mini. Aside from being a man of great intellect, deep erudition and refined esthetic judgment, and who, as of that time, never held a job more elevating than janitorial-custodial work, Norman was nevertheless one of the world's eminent, albeit unrecognized, authorities on matters oenological and viticultural; all this, aside from the fact that his taste for good booze was impeccable. In fact, some years after the war, he put his knowledge to use by writing columns in San Francisco-Bay Area periodicals, as well as raising his own grapes and making his own wine in Napa Valley.

As Nick waved the bottle of Haig and Haig around the circle, a little too quickly I thought, I immediately had a lightning-like flash. In that split microsecond, I suddenly remembered a conversation we once had with Norman on how liquor should smell. He warned me to test a bottle

I'm not too sure of by upending it, rubbing a little of the contents on to the palms of one's hands and smelling it. If the smell is oily and acrid, and a slight oily residue remains on your hands, chances are it's bootlegged and contains fusel oil. That means that it has not been distilled enough and what was worse, could be poisonous.

And so it came to pass that as Nick's hand waved the bottle in front of my nose, and being younger and faster on the uptake in those days, I made a lunge for it and grabbed it. And in so doing, in as calm a voice as I could muster, I asked him to break the seal and let me look at the bottle. I little realized that in doing this I would create an international incident. He dutifully broke the seal and as I upended the bottle and rubbed the contents into the palms of my hands, he led out a yell that could have been heard by the Sphinx some thousand miles away. Needless to say, the stuff stunk something awful. Diluted in a mixed drink, it would probably have gone over not doing too much damage to the iron constitutions of the cash customers, but taken straight it could have been fatal. Later, when we cooled down, we surmised that since all service came from the bar, if anyone ordered it straight, he would have switched it behind the bar to a more acceptable although cheaper, bottle.

In a matter of seconds, after Nick's hostile war whoop, a crowd of people collected; some in native garb, some in Western clothes, all gesticulating and talking in the various tongues prevalent in that part of Egypt at the time: English, French, Egyptian and Greek (recognized by one of the crew). Within minutes, the constabulary appeared, but the gang sat at their tables and placed me in the center. As Nick was explaining in the lingua franca to the constabulary, Buffalo Bill placed himself between them and his tone sounded conciliatory as his hands waived placatingly. Pretty soon they got everybody outside and Nick returned with another bottle, this time, Teachers, another favorite of the day. As a gesture of friendship, Nick offered us the bottle on the house, something I had never seen happen anywhere before or since. I too, then, as a gesture of good will, waived the test and we all accepted graciously.

Meanwhile back at the ranch, Buffalo Bill materialized, this time with a few natives in tow. He explained to us that these men represented a family of magicians and jugglers who were descendents of those who worked for the royal family of Egypt since the first Pharaohs. For a small fee they would like to present their act before dinner. By this time, both Nick and Bill considered me the leader and therefore were addressing me. So I took a vote and we all agreed to watch.

The next hour or so was positively fascinating. A troop of about ten men appeared from the two elders down to a few five- or six-year-olds. They held us spellbound. There were not the usual foolish prestidigitator's card tricks or sawing someone in half so common on the vaudeville circuits. In one act, as I remember, they lined up and started producing pebbles, then stones and finally rocks out of their mouths and piled them up on the floor for all to see and examine. In another act in a take-off on the hidden "up-your-sleeve trick," they were pulling "flags of all nations" (the United Nations was being talked about then) out of their mouths in what seemed like an endless variety of miniature flags, on and on around the room. All these acts were interlarded with various juggling antics and feats employing sharp knives and flaming torches until it became almost impossible to count everything in the air at any given moment. By the time the last act was over, which featured the juggling as part of a human pyramid, they had quite a crowd, got a big hand and made a killing in passing the hat around to the millionaire American sailors.

Sailing time was posted for 6:00 a.m., which among other things meant it was my watch on deck. It also meant that we must be ready for a 4:00 a.m. call to start securing for sea. I therefore informed my watch partner, Clarence C., that he had approximately eight hours to check out the action. Knowing that he cultivated the reputation of a Don Juan, I suggested he be careful in approaching the local women, especially those in *purdah* (originally a Hindu term but used universally throughout the Orient to denote women who wear a veil).

I was not surprised when at or about 3:00 a.m. I was rudely awakened from a deep sleep by the overhead light being flicked on in the focsle. Across from me was Clarence, passed out in his bunk, his previously clean and well-pressed khakis spotted all over with blotches of blood, an ugly gash on his forehead and his knuckles and forearms skinned and bruised. And hovering over him menacingly was a youngish man, clean and well dressed in a uniform, sporting a double bar on his epaulettes. The focsle door was open and a few militarily clad men were in the alleyway. As I sized up the situation, the lieutenant and I engaged in the following conversation to the best of my recollection:

> **Lieutenant:** He's under arrest (pointing to Clarence).
>
> **J. G.:** What are the charges?
>
> **Lieutenant:** Molesting local women.
>
> (It almost all sounded rehearsed.)
>
> **J. G.:** We're sailing in a few hours. Can't we settle this?
>
> Looking around, he closed the focsle door, thereby shutting out his cohorts in the alleyway.
>
> **J. G.:** Will two cartons of Camels do it?
>
> **Lieutenant:** Yes.
>
> So I swung around, opened my locker and fished out the requisite amount. He broke open the cartons and in a flash had the individual packs secreted around his body, like he had done this a few times before.
>
> **Lieutenant:** Thank you, and have a good trip.
>
> And he was out the door in a flash.

Clarence never remembered much about the night before. There really was no way to get an answer to the question over whether he was or wasn't "molesting" native women. And, what's more, nobody cared since he was a perfect setup for a quick two cartons of Camels. Hopefully, the lieutenant was decent enough to dole out a pack or two to his subalterns.

When we got to Bombay there was more improvisation. It was the conversion of the 'tween decks above the lower holds into bunks and makeshift living quarters for the myriad amount of refugees who were in a constant state of transit, pushed and tossed around from pillar to post during the war. One could almost trace their odysseys with the shifting fortunes of the battle lines.

Among others, we had two brothers of some Near Eastern nationality, reputed to be millionaires on their way to New York City. They had been on the run since the fall of Singapore in the spring of 1942. We were now one of the first American ships into the Mediterranean since VE-Day. They would sneak up to our mess room and engage us in conversation by asking such questions as, "Is it possible to have a good time in New York City for a hundred dollars a night?" Which would be tantamount to saying today, "Is it possible to have a good time in New York City for a thousand dollars a night?"

At one point we complained about the coffee tasting lousy, so they volunteered to show us how to make real coffee out of the "floor sweepings," as we used to call it. It turned out their method was the "jungle style" alluded to earlier on in this memoir. They took coffee, milk, sugar and a dab of butter, put it all together in a can and cooked it to a boil. Then they gave it a shot of cold water and the grounds settled down to the bottom instantly. This was the first time since I last tasted a cup of "jungle coffee" just before I shipped on my first ship way back, when I had met my friend Duffy. Both the crew and I were elated and we immediately appointed them official coffee makers in exchange for allowing them to hover around the mess room and cage some food to supplement their diet.

Another character was some third-assistant Brazilian consul who had been trying to get back to Rio de Janeiro since Pearl Harbor Day. He had been shuttling all around the Far East, starting out from Shanghai, and was finally making it at least to New York City. His problem was his obsessive reluctance to use the passenger toilet down in the 'tween decks, which was an army style affair. He would wait until 2:00 a.m. or there-abouts, and sneak up into the crew's quarters to do his toileting, against any and all regulations. Though most of the crew didn't approve of his conduct, nobody hassled him. But it didn't take long for the skipper to find out, at which point, fearing a possible public health problem, he had notices posted all around the ship admonishing all hands "to stick to your own cans."

Last but not least, we had approximately one hundred veterans from the China-Burma-India theater (CBI) segregated away into one of the holds. Ordinarily this was not a problem, but this time around they were under special guard. We were finally told some days after they came aboard in Bombay that they were all "Section 8," that is to say, "psycho-logically disturbed." It was positively forbidden to give them any liquor, in spite of the fact that they did offer all kinds of money for it at all our stops. As far as I know we held to our end of the bargain. These people were out on deck from time to time and though we exchanged some con-versation in the normal course of going about our work, we, none of us, could see what was wrong with them. They sounded intelligent and forth-coming. They wouldn't tell us exactly where they were except to say, "in the interior." To a man they denounced the Kuomintang regime under Chiang Kai-shek, referring to him invariably as "Chancre Jack." Also, the consensus was unanimous that, "Chancre Jack" might have been okay, but "everybody below him was a corrupted thief." As I look back at the situation of the CBI vets whom we repatriated, I am led to believe that they may have been a bit unstable after their experience in the jungle, but who wouldn't be after some of the hair-raising stories they told us. It was obvious to us that the Army Command threw a cordon sanitaire around them so as to keep them quiet and contained until it got them home.

Chapter Nineteen
Christian Sailors

Do not wait for the Last Judgment; it takes place every day.
Albert Camus, 1913-1960

The frailty of the human condition shows up in many ways, especially on passenger ships, and we cannot leave the saga of the SS *President Madison* without speaking about some of the actions of the passengers in certain extreme situations. The setting, it will be recalled, was somewhat as follows: A passenger ship carrying about two-hundred women, children and a few older men, mostly missionaries out of the Orient being repatriated to the United States, is now running the Atlantic blockade of German U-boat packs, totally unarmed but with an ominous looking six-inch "gun" on the stern, actually made of wood so as to "fool the U-boats" as our Chips so succinctly put it. To add insult to injury, the engines are in sad disrepair; the boiler tubes so clogged that the stack spewed forth sparks all night, every night, presenting us as a slow-moving, volcano-like visible target for miles around.

For the first three days out, the skipper—Captain Waldemar Nielson, a fine old Dane from the old school who showed us a lot of class when the going got rough—held lifeboat drills after lunch so as to acquaint everyone with his and her place and task. Passengers were shown and told how to grab their kids, places were assigned in each boat, and crew and officers discussed the situation with them thoroughly. The boats were all swung out suspended in their davits, and lowered to the promenade deck lashed to the railings in anticipation of lowering away when the order was to be given. What with all these preparations, and the sky pilots (an old Wobbly expression referring to Christian ministers who punctuated their sermons with their hands raised skyward) holding various services during the day, plus the hymn singing almost continuously, we all felt well accounted for in the eyes of the Lord and safe beyond concern. One particular practice that irked the crew no end was a daily sunrise service (5:00 a.m.), which began with a hymn-like exultation:

Oh the best book to read is the Bible,
Oh the best book to read is the Bible.
If you read it every day,
It will help you on your way,
Oh the best book to read is the Bi-i-i-ble.

The last "Bible" was long and drawn out. After which they immediately launched into another one:

Be careful little eyes what you see;
Be careful little eyes what you see;
For the good Lord above
Is looking down on you with love,
Be careful little eyes what you see.

It then switched to: "Be careful little ears what you hear," and "Be careful little tongue what you say," "Be careful little hands what you touch" and some others I have since forgotten. As one of my watch partners remarked to me one morning, "Just what *can* these poor kids do, anyway?"

After a hiatus of a few days with things settling into a routine, the old man walked into the wheelhouse about eleven o'clock at night and pulled the general alarm. To all those who never had the dubious honor of hearing a general alarm, be forewarned that it could be a most unnerving experience. It is an extremely loud, continuous bell-ring that permeates and penetrates every inch of space of the ship's interior, not to speak of one's psyche. In short, it wakes up the dead. The hysteria and confusion that followed was indescribable. All of the good God-fearing Christians, forgetting all the good training we thought we imparted to them, stepped all over each other, in some instances trampling over children, as they made their way to the promenade decks. Many of them were climbing into the boats which were still lashed to the railings, which they well knew was a no-no, and almost all of them were carrying suitcases and small parcels of belongings, as well as armfuls of clothes, expecting a first-class window seat in the lifeboats—and all of this to the accompaniment of hysterical screaming and children crying. When some of us ventured to ask them just how many seats they think they needed in the boat, they stammered that they thought it "wouldn't take up too much room." By the time the captain rang the dismissal signal so as to end the farce, many embarrassed men and women of God were seen shamefacedly shuffling back to their cabins, clothes, suitcases and all, avoiding our eyes and totally subdued.

At noon the next day the following notice appeared on the ship's bulletin boards under the Captain's signature:

The late night boat drill just held showed that we are not prepared to abandon ship, if and when necessary. Please keep in mind that, God willing, it is most important to save our lives first and all earthly goods can be replaced later. We may have another drill real soon.

As it turned out, we never had another drill and life resumed its hymn singing and praying routine. And they, none of them, ever missed a meal. This dismal story of man's jungle-like behavior has its saving grace. One of the other passengers, neither Christian nor a sky pilot, showed up at the proper time and place, dressed in shirt, shorts and sandals, carrying a pocket-sized book of poetry in his hip pocket and some chocolate bars in his shirt pocket. He helped the boat captain, who happened to be my watch partner, calm the women and children and carried himself in a dignified and decorous manner, although crippled and unable to move swiftly. His name was Sir Victor Sassoon, past the age of seventy, we were later told, and probably one of the world's richest men in those times. He later commended the crew to the captain and sent down a couple of quarts of Scotch to the focsle. A gentleman to the manor born.

✳✳✳✳✳✳✳✳✳✳✳

Long-haired preachers come out every night,
Try to tell you what's wrong and what's right;
But when ask'd how's 'bout something to eat
They will answer in voices so sweet:
You will eat bye and bye,
In that glorious land above the sky;
Work and pray, live on hay,
You'll get pie in the sky when you die.
"The Preacher and the Slave," Joe Hill, 1882-1915

Chapter Twenty

Gospel Values

The worst vice of a fanatic is his sincerity.
Oscar Wilde, 1854-1900
Fanaticism consists in redoubling one's efforts
when you have forgotten your aims.
George Santayana, 1863-1952

A staple ritual of Sailors' Union procedure from its very beginning was, and probably still is, the "Quarterly Finance Committee." A committee of five members was elected from the floor at a regular Monday night meeting, four times a year, to go over the finances of the organization with the public accounting firm and the union auditor in attendance. It was on such a Monday night, sometime towards the end of the war, that I allowed myself to get hornswaggled onto this committee, and at its first meeting I met our new auditor, H. S. Corlett. And as I look back at the incongruity of our meeting, again I marvel to this day at the many patterns we draw with our comings and goings, random or by design, and from the many different directions from which we come together.

Whatever preconceptions and presuppositions of "pencil pushers," accountants and related types I might have had, they were shattered immediately by our first encounter. This was not the little mousy guy with the starched collar whom Dickens placed in the counting houses of London in the early nineteenth century. Rather, we saw a medium-built, white-haired man with silver-rimmed eyeglasses, whose constant uniform of the day was a shiny old black suit, white shirt and dark tie, in the manner of a Roman Catholic lay brother.

In fact, for those who can remember that far back, he was a dead-ringer for F. D. R.'s Vice President, Henry Wallace. He spoke in a stentorian tone at all times using barbed witticisms and sermons in equal proportion. On rare occasions, he would speak politely, but only to older women. And one of his unforgettable characteristics was an unmistakable laugh, which was part hilarious, part hysterical, and part maniacal.

At the drop of a hat, or for that matter anytime he could get the word in, H. S., the name by which he was universally known and referred to, gave you his "full-bore sermon," as he used to call it. H. S. was, as I look back at it now, a liberation theologian years before anyone ever heard of eceumenism and Vatican II. Other than Dorothy Day—who ran the Catholic Worker Mission down on the New York Bowery, a free soup kitchen for the unemployed and homeless (yes, even in those days there were lots of each); and Peter Maurin, whose underground worker-priest movement was popular in Europe in the early 1930s—H. S. was the only one of his kind who preached the Gospel of Christ, the working man or "Jerusalem Slim," as the old Wobblies used to say. He considered cooperative living the only form of social organization worth having so as to bring the kingdom of God to earth and demanded that the Catholic Church declare itself for Christian Socialism, immediately, if not sooner.

H. S., it turned out, had a checkered career. He was educated as a Presbyterian minister, but he never spoke about his break with Protestantism. He wound up in California in the middle 1930s and, being among other things an accomplished violinist, made his living playing in the pit, in theater orchestras and at weddings. He used to tell me that as a musician's union member, he would go out on a job to the theater and sit down at the music stand in the orchestra pit. The conductor would signal and they would open the score. On the downbeat they would start to play. Two mistakes were allowed and on the third you were replaced the next day, or even between the acts if you were bad enough. He perfected his playing and was able to make a living.

I remember telling him—I thought jokingly—that in some reading I was doing in early labor history, I discovered that in the first Musicians Union Local in New York City one hundred years ago, there was a strict rule that all meetings were to be conducted only in German. He answered me by launching into a discussion in German, that it wouldn't bother him one bit since he could also speak all the Romance languages as well as Esperanto!

Somewhere along the line, he picked up bookkeeping and accounting via correspondence school, a popular method in those days. Soon he made the transition and wherever he went he preached unionism, Socialism and his newfound Catholic faith. Since a combination like that wasn't very conducive to full-time employment, he kept drifting around until he landed at the Sailors' Union office. And accompanying him on all these strange peregrinations was his wife Hilda, an almost silent, soft-voiced, all-suffering, all-admiring, flaxen-haired blonde who worshipped him and hung on his every word. She too got a job in the office and they worked admirably well as a team, he giving all the orders and she doing all the work.

The union at the time was exploding with new members, all paying dues and assessments, and our Secretary, charged with the responsibility of hanging on to the money, was making some dubious choices for business agents and patrolmen, as our representatives were called. H. S. was hired in this difficult period to set up a system to "keep everyone honest;" at least that's what our secretary told me some years later. "He's an honest man, but a little screw-loose," he added.

Among other things, and there were many, H. S. was an apostle of a little known scheme known as credit unions. These were essentially small-scale cooperative banks, limited to a specific field of membership. The membership operates on a shoestring out of the company offices, sells shares to raise capital and make loans to themselves. The interest charged after expenses are deducted goes back to the membership as dividends.

In those days, there were many such small scale banking arrangements; in old established neighborhoods, federal and state civil service offices, single factory plant facilities and a sprinkling of labor unions. Today, some credit unions are large, thriving and wealthy, and rate honorable mention on official Federal Reserve Board reports. H. S. managed somehow to organize a credit union in one of our Seafarers' affiliates in the fish canneries.

At the first meeting of our Quarterly Finance Committee, H. S. took us aside and pointed out to our untrained eyes that there was a "shortfall," as he called it, between the dues receipts issued and the money collected. He further informed us that a "five-fingered defalcation" had occurred. We all knew what he meant and exactly whom he was referring to. Before the committee adjourned a few days later, he had succeeded in floating a loan from the fish cannery credit union, thereby repaying the Sailors' Union "shortfall" and placing the erring brother on a firm repayment schedule, which H. S. himself monitored and saw to fruition by the simple expedient of handing out the paychecks every Friday and being there to cash his check.

H. S. was very aware of his eccentricities and was dead serious about his ideas. He did not suffer fools gladly and worst of all was his treatment of his co-religionists who didn't agree with him. For them he reserved a singular dosage of his barbed wit. He had various names for different people, mostly uncomplimentary. A swaggering, Mafioso-Napoleonic type was known as "the Little Caesar of the waterfront," and co-religionists who disagreed with him were referred to as "the knees of whose pants were baggy from genuflecting twice daily."

After H. S. got settled into his new job, it didn't take very long before he started a low-level agitation to organize a credit union among the Sailors' Union membership. To this, our Secretary was firmly opposed, and for good reason. He didn't think that we should get involved with the personal and financial problems of our membership, in spite of the fact that it would be a separate organization. One way or another, since the membership would be the same, the proposed credit union would become identified with the Sailors' Union. What was more, a strong, strict hand was necessary to guide and operate the organization, considering some of the element that would want to partake of its benefits.

The argument was very reasonable and, as fate would have it, our Secretary's misgivings turned out to be both prescient and prophetic. But if he didn't realize it then, he soon found out that he wasn't dealing with a reasonable person but rather with a fanatic who was blinded by a recently acquired faith. Like reformed drunks who have seen the light, they're the hardest to deal with.

Like many others before me, I have thought long and hard about this particular phenomenon we call fanaticism. In the world of the 1930s and 1940s, the world of totalitarianism, of Hitler and Stalin, it was a popular subject. When does a "considered opinion" become a "firmly held view?" And when does this "firmly held view" become "cast in concrete" to the total exclusion of any and all compromise? But I think Finley Peter Dunne's Mr. Dooley said it best for H. S.: "A fanatic is a man that does what he thinks th' Lord wud do if he knew the facts iv th' case."

Like Savanarola challenging the Medicis to clean up Florence, H. S. went on a crusade to establish a credit union for the Sailors' Union membership. He single-handedly overrode all objections and did all the work required to get it organized, off and running. He dragooned some of the officials to serve on the Board of Directors; got the charter from the State of California; set up the office and installed the phone; got all the paraphernalia and stationery together and was in business—and all this time, dragging everyone along in his wake.

When I was in my breaking-in period I once asked him if he could stop long enough to explain something to me. His answer was revealing: "I'm afraid if I stop, this whole enterprise will fall apart." In other words, H. S. believed in the doctrine of indispensability. Nobody else could either do it at all or do it better than he. When such self-centeredness combined with a touch of paranoia, the volatile result in the world of the 1930s yielded some disastrous results. Our leader was now leading us back into the forest.

I do not wish to leave the impression that H. S.'s credit union plan didn't get some favorable response. In some quarters he was well supported; to be precise, from all those who thought it "was a good idea," to those who wanted to borrow money as soon as the doors were opened. The way I saw it, a credit union was a natural at the time. Towards the end of the war and immediately thereafter, shipping was still good and many of our members were fully employed. Some had a pretty good stake salted away, as we used to say it. More and more, seafaring men were getting married and looking for homes and cars.

Done correctly, the membership would have benefited from a self-directed cooperative bank promoting cheap loans. But this was not to be. What with twenty/twenty hindsight, the best laid plans of mice and men "doth oft gang aglay." Instead of using discretion and tight rules in the beginning so as to screen out the "working class cons," as we got to call them, the doors were thrown wide open to any "full-book member" who could muster up the entrance fee of one dollar.

The Gospel According to H. S. held that there is a fundamental goodness in all human beings and, that given the proper opportunities and conditioning, a new person would be nourished into the world and would march on to bigger and better things. Since everybody half agreed with him, it was hard to argue, but the key, of course, was the proper opportunities and conditioning. And the way H. S. went about it was ridiculous from the start. A prospective member walked in the door and within a few minutes, on the strength of his own signature, walked out with a check for ninety-four dollars. He didn't really need his entrance fee of one dollar, since H. S. incorporated it into his loan together with the five dollars for his first share—instant credit instantly arrived at. For larger sums, collateral was asked. This, too, was a joke, since none of it was documented or recorded correctly.

I too showed more than a passive interest. I joined and became a charter member. I firmly believed that cooperatives were a step in the right direction, a step towards some utopian-socialistic idea I gave lip service to in those days. Today, the right-wing idealogues call it "secular humanism."

There are times in a person's life when a number of things come together and create a new situation. This was the period in my life when I began thinking seriously about quitting the sea. It was also a time when H. S. was getting fed up with carrying the credit union on his back (about a year after it got under way), and his enthusiasm for his job at the Sailors' Union began to flag. I soon discovered that it was in the nature of things with these types of people, that they couldn't stay on one job too long. His liberation theology however, never diminished.

One day, while waiting for a ship, some members of the board cornered me up at the hall and asked me to attend a meeting with H. S. and see if I would be interested in the job. Succumbing to their blandishments (nobody had ever sought me out before to offer me a job), I went to the meeting, in spite of the fact that the pay was almost non-existent and I knew absolutely nothing about keeping books. In retrospect, I remember rationalizing it all by saying that it costs money to learn. I was avidly looking for a new life ashore and H. S. needed someone, maybe anyone, to grab the tiger by the tail. After a break-in period of about a week, with H. S. dashing madly in and out of the office and finishing up across the street at the Seafarers' Union office, I became the treasurer/manager of the Pacific Seafarers' Credit Union, a wholly membership-owned-and-operated cooperative bank "serving the Sailors' Union members but in no way officially affiliated with it." The last statement was a must if we wanted cooperation from the union officers.

I saw H. S. one more time, when he came down to visit us at the ranch in Pescadero some years later. Needless to say, he was busy with another cause, this time a cooperative housing community within an all-black, Catholic congregation in the Fillmore district of San Francisco. He was very taken with the new Pope, John XXIII, and Vatican II. He said the reforms were going in the right direction but hardly fast enough. I often wonder what he would be saying now, some thirty years later, what with Christian-based communities all over the third world, priests bearing arms in guerilla movements and serving in the Sandanista government of Nicaragua. Chances are that he would be laughing uproariously at Pope John Paul and castigating his counterreformation with some of his choice barbs.

The visit was not without its incongruity. At one point, with a number of friends and visitors present, he mentioned that he and his wife were trying to have a child with a singular lack of success. "We're doing everything the doctor told us to do but still, nothing's happening," he complained. Whereupon a voice was heard from the back of the room saying, "Yes, but did you try having intercourse?" H. S. was always the butt of these kinds of remarks, but he took them all in stride and with good humor.

My first foray into the unknown world of shoreside employment turned out to be something radically different from what I was accustomed to. My old ex-Wobbly friends began calling me a "white-collar stiff," that is, an office worker, and when I began getting into the accounts and records, I discovered a monumental mess; it was like opening a can of worms. As stated previously, lending money to seafarers who have no permanent address ashore other than a next-of-kin somewhere inland who likely wouldn't know where he could be found at any given time could be a very risky proposition.

This in no way seeks to cast any aspersions on the character of former shipmates. It is just to say that the life we lead conditions us towards a type of behavior, modified, to be sure, by early family training, beliefs and customs. But as the years go by and one doesn't see much progress made, a sense of responsibility takes a back seat; in fact, it's the first thing that goes. And, as what happened began to sink in, I realized that it was incumbent on me to salvage what I could of the membership's money and try to keep the doors open—a rather formidable, not to say contradictory task.

Let us consider the case of Mathew J., a true son of the working class. He was fond of being addressed by the name of the apostle after whom his devout mother named him. He grew up back East, the son of a machinist who learned his trade in the old country. When Mathew graduated high school, wanderlust set in and he drifted down to New Orleans looking for work, and started sailing merchant ships. He met a woman in a bar in the French Quarter who was a part-time prostitute, married her and began to act as her pimp. The mob (her previous employer) had other ideas, and beat him up enough to scare him out of town. This brought him to San Francisco without her. As life would have it, I shipped on the SS *Mahimahi*, and it was there that I met Mathew J., my future watch partner for the next six months.

As a shipmate and watch partner, Mathew J. was exemplary in his work habits, seamanship and personal conduct. With a little bit of prodding on my part, he began studying navigation and cargo stowage from some books we found aboard with the intention of upgrading himself. He had intelligence and showed concern for his shipmates. I had great difficulty reconciling his story about pimping his wife with his church-going background, until we went ashore together in Honolulu, our first stop, and he showed a definite number of weaknesses, one of which had to do with his inability to hold his liquor. In fact, whenever he started drinking he got loud, boisterous, obnoxious and obstreperous. And this type of conduct always attracts a similar type and a fight invariably ensues.

When we returned from our six-month shuttle run in the South Pacific (a shuttle run is when your ship is sent island-hopping for an extended period of time, in some instances for as much as a year), he immediately left for New Orleans "to either straighten out my marriage or get a divorce." Approximately a little over a year later, we met again in San Francisco, and though the divorce came through (he had changed his mind about straightening out his marriage), a new calamity had befallen him. He met and married a sweet young thing who was hysterically afraid to go to bed with him, notwithstanding the cajoling, beseeching and entreaty placed on her by her family and the psychiatric help they consulted. It began to look to me that Mathew J. was a loser whose choices were akin to the wild swings of a pendulum. Whatever were the psychological ramifications of his conduct (for example, why did he have to keep *marrying* these women?) he apparently was destined to have many more such misadventures.

We are now some years downstream and I am sitting in the credit union office looking at the loan portfolio, the collection for which I have just become responsible, when I am confronted with a note for one-thousand dollars signed by one Mathew J. Covering the note was a mortgage instrument (as the bankers like to call it) reciting a few roomfuls of furniture. The account was now over a year old and not a single payment was ever made on it. His share account was five dollars. A quick check through the union grapevine told me he was in bad standing for non-payment of dues and his whereabouts were unknown. The rest of the story was another disaster. Some months later I received a petition from a bankruptcy court somewhere in Southern California listing the credit union as a creditor in the matter of Mathew J., and we never heard from him again. I wonder to whom he's married, now?

This rather extended story illustrates among other things the damage done by too much faith in the goodness of man as preached by H. S. It could be that placing temptation in front of some humans, who do not have the proper constraints nor the strength to withstand it, becomes an enormous burden for them and consequently an invitation to disaster.

Slowly but surely I began to notice an interesting thing about myself: my attitude was beginning to change, subtly but perceptibly. Instead of interested observer with total empathy for my seafaring brothers, I began to rearrange the world and modify some categories. Though the old class struggle remained between "us and them," we now had a new category of "working class con artist." There are "responsibles" and "irresponsibles." People can be depended on only in very limited ways and circumstances. Some repay their debts and others do not, just as some show up for appointments and others do not. To stay the hand of temptation and human failing, we need constraints against anticipated abuse. And the constraints must be derived and imposed democratically or the game isn't worth the candle. And the same applies to society.

There is yet another subtext to this problem of responsibility, which at the time rekindled an ongoing debate that waxed and waned through the years and to all intents and purposes will probably never be settled. I refer to the seaman as "ward of the court" argument. What this means is that in law scholars have traced back to the Phoenecians circa 400 BCE, the seafarer cannot take care of himself or his finances, so the court of the land intervenes in his behalf and protects him against scoundrel-masters and all others who try to attach his earnings. Through the eons of time that have transpired from the Phoenecians to this very day, an assignment of a seaman's wages is not permitted other than for support of an estranged wife and/or a minor child.

In spite of the fact that lots of enabling legislation passed through the years, such as the previously mentioned La Follette Seamen's Act signed into law by President Wilson on March 4, 1915, and practically written by Andrew Furuseth and hailed as a great milestone in our emancipation; as I say, in spite of all such statutes on or off the books, the seafaring man to this very day remains a "ward of the court."

To bring this whole thing home, if I had a dollar for all the times members of the credit union came up to me and informed me of the fact that I could not attach their wages no matter what, other than for the above-mentioned exception, then I could spend a good day at the racetrack.

None of the above does in any way apply to all those who established themselves ashore, albeit still following the sea, since they started accumulating assets such as cars and houses and joined the American dream. These assets, after all, are attachable. And it has been and always will be my contention that so long as the seafaring man remains a "ward of the court," there will always be that certain percentage of "irresponsibles" in his midst. But since there are so few American seamen left and their future looks even bleaker, the whole subject is rather moot.[15]

✳✳✳✳✳✳✳✳✳✳✳

My relations with the officials of the Sailors' Union in those days were good in that they were always respectful but at arm's length. Since I was always some sort of independent thinker, though not a militant up-front maverick type who wore a hair shirt, nobody ever suggested that I run for office. However, I did fill in from time to time on request, in the front office and at the dispatcher's window, when the action required, and purely on a voluntary basis. The committee work was also momentary and voluntary between ships, although a few dollars per diem were involved in some of the more time consuming assignments such as the Quarterly Finance Committee.

When I took the credit union job and found myself confronted with all the delinquent accounts (non-working accounts, the bankers like to say), I felt I had to take special measures to tighten up the lending aspect of the organization. In doing so, I had to discreetly but firmly step on some official toes, since some of them were always "short" at the end of the week. I therefore got the Board to place a tight cap on weekly loans; none were issued until previous ones were repaid. The difference between the credit union and East Coast waterfront loan sharks was in the interest rate. We were very reasonable. Apropos of all this, an incident took place that shook us all up and resulted in contributing in great measure to my lifelong condition of insomnia, not to speak of premature graying at the temples.

One of the more fundamental weaknesses of many seafaring people in my day, referred to a number of times in the course of this manuscript, was a peculiar sort of love affair with racehorses. Many were the seafaring men whose undoing took place, not so much by fast women and nimble-fingered bartenders, as by slow horses and quick talking "turf consultants." Sailors bet on horses with a passion. On the beach they went to the track. When this was not feasible, they utilized the services of a bookmaker, otherwise known as a bookie, in time-honored tradition.

Soon after I came to work, I developed the habit of having coffee at a favorite cafeteria on the waterfront known as Foster's, one of a large chain scattered throughout the city. I particularly noticed a rather well-dressed man in a business suit, white shirt and colored tie, sitting not too far from me and a somewhat steady stream of Sailors' Union members, as well as officials, all of whom I knew, engaging him in conversation as he made notations in a small notebook. This immediately identified the local bookie, soon introduced to me as "the Colonel." The appellation, it turned out, referred to his place of birth, Kentucky, and he sported a tiny official Masonic emblem on his lapel at all times. To round out his image, it was said that he drank only Mint Juleps at the local watering holes.

A number of weeks after we met, he walked in on me late one evening just before closing time. He sat down and pulled an envelope out of his inside jacket pocket, threw it on the table and asked me to look inside. Knowing immediately what it was, and anxious to know what he thought I was worth, I availed myself of his invitation and peeked inside. It was what appeared to be (I never counted) ten brand new, crisp, hot-off-the-press one hundred-dollar bills. He explained to me, matter-of-factly, that I could have one of these a month, if I would allow him to install another phone for his exclusive use. With the credit union as a front, it would be a perfect cover, and nobody needed know but us two, not even the Board of Directors. And when I was ready to quit, he would pull the phone. I thanked him for his interest and good taste in choosing me, and respectfully declined his kind and generous offer.

I think about the incident from time to time, especially when I think of bribery, be it outright payoffs or large-scale political campaign contributions. Where does one end and the other begin? I also keep thinking about the many excellently thought out rationales that I could have used in accepting the offer. But I instinctively reacted against it by moral choice. To this day, I might add, I am paranoid enough to feel that somebody in the Sailors' Union officialdom tried to set me up.

The saga of the horses is not without its ridiculous overtones. Approximately halfway during my tenure, a certain small-time steam schooner operator was engaged in negotiating a new agreement with the Sailors' Union. Along with the steam schooners, he had some interests in lumber and paper mills in Oregon and Washington. But known only to a chosen few on the inside, mind you, was the fact that Mr. L., the man in question, was also the proud owner of a string of racehorses, all of whom he was "bringing along," as the turf consultants refer to the various stages of preparation for the big money races. And the jewel in the crown was one called Diamond Lil.

To the uninitiated, it must be explained that it is a fact of life that the owner or trainer usually instructs his jockey just exactly what he expects out of a certain race. Is it to win, place or show? He then places his bets. Of course, this may all be illegal, but no matter. Since the general run-of-the-mill bettor doesn't know this, a large-scale industry has arisen consisting of newspapers and textbooks, involving pedigrees, geneologies, mathematical odds and averages all supporting the business of "handicapping," as this is called.

The purpose of this long-winded explanation will begin to make sense if we realize that the negotiating committee, as well as the inner councils of the Sailors' Union, seemed to be more interested in getting some sort of glimmer from Mr. L. as to his intentions regarding Diamond Lil, rather than attending to the negotiations in progress. It seems that at one point in the bantering around the table, he judiciously let slip the fact that he intended to enter her real soon.

When the appointed day arrived, as I entered the office in the morning, the telephone was ringing off the hook. Suddenly, most of the negotiating committee and the other pie-cards from the out ports as well, needed hundreds of dollars worth of loans. (The term "pie-card" originated with the old-time Wobblies who used it instead of "union official" or "labor executive," as the establishment likes to call them, or "pork chopper," as I've heard in recent years.) Only after reminding them that our state charter requires that all loans must be made only "for provident and productive purposes," and they assuring me that that was so, did I get the required amounts together totaling approximately two thousand dollars

spread over ten to twelve individuals, all swearing on their mother's sancti-
ty as to the "sure thing" they had in hand.

We needn't prolong the agony. Diamond Lil barely showed, placing
somewhere towards the back of the pack, our wayward brothers betting to
win. Not since Casey had struck out on that fateful day in Mudville did
anything as cataclysmic happen. I didn't see any of our borrowing brothers for days. Some of them bid me a hasty "Good morning" in Foster's
but moved on quickly. As time went on and the decent interval period of
mourning ended, I began to break the ice by suggesting a repayment
schedule, as painless as possible to be sure. There were lots of promises
but not much tangible evidence on Friday night when they got paid. After
all, wives were waiting at the door and kids had to be fed.

After a month or so of this type of no-action, I collected the notes in
question, made an appointment with our union Secretary, and on the
appointed day and hour, with no one else present, sat down and confronted him with the goods, as they say it in the underworld. He turned col-
ors. He felt called upon to apologize for all the trouble and problems
caused by "those bums" and assured me that he would call a meeting
"tonight in the front office" and see to it that "this thing is taken care of."
So, heartened by his interest, I in turn thanked him and as I rose to leave,
inadvertently dropped what turned out to be a bombshell. I told him that
if worse came to worse, if I saw no significant change in the next thirty
days, I would initiate suit against each of them and have the Sheriff attach
their wages every Friday night until the debts are cleared up. This is
known as a garnishment and is not appreciated by a front office anywhere
since it requires a double payroll: one to the Sheriff for the sum stated and
another to the employee for whatever is left. His parting shot was, "I can't
tell you your business, but it had better not come to that."

I remember thinking long and hard about that last rejoinder to my
rather open but well-meaning threat. It occurred to me that I had never

used such language before and wondered whether I'd have the nerve to carry it out. My colleagues on the board, the only other ones privy to this whole affair, jumped for joy and congratulated me, all hoping they could be around "when the shit hits the fan." As the month drew to a close and as we all suspected, it began to look like some sort of showdown at O.K. Corral was about to ensue. I realized that once I lifted the phone and requested our attorney to start proceedings, the die would be cast, and though some of us might live to regret it, it was a matter of self-respect, both personal and organizational.

The dénouement came on schedule. The Sheriff's deputy, who does these things, served the papers after 1:00 p.m. on Thursday afternoon, which disrupted the payroll procedure as anticipated. The Secretary got me on the phone, livid with rage, and cussed out a blue streak (expletives deleted), directed toward the credit union, me, and my predecessors, wished us all into oblivion and ended by telling me rather succinctly into which part of my anatomy I could put the credit union. I held the receiver about two feet from my ear and when I heard the phone crash into its cradle on the other end I too hung up and breathed a deep sigh of relief. Within the next thirty days or so the money was all collected, voluntarily, and as word of what happened got out I became an instant hero on the waterfront. It took a little bit longer for the pie-cards and the Secretary to start talking to me again.

One more incident deserves honorable mention. Mike K. was nobody to fool around with. He was built like a solid square block of concrete on a five-by-five frame. I was told on good authority that he could hit the same way. In fact, as was once told me by an old shipmate, "If you get into a beef with him, you had better get a good one in first because if he hits you, you're finished." He had no record of ever being on a ship anywhere, but he carried some sort of full book in the Seafarers' International, our parent organization. It was understood that he was a goon, doing muscle work and "riding protection" for some of our lesser physically able officials. Upon meeting him, in the comings and goings of daily existence, he always had a wise remark and/or dirty joke. It was his mask against the world.

One day, while sitting up in the office, I got a call from our secretary claiming that Mike K. was on his way over and needed some money rather urgently. Would I please do something for him and "I personally will see to it that he makes it good." I no sooner put the phone down when in he came, resplendent in suit, shirt and tie, a gold watch on his wrist, and a solid looking rock on the third finger of his other hand. For once he had no wisecrack. The urgency the secretary described looked more like desperation. Without my asking, he pulled a pink slip out of his pocket made out in his name and showing ownership of his late model Cadillac. He needed two thousand dollars for personal reasons. I got him to sign a mortgage agreement and the usual promissory note with scheduled repayments.

A week later he came over to me at Foster's and thanked me again, "You saved my life," he said. I accepted the remark as an expression of gratitude when a few days later, while visiting with a former shipmate and friend who owned a bar in the Tenderloin, my eye drifted to the back of the room and I caught sight of Mike K. in close conference with a pair of hoods. I questioned my friend about Mike and he told me, "He leads a charmed life. Recently he owed a few thousand bucks he dropped in a card game with the mob, and was given twenty-four hours to come up with it. He got it from somewhere." Needless to say, he drove around town with impunity and never once came by to make any payments. Eventually he too was caught in the dragnet with the horse racers.

Another interesting aspect to my job was my belated discovery that from time to time little things have to be done over, above and beyond what the job description states.

Early one morning, while plotting my day and checking out which ships were paying off, the phone rang and on the other end was a member I knew rather casually, calling from the Hall of Justice. Sparing me the details, he said he was allowed this one call and asked would I please take one hundred dollars out of his account and come down and bail him out, and, what was more, they demanded cash. Never having done this in San Francisco, I took the requisite amount out of the till and went uptown to the local Bastille. I surrendered the cash to someone behind a grilled window but he refused me a receipt. "Sorry, we don't issue receipts," he told me. " It's just like shooting craps," he explained. The brother in question showed up later that afternoon, profusely apologetic and very hung over. I told him that I really didn't mind bailing him out, but was rather disturbed that I had to bring cash and didn't even get a receipt. Didn't they trust our check?

It suddenly dawned on me that a few years back on the old SS *Waiamea,* I was watch-partners with Jack M., who, before he went to sea was a plainclothes man in the San Francisco Police Department. I thereupon placed a call to Headquarters and sure enough, they had an Inspector, Jack M., who returned my call the very next day. Yes, he certainly did remember me very fondly. And so I asked him about the requirement for cash and he told me he would see what he could do. A few days later, I received a call from him telling me that the credit union is now on the select list with bail bondsmen, and other such important operators, and our checks will be recognized. All told, I was called upon a few more times and our checks were honored. It pays to have connections in high places.

Our membership at its height ran to about five hundred, and as I tackled the worst-case scenarios, I began to slowly see a turn-around. More solid citizens became members and the freeloaders, pie-cards, and other assorted no-goodniks and dipsomaniacs started falling away. We used to receive many thank-you notes from wives and family members. In one instance, we got a letter from the mother of a member signed with an "X," written by the parish priest and thanking us profusely for keeping her son out of trouble. One member apologized for his tardiness and wrote, "My wife was in the hospital having all her female gear removed." Another old country type came in one day and insisted on giving me a ten dollar bill for some little favor I had done for him while he was out to sea. By-and-large, I noticed that spending a little time with a member and lending a sympathetic ear to his story while helping to assist him with his problem, not only made me feel good, but simultaneously built a reservoir of good will all around.

The rest of the story is anticlimactic. I tried to clean up the mess left by the Mathew J.'s of the world as well I could and keep the wolf from the door, that is, keep the State Examiners satisfied. Technically, they were supposed to examine us twice a year but I don't think I saw them more than twice in the two years I was there. I had promised the Board I would stay around for one year, so when the time came, I started looking for a replacement. That wasn't so easy. After a diligent search and a little bit of luck, I ran into a likely candidate, a young man, Dave A., who needed a job. He was full of nervous energy and just nutty enough to be willing to try something new and different—just like somebody else I knew a few years earlier. Before he could change his mind, I introduced him to the board and after a short break-in period he was aboard.

I realized that as a non-member, Dave would never have the entrée to the Sailors' Union that I had, so I approached the Secretary for a spot on the agenda at our regular Monday night union meeting, and told him exactly what I wanted to say. When my turn came, and I had seen to it that the word got around about what I was going to say, the Hall was packed and ominously quiet when I got up to the mike. I took a minute or so to review the past, reminding them of how many were helped when the chips were down. I then reminded them about the open secret that the "con artists" among us are giving the organization a bad name regardless of our unofficial connection. I finally told them that there are some monies still outstanding that should be collected and though I wasn't going to mention any names publicly, I thought the time had come to turn over the names on my little list to the business agents who make the ships and collect the dues, so as to bring a little moral suasion to bear on our wayward brothers in order to get them to do the right thing. This, I told them, was the only way to save the good name of the Sailors' Union and keep the State Examiners from shutting us down.

The speech was a huge success and my motion carried unanimously. I received many congratulatory comments and handshakes. Eventually, not all of the outstanding money was collected and only a small reserve was available to take care of the real bad ones, and the credit union finally expired about a year later. Some money was lost but it was not half as bad as it could have been. Within a few days after my swan song, I was out to sea, earning the first decent paycheck since my last ship two years before.

Some philosophers have it that the very essence of maturity, not to speak of life, is the ability to respond to challenges and situations not in the textbooks. In a sense, the essence is in the handling of the problem. It's the nitty-gritty of the actual performance down on the firing line where it all happens, and where it counts. As my mentor and friend Duffy used to say, "You get your kicks in the doing, not the talking."

Chapter Twenty-one
The Foreign Legion Run

Another well-known run in the decade before the war was the "Foreign Legion" run. Highly popular, it got its name by virtue of the fact that though its basic itinerary was known, nobody knew the exact sequence of ports until you were a few days out to sea. It worked somewhat as follows. Starting from San Francisco, you took general cargo to Honolulu; picked up bulk sugar and case pineapple around the islands with such exotic names as Hilo, Kahului and Hanapepe, and back to Honolulu. This was known as the "Hawaiian Loop." Thence, southeast to the Panama Canal wherein, a few days on the other side of the canal, you were radioed your first East Coast port. Assuming it was New York, once you got there and discharged, they sent you on an "East Coast loop" touching any number of ports like Boston, Philadelphia, Scranton, Baltimore, etc., and thence back to New York, discharging and loading anew as you went, and finally back to San Francisco, where it started all over again.

Many sailors liked this run. You were out to sea as much as in port, and it was a most interesting variety of ports. On the other hand, it was a constant turnover of crews on the various loops for any number of reasons, mostly having to do with inability to stay out of gin mills long enough to make the next port. An example of a common type (thankfully in the minority) who shipped on these loops was a character who had put in a hitch in the U.S. Army and was referred to as "Yardbird." The title had nothing to do with rank but rather everything to do with status. In fact, I had already been shipmates with a number of ex-"dogfaces" and all of them were exemplary. However, in this particular case, it was fairly well known by our Hawaiian shipmates that he was a lowly yardbird who never quite made Private First Class, for all the time he was ostensibly defending our country's far-flung interests in the Pacific.

The scuttlebutt had it that he was discharged from Schofield Barracks some years before, obtained his shipping papers from the Shipping Commissioner in Honolulu and had not yet, as of then, gotten back to the mainland. Yard bird's operation was simple. He would ship aboard in Honolulu with an intense hangover and make a pretense at working for the first few days. This was necessary so as to build up a backlog of a few days' pay. When we made our first port on the loop, he would be entitled to draw at least half his pay, which he promptly did, and disappeared ashore, returning a few minutes before sailing time. He repeated this performance in each port, and quit in Honolulu, a *wahini"* (island girl) waiting for him on the dock.

Yardbird had another unique aspect to his personality. Hard as it was to believe, he was slightly handicapped in that he had lost some fingers on one hand. We assumed this happened either as a result of an accident while serving or some time after his discharge since there was no way he could get into the Army with such a handicap. When he shipped aboard, it was lunch time and he no sooner was seated at the table with us when he off-handedly called attention to his handicap by asking to pass a pitcher of milk down from the other end of the table ostentatiously waving his partially fingerless hand toward the pitcher. This was accompanied by a remark about handicapped people being just as good as any others. We soon discovered how correct he was, for when he was at the end of a guy-line (there were some rare moments when he pitched in and helped us secure for sea), he didn't need any help. His grip and pulling power were the equivalent of two. Like many handicapped people, he felt the need to overcompensate so as to prove his worth. Whatever demons he couldn't face, his inner drive to have to become paralyzed drunk every chance he got, remained a mystery and no one asked him any questions. However it would not be an understatement to say that we were quite relieved when he quit. This situation was not very conducive towards getting to know your shipmate.

****

Sometime in the spring of 1941, I joined the SS *Mahimahi,* a Matson Line freighter, and stayed on it for two entire round trips, approximately six months. When Yardbird quit, we picked up an AB whom nobody knew or had been shipmates with before. He was very quiet and unassuming, and looked to be in his mid-forties. When he spoke, we detected a slight Teutonic accent that was of no consequence on an American ship since almost everyone had some sort of "foreign" accent in those days. One evening, when coming off watch, a big discussion was going on in the mess room about F. D. R. and whether we're going to get into the war or not.

The discussion was apparently triggered by a rather strange incident the night before. It will be remembered that the war in Europe was now a year-and-a-half under way. British and Allied shipping were running under black-out while American ships, ostensibly neutral, were running with "lights abright." That previous midnight, in the Caribbean, a ship under blackout, no running lights showing, suddenly materialized a little too close for comfort and caught the lookout completely unaware. All hands became a little unnerved at this and immediately concluded that she was a "Limey" (British, that is) and deliberately came that close so that if a German submarine plying the area launched a torpedo and hit *us* instead, it would create an international incident. All hands were unanimously convinced that the British Admiralty devised this cunning little stratagem to get us into the war.

This discussion was under way when I got off watch so I thought I'd hang around and listen. It wasn't very long before this man with the accent stood up and like from out of nowhere delivered a homily somewhat as follows:

The other day I was reading an article in which the author says that all wars are fought for money, and if you look around you will see that most of the money in the world is owned by Jewish international bankers, so regardless of which side wins or loses, they will always win. And I can't help agreeing with him. Sooner or later, Franklin Rosenvelt [sic.] will get us into the war.

As soon as he finished I suddenly realized that this was the first I'd ever heard of any Nazi-like talk (and the last, as I now realize) in a ship's mess room. The reference to "international bankers" and the deliberate distortion of Roosevelt's name, a stock-in-trade at the time of the German Propaganda Minister, Joseph Goebbels, was a giveaway as to where he got his information. Interestingly enough, some of those present took issue with him and so did I, but it was a waste of time as far as he was concerned. I joined the discussion only to make sure that the other side of the question was aired to the listeners. The discussion was never alluded to again and he paid off at the very first East Coast port and I never saw him again.

As I recall this incident, I reflect on the fact that there was very little of this type of talk in the focsle, in fact it was almost nonexistent. Of course, from time to time, the usual bantering, semi-kidding, nation-baiting slurs would be heard; anti-Italian, anti-Jewish, and anti-whatever. Nevertheless, as a Jew, and a minority of one pretty much most of the time, I found myself face-to-face with the problem on those rare occasions. How does one react to bigotry? How does one handle openly expressed anti-Semitism? Maintaining silence for the sake of "keeping the peace" may be the wrong thing, since it leaves the field to the bigots. Raising your voice, when called for, must be done judiciously or you lose the whole effect. The mess room speaker was just tolerated. Nobody paid him much mind. But one must remember that when such banality achieved a position of power, the Holocaust was loosed on the world.

How did I accost it? For openers, it should be said that I never advertised. Since I wasn't a person of color, I didn't stand out. The fact of the matter was that I usually blended in as just another wage slave in the focsle doing a job, pursuing the sea, in good standing in the union and trying to be a good shipmate. It was only when discussions started and I felt confronted, that I volunteered my background. All told, I said what I felt called upon to say, and I don't remember a single instance of ever being reprimanded or denigrated. As for alienation, other than what was built into my psyche—the baggage one carries around from birth that is—I seldom felt it in those days, but since the Russian and German holocaust, I've changed my mind.

One of the strangest things I encountered was a little touch of bigoted anti-Semitism in my own community on the left. I think back that almost every IWW member—both ex- and dues-paying—I ever met, at one time or another stereotyped all "international bankers" as Jews and/or vice versa. And when confronted by me they were surprised to realize the contradiction. In doing so, I found that personal relationships counted for more than political opinions. And as mentioned a number of times in these memoirs, personal relationships were made on the job and in the focsle, and they transcended all other relationships with the possible exception of marriage and immediate family.

We cannot leave the subject of bigotry without talking about racism, discrimination in terms of color rather than nationality. I think I am safe in making the point-blank statement that the Sailors' Union of the Pacific, as well as the Seafarers' International Union, practiced discrimination in employment against African-Americans, or Negroes, the preferred term in those years, despite all their protestations to the contrary. As a matter of fact some of us enlightened ones all but took our lives in our hands when we even alluded to the subject let alone bring it up point blank. This in spite of the fact that President Roosevelt issued his Executive Order # 8802 on June 25,1941 (a full five months before Pearl Harbor) which came about, as was well known at the time and has been fully documented since, by the threatened "March On Washington" led by A. Philip Randolph of the Brotherhood of Sleeping Car Porters. The very threat of this march brought about the Executive Order.

This was not the case with all people of color. The Hawaiian Islands in those days were and probably still are a living laboratory for ethnologists. The Sailors' Union, by the same token, contained a strong percentage of Hawaiian, Chinese, Japanese, and Korean, mixtures as well as "pure"; various kinds as well, of South Sea islanders, a sprinkling of Latin Americans with Negro characteristics, but no African-Americans. The reason for this was pure prejudice. The same reasons heard against voting rights and lunch-counter integration in the South during the 1960s were used by the membership as far back as I can remember, to keep African-Americans out. This position was reinforced by the Armed Forces, all of which practiced segregation during the War since Roosevelt's Executive Order applied only to civilian employment. To round out the picture, it wasn't until President Truman issued his Executive Order #9981 on July 27, 1948 integrating the Armed Forces, that some progress was made. However, none of this applied to the U.S. Merchant Marine with its privately-owned ships and autonomous unions.

This is not to say that there weren't any African-Americans sailing West Coast ships. Other than the handful I knew in the Sailors' Union who "passed," those that did not were in the Stewards Department and members of a small Communist-controlled union, mentioned somewhere above, known as the Marine Cooks and Stewards Union-CIO. And though the antagonism between us and them was on the one hand highly political, on the other hand there was a mean, ill-spirited, bigoted current of racial hatred that, though never talked about officially, was nevertheless audibly voiced unofficially in many ways, and by many of my brothers. In these conversations, when I was present, no amount of mitigation on my part was to any avail. In fact, some of my mildest questioning was overcome with such wild expletives as "nigger lover." Looking back at it now, I must say that the worst race baiters were the Hawaiians and Latin Americans; in other words, those closest to the African Americans on the color spectrum. Perish the thought that they should ever be taken for Black!

As a matter of fact, I was once witness to a violent scene in a bar in Jacksonville, Florida, when we put in there overnight on one of our "Foreign Legion" runs. One of our crew, Jim J., a Portuguese-Hawaiian with some of the usual Negroid features, entered a bar with us and sat down for a drink. The yahoo-rednecks present insisted that he was "colored" and that he go to a "colored bar." Jim, grossly insulted, was no slouch in these kinds of beefs, and so a fight broke out immediately in which both benches emptied, so to speak, we being vastly outnumbered. I too, a normally peaceful type, had to take a few and give a few before we got him out of there alive, into a taxi and back to the ship.

It should be mentioned that there were very few "pure" Hawaiians. Pretty much all Hawaiians, as well as many South Sea islanders (as we called those of the Marshalls and Polynesia), were some mixture or another, usually Hawaiian-Portuguese, since Portuguese sailors and traders were the first large group from Europe to settle in those parts and intermarry. The Portuguese themselves were not so "pure" either, so that the color lines were all mixed up.

I am sometimes questioned as to how this came about. Why did the Sailors' Union accept every other person of color except African-Americans? The reason is that during the great strikes of 1934 and 1936, the Hawaiian islanders already had a foothold in the union. They banded together, albeit as a minority of the membership and, literally and figuratively, not only held their ground as good union men, but opened the door a bit wider to the point where they got one of their own, Maxie Weisbarth, elected as a patrolman (the patrolman met all ships putting into port and helped settle as many beefs as possible, whereas the Business Agent handled the wider issues with the ship owners and the community) in the port of San Francisco and soon after in Honolulu. When they showed themselves as good and sincere fighters, they won the respect (maybe reluctantly) of the general membership. Had there been such a core of African-Americans sailing West Coast ships in the period from 1934 to 1936, the same would have happened with them.

Nor can we leave the issue of bigotry without mentioning the anti-Japanese xenophobia and hysteria that gripped the country after December 7, 1941. Many may still remember and those who were not yet on the scene must have heard about the shoddy treatment handed out to our Japanese co-citizens and non-citizens, native-born and naturalized. If December 7 was F. D. R.'s Day of Infamy, then May 5, 1942, the day he allowed the forced relocation of all Japanese people on the West Coast to what were euphemistically called "relocation camps," was equally infamous. The Sailors' Union was taken aback at this, since we had many members of Japanese ancestry. Those living in Hawaii were allowed to remain there, but some thirty-five to forty of our members were on the beach in various West Coast ports and they got caught in the dragnet. It is to the everlasting credit of the Sailors' Union that its Secretary and its New York port agent went to bat for these men and succeeded in prying the War Shipping Administration bureaucracy loose so as to liberate them and allow them to transfer to the East Coast and Gulf and continue in their chosen trade. I had been shipmates with at least three of them, and I was happy to see them back on the West Coast after the war.

Anyone reflecting on the tenor of the times these days will notice that disparagement and denigration of things oriental is still very much with us. Since the middle of the nineteenth century with its "Oriental Exclusion Acts" to this very day of Japan-bashing, rightly or wrongly, the Caucasian people tend to look down on and devalue the achievements of the Orient.

The American focsle in my time was no exception. As I think back on the attitudes of most of my shipmates, they invariably equated almost all goods coming out of the Orient as "junk"; in fact the term "Japanese junk" was the commonly accepted phrase. One popular piece of mythology had it that the inscription, "Made in USA," referred to a city in Japan, whereas "Made in U.S.A." was the real thing. A very popular story, oft-repeated in many a mess room, ran something like this: At the turn of the century, the Japanese Navy sent a delegation to the Clydeside in Scotland to learn about shipbuilding. The Scottish engineers turned a set of blueprints for a battleship over to them, whereupon the delegation went back to Japan and proceeded to lay the keel. When the hull was finished and launched, it slid down the ways, capsized and sunk. The explanation was that the wily Scotties drew the plans one-quarter inch off and pulled a fast one on the hapless Orientals. Although all this ridiculous talk came to a screeching halt on December 7, 1941, it didn't necessarily put an end to anti-oriental bias to this very day.

****

Starting with the "Foreign Legion" run and many times thereafter, I got to be a frequent visitor to the Islands. Since quite a few who shipped on this run were natives, I became friendly with a goodly number of them. Much to my surprise, I found very little sophistication in their attitudes; they were rather simple in their reactions. They either hated you or loved you and there were no gray areas in between. Many times I was invited to their homes, when we put into the various island ports and even participated in their *luaus,* as they called their family gatherings.

On one such occasion, my watch partner, Joseph Holomalea, known in certain parts as Jojo (one of that rare breed of "pure" Hawaiian), took me to his sister's house for a family luau somewhere on the island of Hawaii, just outside of Hilo. This was Friday and we negotiated with the chief mate for a few days off. In the focsle, especially on arrival in homeports, all sorts of negotiations used to take place, trading days with each other. Jojo's sister and her husband met us at the gangway in a jeep and started taking us up Mauna Loa.

At first I thought they were giving me the Deluxe Cook's Tour, but I soon found out differently. Somewhere around the eight- to ten-thousand-foot level, Jojo's brother-in-law stopped the jeep and reaching under the seat, pulled out a rifle, cocked it and aiming for what looked like thick brush on the mountainside, pulled the trigger—my ear drums nearly bursting. All three of them, big and overweight as they were, dashed out of the jeep and plunged into the brush. Following in their wake, I soon realized that he brought down a huge wild boar that was to be the main staple of the upcoming luau.

I was enjoying this escapade no end, until it came to hauling the thing aboard. It must have been some combination of the rarified air at a high altitude and the steady sipping on a bottle of Jim Beam that Jojo's brother-in-law brought along for the occasion, coupled with the fact that in those days many of us were still smoking, that made us have one heck of a time wrestling that dead boar aboard. I still don't believe it, but it took the four of us at least two full hours to drag that thing one hundred feet or so and get it up on the front hood of the jeep.

When we finally got to their house, other members of the family had everything set to go. The pit was ready and the fire was going. After some initial preparation of the carcass, they trussed it up on a spit, while a small electric motor was hooked up to keep it continuously turning.

One of the many things Hawaiians joke about is something called "barking pig." This refers to the many stories told about Oriental people using domesticated dogs as a protein staple in their diet, usually camouflaged to make it seem like a young porker. Whatever the truth of the matter, I can personally testify to the fact that the menu at this luau was the real thing—wild pig.

The following evening, some twenty-four hours later, the crowd was there, well oiled, along with a ukulele/Hawaiian guitar combo to furnish the music. Apparently, half the island was in his family and, although I was supposed to be an honored guest, the party was really for his sister whose birthday it happened to be.

I soon began to realize that for most Hawaiians, in those days, it didn't take much of an excuse to throw a luau; Jojo's arrival coinciding with his sister's birthday was enough. She had a large family and his brother-in-law had a good job on the waterfront. The party lasted all night and everybody was your instant friend. We sat around in circles on the ground and passed around a bottle of stuff called "kava juice." It was a ground root, grown all over the place, that when fermented into a liquid turned out to be about 180 proof. Custom dictated that when the bowl was passed around, refusal was not acceptable, so you just touched it to your lips or tongue, maybe tasted it and passed it on. Sooner or later, and with me it was sooner, it gets to you and I suddenly found myself unable to get up off the ground. Two of the men, realizing my difficulty, moved over towards me as if on signal, and placing a hand under each of my arms, lifted me straight up and guided me towards the outdoor toilet on the edge of the field, trucked in for the party. I never would have made it without them.

Two other men with long butcher knives were cutting strips of meat off the carcass and passed them around, while a couple of women were skinning pineapples, slicing them and passed them around the other way. Bowls of poi also made their appearance from somewhere and we scooped up the stuff with our fingers, in traditional Hawaiian style. Poi is made from the taro root, ground, baked and mashed, and then mixed into a paste and fermented.

Meanwhile, ukuleles and guitars were strumming away, with musicians spelling each other off, as the night wore on. It seemed to me that almost everybody there took a turn as musician. Singing and dancing was continuous—that is, if you could get up off the ground—while all sorts of comings and goings were occurring in and out of the main house as well

217

as the fields beyond. Along about 4:00 or 5:00 a.m., they piled Jojo and me into the jeep and drove us back down to the ship, barely making it for a 6:00 a.m. departure. Though my hangover stayed with me almost to the Canal, I must say that I never tasted a better piece of pork or had such a wild time either before or since. I came to the conclusion that everyone should try something like that at least once in a lifetime.

Some days later, when things cleared up a bit, I asked Jojo about something that had been bothering me since the party. In visiting the Bishop Museum in Honolulu and according to some stories I had read in the past, the natives, in organizing a luau, would dig an *"imu* pit" and use a local wood called *kiawa,* as well as chunks of basalt to light and keep their fires going. The latter was readily obtainable from the volcanic rock in such plentiful supply there.

Jojo laughed at the innocent question that only a *Haoli* would ask. (This word, pronounced "howly" is well known around the Islands and simply means visitor, or a Caucasian mainlander. There is also *Hapa Haoli,* which means half-white/half-Hawaiian.) His answer was straight-forward as usual. "That stuff is for the tourists. We live in the twentieth century, and we don't bother with that anymore." And today, with the Islands converted to a great big tourist trap, some of my friends who've gone over recently tell me that they don't even do it for the tourists anymore.

This reversal of roles goes on everywhere in the world where "progress" is encroaching. By the same token, the Eskimos in the Arctic now use snow-mobiles and high-tech harpoon guns in pursuit of their food and livelihood. And it all has to do with making life a little easier and more bearable. The loss of one's heritage and the adoption of the white man's culture is just one of the consequences that ensues. Whatever conclusion one comes to, the fact of the matter was that we had one great time at that luau.

❋❋❋❋❋❋❋❋❋❋❋

Among the many things occupying a seafaring man's mind, plotting a life after the sea is quite common. With many of course, it's pure fantasy but with others it's a reasonable goal, either in the planning stage or well under way.

Kenny W. was a mild-mannered Islander, soft-spoken and easy-going, aged somewhere in his young twenties. He possessed a ready smile and his countenance radiated peace and serenity. While working on deck he was both knowledgeable and handy, never wasting too many moves or gestures. Kenny was my watch partner on the SS *Hawaiian Packer,* a C-3 type ship twice the size of a Liberty ship and therefore requiring twice as much work. But since he was a damned good shipmate, it made life much more tolerable.

On this ship, again on the Foreign Legion run, we carried the usual deckload covering all the hatches, but on the number four hatch, behind the midship house and thereby somewhat sheltered, a small space was reserved for a consignment of a dozen or so cages containing chickens. On closer observation they turned out to be roosters all individually compartmentalized, one to a cage. They pranced back and forth and made a lot of noise, not the least of which was the incongruity of a cock crowing at daybreak on the high seas. To the uninformed eye it seemed like just another piece of general cargo, consigned to someone somewhere in the Hawaiian Islands.

One evening on our watch below, with both of us stretched out on our respective bunks, curtains semi-drawn and I with my nose in a book, I heard the rather familiar sound of steel passing back and forth, slowly and steadily, across on what sounded like a whetstone. I assumed Kenny was sharpening his pocketknife, since a basic requirement of all sailors in our day was to carry a pocketknife. (An oft-repeated axiom among the iron men from wooden ships was, "A sailor without a knife is like a whore without a cunt.")

Something, however unexplainable, impelled me to take a second look. It was not a pocketknife at all. It turned out to be a small, short-handled exacto blade as those used by artists for paper cutting. Finally my curiosity got the better of me and I asked Kenny just what one did with an exacto blade aboard a ship?

"It's a knife, not an exacto blade, " he answered. " I use it on my chickens."

"Your chickens? What chickens?"

"Yes. You know those cages on the number four hatch? They're mine."

"Really! What do you do with them?"

"I train them to fight," he answered in a matter of fact tone. It suddenly flashed on me that here was a guy akin to a fight promoter, using animals instead of people.

"So this is a sideline with you?" I went on.

"Oh yes, but I'm trying to make a go of it full time," he patiently explained. "My sister and her husband take care of things for me while I'm away. They feed them, keep them clean and watch over them, and I buy and sell and promote fights stateside."

"So when and where do these fights go on?" I asked, still half-doubting what I was hearing.

"Mostly in the Filipino community around Stockton and San Jose."

"Do you think you could explain to a dumb bunny like me, just how these things work?"

"Well, if you want to fight your chicken, let's say," he went on patiently (invariably Kenny used the word chicken in referring to his fighting cocks), "you line up a fight with another guy, and you bet on it, let's say ten dollars. Then you exchange chickens and feel them around real good. Only one razor is permitted tied to one of his legs. Then you go to your corner just like in a regular prizefight and when the referee rings the bell, you let go of your chicken. They mix it up and the one who draws the first blood usually is left standing and wins. Of course lots of betting is going on all around you since these fights are well attended and you have to pay to get in, just like real fights uptown."

"So, how long does a fight last? And how long does a chicken last?" was my next question.

"Oh, about a few minutes or so, maybe two fights but almost never more than three."

"So, how much of this is around anyway?"

"Oh, they're all over the place. Here, look at this book," he said, as he reached over to his shelf and handed me a small magazine in a *Readers Digest* format and equally thick, characteristically named, *The Pit*. As I leafed through the magazine I was amazed to discover this whole other world that I had known nothing about. The major part of the copy was taken up with advertising relating to dietary formulas, cages and paraphernalia, but most importantly to nasty-looking knife blades of every size shape and description having to do with fitting on a rooster's leg and sold openly at locations all over the United States. The pit, of course, was the equivalent of the boxing ring, and to my further chagrin, I discovered that dogs as well as roosters were trained to this calling. I also surmised where the term " pit bull" came from.

So I asked Kenny why he didn't use dogs, and he answered rather quickly, "Oh no. Not dogs. I couldn't stand to see them suffer and die that way."

"But chickens?"

"Oh, well, chickens," he sighed. "They're so dumb ... Nobody misses them ... But I'll tell you what I'm really looking for," he went on. "I'm looking for a chemist."

"A chemist?" Why a chemist?"

"Well, you remember when I told you about how we exchange chickens before the fight, and feel them all around for hidden knives?" he continued. "If I find a chemist who will invent a secret poison formula, say a colorless salve or liquid, where let's say I can take some in my hand and rub it into his chicken and it catches on right away, so by the time the fight starts in a minute, his chicken is half dead ... Boy, I'll betcha even if I cut him in for half, I could make a million on it .... "

I thought I'd heard enough by then and thanked Ken for his patience with me as I went back to my book. I have thought of this conversation many times since then. We have already discovered that once upon a time it didn't take much to push this attitude one step further and apply it to people. After all, you can always make an exception for dogs. But I still can't figure it out. Like I said earlier on, Kenny was such a nice guy and one hell of a good shipmate.

Chapter Twenty-two
Unquiet Souls

The rebel's quarrel with society has neurotic roots.
Arthur Koestler, 1905-1983

I n my enforced peripatetic comings and goings around the waterfronts of the world, I often heard reference to an aphorism that rang true. It went something like this: On any given waterfront anywhere in the world, you will always find:

> A British rustbucket tramp
> A Norweigian beachcomber
> A French whore
> And Swedish matches.

Be that as it may, on the waterfronts of the world, not all the people you meet have a direct connection with you in the focsle. Like many such cross-roads, all sorts of people meet in many other ways other than being ship-mates. That special connection you have to another due to bonding as ship-mates doesn't always mean that you own each other forever. Rather it means that at a certain point, due more likely than not to random selection, you were thrown together and had to make it work. In most instances it did, but sometimes it did not. When word got around that so-and-so was a lousy shipmate, or as one would occasionally hear in that connection, "a miserable bastard to live with," it didn't take long for him to realize that he either would have to change his ways or go find some other way to make a living.

Most seafaring men, especially those who failed ashore rather than those who came in and left due to World War II, were in the nature of things independent and rebellious and, as stated a number of times now in this narrative, many of them succumbed to hard liquor consumption as a way out of their difficulties with themselves and society. And all the more amazing was it that many of them "saw the light" and quit of their own accord. Furthermore, the fact that they would allow themselves to be organized and molded into a functioning unit when the opportunity presented itself was the greatest story of all.

Fred Liere was one such person. A former Wobbly, he had mastered a drinking problem some years before we met on a stand-by job on a steam schooner, the SS *Edwin Christensen,* preparing her for sea. He had left Rotterdam where he was born and made his first trip as a cabin boy at the age of thirteen on a topsail trading schooner on the North Sea, just before World War I. His father, an ex-skipper, ran a combination hotel and bar on the waterfront and as Fred said, looking back, he probably "did his share of crimping, pimping and shanghaiing." When the war was over, he found himself on the New York City waterfront, broke and on the beach.

In those days the U.S. Army had a deal. Sign up for a three-year hitch and you are guaranteed citizenship. Since he told me this story, I have met many people who availed themselves of that opportunity. In the Army, with just a smattering of English, Fred was sent to somewhere in the Midwest and assigned to the Cavalry; this, in spite of the fact that he "didn't know one end of a horse from the other," a situation that army recruits face to this day. Nevertheless, Fred became an expert horse handler, as well as a mule skinner, since the army still had mules. In later years, we went out to the races together a few times and he walked me around showing me what to look for in a horse. This, needless to say, didn't prevent him from losing just about every bet he placed.

Fred carried out his end of the bargain and obtained his citizenship, but being of a rebellious temperament, and having been conditioned by some hard knocks at an early age, his army discharge was "less than honorable" rather than the usual "honorable discharge." This haunted him in his later years when he began to realize that although his complaint against society was valid, he would remark, "I was a headstrong kid."

Fred drifted to the West Coast, went back to sea and joined the IWW. When the 1934 strike was called, he was one of the first to answer the call and helped tie up the ship he was on. He maintained his militancy for the next few years, engaging in many job actions. A few years before Pearl Harbor he became ill, was hospitalized and underwent a series of operations, all of which in later years (when psychosomatic illness was the vogue in pop-psychology) he blamed on his "neurotic inadequacies," as he put it. He never married though he had a woman friend interested in him. At the last moment he backed away from marriage, claiming, "with the life that I've led, I could never do a woman justice."

One morning sometime in the spring of 1950, upon his return from a trip, we went downtown to the Post Office to pick up his mail. Many seamen kept a box in the old Rincon Annex in San Francisco. There was a letter postmarked Rotterdam. He looked at the envelope for what seemed an eternity and I couldn't help but notice the return address in the upper left-hand corner. It was his surname. Silently, he opened the envelope. The letter was written in his mother tongue, Dutch, which he miraculously was still able to read. It would seem that, most miraculously of all, his older brother had survived the war. He lost a wife and child in the starvation winter of 1944 and was now remarried. His new wife pressed him to start looking for his long-lost brother. Together, they had written to every port in the United States on both coasts and to all the seafaring unions they could reach, as well as all Dutch consuls in various seaports. In San Francisco they hit pay dirt. After some discussion and an evening of soul searching, Fred sat down and wrote his brother that he was coming over to visit him. Within the week, he bought an entirely new outfit, a suitcase full of clothes and an open-ended round-trip ticket, and away he went, closing the circle opened some forty years and two world wars ago.

Two weeks later he was back on our doorstep. Yes, he visited with his brother and sister-in-law. All she did for the entire time was "cry, bitch and moan about how they needed everything and you Americans have so much money." (Considering that the Marshall Plan was implemented at about this time, the argument per se, made sense.) After visiting around the scenes of his childhood, in which among other things he found a boyhood friend, a Jew, who had been hidden during the entire German occupation, he gave all his money, his life savings of a few thousand dollars to his brother and left for home. In the next few years a few more letters were exchanged, the last one announcing his brother's death and that ended the rebirth of a possible new beginning.

After Ann and I got married, Fred became the surrogate grandfather to our children. When he came over (invariably with a loaf of sourdough and a bottle of red wine) he devoted himself completely to the kids until they went to bed, in spite of the fact that he was becoming progressively deaf. They remember him lovingly and to this day they keep his picture around. Fred managed to get a pension, one of the first issued by the union pension fund, although he always maintained he'd never live long enough to collect the first check. In fact, he lived for ten years thereafter "on the rocking chair," as sailors referred to pension and unemployment insurance checks. A sailor's sailor and a man of uncompromising integrity (a famous old Wobbly slogan was "No compromise, no surrender"), he managed to live his life according to his own principles and as he saw fit, within the limits allowed him by an otherwise hostile world.

****

The days we write about were days of intense social upheaval and political activity in the country at large as well as on the American waterfront and they drew many characters and personalities into the maelstrom of events. The savants tell us that history brings people up from the depths to center stage; they play out their part and either depart willingly or are pushed aside. And those who manage to hang on to this locomotive of history, grab onto a piece of the action and, if lucky, stay with it long enough to make a contribution, as well as in many instances making of it a career and/or building an empire.

The years of the mid-to-late 1930s offered many examples of such people, driven to the edge of despair by the conditions they found on American ships and by the frustration encountered in changing them. By putting themselves forward, they were in effect offering to take the lead. In some instances it was received and accepted, but in others it went against the grain of the times and fell by the wayside. There were many people around the waterfront in those days, some highly political and others totally innocent, who fell into one or another category on the spectrum. One among them, Henry F. Jackson known universally as "Blackie," had a profound influence on me. It should be explained that seafaring men many times refer to each other by the color of their complexion. Dark-haired people were called "Blackie," blonde and light-complexioned ones were known as "Whitey," and then of course there was "Red."

People come to political and social consciousness in many different ways. In those days, if they became radicalized before entering the job market, they were known as "colonizers." But if they achieved political consciousness while on the job, in this case within their sea-going years, they were known as "indigenous." Of the former there were many; of the latter there were very few. It was to this latter category that Blackie belonged.

Born in the Czech-Bohemian section of Cleveland, Ohio, he came of age in the depression years. His childhood was wretched. His father, a skilled machinist, drank heavily and beat him, his siblings and his wife regularly. As an acolyte and altar boy he attended church, but as a thinking individual he was dissatisfied with its answers. Early on, he developed a stutter that he couldn't control. One day in his late teens, his father tried to beat him up once too often, but Blackie turned the tables on him, beat him up instead and left home. He ran away to Baltimore where he managed to get aboard a ship on the Isthmian Line, a well-known ore carrier in those days.

Some years later, after we got to know each other, he would tell me of these childhood and adolescent traumas and avidly justify and rationalize his assaulting his father as "self defense," although it could easily have turned into patricide. Thinking back on it now, his mentioning of it from time to time seemed to betray a deep guilt feeling with which he could never quite make his peace. However, it is interesting to note that when I knew him he never stuttered.

In those days, on many Eastern seaboard waterfronts, a paper union called the International Seamen's Union (ISU), run by careerists and gangsters and adhering to the AFL, was in control of labor politics. This meant that if you got a job, they would try and get you to join the union and pay dues. That's where it ended. Their contracts, if any, were meaningless and unenforceable.

After a number of trips, Blackie got on a ship where the mate and bosn demanded that the sailors go over the side on stages while at sea and paint the hull. Sailors painting the hull in port was very common, but unheard of at sea. Even from a selfish, self-serving company point of view, it was too dangerous. Blackie aroused the crew and they refused to do any such thing. When they got back to port he found himself blackballed, and the union not only refused to defend him, but barred him from the hall.

The next day he sneaked into the hall, and surrounding himself with some men he could trust, jumped up on a card table and proceeded to denounce the collusive union bureaucrats as tools of the ship owners, which is exactly what they were. The members became so inflamed, that they drove the officials out of the hall and held possession of it for two days. Eventually the police arrived and restored the hall to the officials. Realizing what he could do gave Blackie a new lease on life, and after the incident he went into an extended period of reading, studying and devouring every and any book he could lay his hands on covering just about every subject he could think of.

He made his way through the political maze of the various tendencies on the waterfronts up and down the East Coast and, sometime in 1936, took a ship around to the West Coast and joined the recently declared strike. Somewhere in this time frame he had made his way into the Socialist Workers Party (SWP), thereby becoming the first Trotskyist in the SUP, as well as the first SUP member in the SWP. He was very active in the strike and became very well known in the union.

This was the first and only political organization that he ever joined. Tortuous as it may sound, it is worth digressing to explain the workings of some of the waterfront politics of the day. There was a problem. The organization known as the SWP was a Bolshevik/Leninist sort of organization, and required a form of discipline that Blackie was unprepared to give. Basically, all these organizations operated from the top down. Orders and directives were issued down a hierarchical ladder, and execution of these directives was left to the locals on the scene. But when the ranks started sending their input back up the ladder, it usually got lost somewhere along the way and/or fell on deaf ears. Ostensibly, once a year, a certain time frame was set aside for "open discussion" in the safe confines of the party. After a while, it was turned off and things went back to status quo, ante bellum. The better-known Communist Party (CP) operated exactly the same way, except even a little more rigidly and totalitarian.

Both these political groups were attempting to do the same thing—to become influential enough to impose its own agenda on the Sailors'

Union. The SWP opted to support the SUP against the CP. In this intense situation, the SWP submerged itself totally to the aspiring leadership of the Sailors' Union. Blackie and some other independent spirits, though agreeing to prevent the CP from imposing its hegemony on the West Coast, didn't see fit to accept a non-critical role towards the union leadership and the machine it was building. Given his personality, it is surprising that he lasted the few short years that he did.

Blackie liked to sail quartermaster on the American President Line ships running to the Orient. When the war broke out, this option was foreclosed. By now married and with a new baby, he didn't want to go to sea (where, as previously stated, we were "frozen" by executive fiat), but the draft board threatened him with military service, a fate we all thought of as a worse case scenario.

About a year after Ann and I were married (1943), we were sitting around one Sunday morning, I on the beach between ships, when we got a phone call from Blackie asking us if we could come over for a little while. When we got there, he sat us down and explained to us that within the last few weeks, a buildup of some inner tensions had taken place and he had what could best be described as a "nervous breakdown." He had quickly made his way to a local clinic seeking help and was assigned to a resident woman psychiatrist. Thus began a series of bizarre incidents that threw him into an anxiety panic.

The psychiatrist, Jean Tatlock, apparently must have had troubles of her own, because a few sessions downstream, the morning newspapers announced her suicide! Spread all over the front pages of the local newspapers was the fact that she was the former paramour of one J. Robert Oppenheimer, a brilliant physicist at the University of California (who, as we learned much later, had been assigned to the Los Alamos Laboratory to work on the atom bomb). Blackie was then assigned to another therapist, a certain hyphenated Cavendish-Moxom, who after a few sessions suggested that he do political work on the waterfront, with an oblique reference to working with the Communist Party!

What with all this trauma, he kept his stability long enough to get out from under these crazy shrinks, and was at the moment in a bad state trying to decide what to do. He described to us rather vividly (his descriptive abilities were superb) all his symptoms and reactions and it seemed his most immediate worry was how to keep working ashore, since he couldn't get himself to ship out just yet, and still satisfy the requirements of the Draft Board so as to keep his "vital industry" deferment. He could count on the union's help but he could never count on the communist shrink at the hospital, whom he justifiably thought was quite capable of making life miserable for him in view of Blackie's strong anti-communist views.

In later years, when we'd get together, we would talk about this incident and marvel at the interlocking, albeit circuitous paths, our lives took and how our lives intersected with history. Also, we realized that this was our first exposure ever to this type of phenomenon, and Ann and I felt extremely sympathetic and scared as hell as to where this all would lead.

As luck would have it, our secretary decided just about then to inaugurate an organizing campaign at the Standard Oil Company in Richmond. This was a fleet of about a half-dozen coastwise tankers, all of which were anchored offshore and totally obnoxious to work on, for all the reasons mentioned elsewhere in this memoir.

Blackie was asked to join a hastily put together core of organizers to go across the Bay and try to organize the tanker crews into the Sailors' Union. He then asked me to help him. I shipped on one of them for one month, signed up the majority of the crew and turned them over to Blackie who was the contact ashore. But it was all a thankless task. Most of the crews turned over so fast that they never got enough of a majority for a National Labor Relations Board election. And to top it off, the chief organizer was a petty gangster and shrewd operator named Hal Banks, who in later years achieved notoriety on the Canadian waterfront. Neither Blackie nor I could tolerate him. I finally gave up and fled back across the Bay to catch a freighter.

After a few months, when Blackie was about to explode, another minor miracle happened. The New York Port patrolman's job was open, and our business agent asked for him. Blackie accepted the job, picked up his family and moved to New York City.

In those days, the latest fad in psychotherapy was a thing called "Vegeto-therapy," as advocated and practiced by Dr. Wilhelm Reich, a former disciple of Dr. Sigmund Freud. Blackie enlisted in this new cause; that is to say, he threw himself into this movement with the same avidity and energy as he did in his previous union and political life, complete with textbooks and message, chapter and verse.

Soon thereafter, I caught an inter-coastal ship and visited him in New York. I remember coming away with an armful of books covering an assortment of Dr. Reich's writings, the political-philosophical ones of which I thought rather highly and the psycho-technical ones I barely understood. The long and short of it all was that Blackie submitted himself to a "depth therapy" for the next few years, the result of which seemed to be his total emotional unhinging. That is to say, they stripped away his "character armor" (a term they were fond of using) and put nothing in its place to support him while acquiring a new personality, or whatever it was you were supposed to acquire. One of the aspects of "Vegeto-therapy" was the presence of a rectangular metal-lined plywood box that Reich called an "Accumulator." You were supposed to sit in it and absorb certain thermal currents. It wouldn't be so funny when one stops to realize that some years later, many people had tried it with varying effects—from feelings of warmth to no feelings at all.

Unbelievable as it may seem, Dr. Reich died in jail serving time for interstate transport of the box—a supposedly illegal act and a picayunish and demeaning charge avidly pursued by his detractors (some of whom were known Communist fellow-travelers) and some avid government bureaucrats out of the Food and Drug Administration. Probably one of the best-kept secrets about this little-known case is that a Nuremberg-like book burning incident took place at the conclusion of the case. By law, since the "Accumulator" was judged to be a quack-type gadget rather than a therapeutic-scientific type healing instrument, all copies of the box, including all literature associated with it, were ordered destroyed. And since all his books and articles made some reference to the "Accumulator," they were all collected and tossed into a big bonfire by federal marshals and destroyed! This happened in 1956 in the United States to a man who had his books burned in Germany in 1933.[16]

It would be less than fair to leave the subject of Dr. Reich and his therapy without mentioning that at this late date, at the beginning of the 1990s, more and more people are showing an interest in his work and life in spite of its tragic ending. Today, entire groups of healers are using types of massage and acupressure in alternative schools of therapy and many traditional health workers are recommending them in conjunction with their own. Lastly, I venture to say, that the latest theories encompassing the electro-chemical concept of the human brain as the seat of directed human activity can be traced to some of Reich's ideas, among others. Much is being written about Dr. Reich, not the least of which was a full-scale biography which received national attention in the literary reviews a few years ago.[17] As the apostle Mathew would say, "A prophet is not without honor save in his own country."

At about this time the union job was over, and Blackie got the idea that a complete change of life might be possible, and for some reason which I was never able to fathom, he started taking an interest in agriculture. Some years later, I broached the subject and the only thing I could come up with was that he was trying to find a niche as far away from the sea as possible. As we laughed about it, some years later, it even got funnier when we remembered a ditty we used to sing, "Farmers and Tailors Make Dollar Line Sailors" to the tune of "Blow the Man Down." The Dollar Line was the predecessor of the American President Lines on which he liked to ship as quartermaster.

He enrolled in an agricultural college somewhere out on Long Island which he attended for two years. As usual he was in constant friction with the authorities. One story he told me had to do with a final exam on which he scored a ninety-eight percent. When he got his paper back, he realized that the two points had to do with a factual item. He immediately went back to the textbook, and found the answer could have gone either way. After a heated argument with his instructor, he forced him to change his grade to one hundred percent.

In retrospect, I feel that such compulsive behavior went a long way towards undermining Blackie's own effectiveness and ability to cope in life. Nothing much ever came of this agricultural experience. He got a job managing a dairy farm for a weekend gentleman farmer who wanted to make it pay. Needless to say, there was disagreement and the job lasted a very short while. That was the end of the farming life.

Soon after, needing a job, Blackie went to look up some of his old union buddies in the Painters' Union. Lots of sailors who went ashore got into house painting, since so much painting was done at sea. The Painters' Union had contracts with the City of New York to paint and maintain its various housing developments scattered around the city. He went to work in these buildings. Mentally and spiritually this was stultifying, but it was a port in the storm for however long it was necessary.

While all this was going on, his wife Leona, working full time as a schoolteacher, was trying to keep the family, by now increased to three children, together. But when the Reichian therapy wasn't working, for whatever reasons, and Blackie's personal problems remained unresolved, he took more and more to drink and they separated. Somewhere in this time frame Blackie made one more trip, again as quartermaster on an American President Lines ship. This was to be his last.

The alcoholism and painting kept going for a year or so when he met Mary D., who steered him towards Alcoholics Anonymous. Apparently the AA meetings and Mary's help were effective in de-toxing him long enough to allow them to get married and set up a normal married life, when a routine medical exam came up with the diagnosis of Parkinson's disease. As the disease spread slowly but insidiously within a year after they got married, Blackie had to retire from all work and go on permanent disability.

Throughout all of this, Mary worked full time as a social worker and tried to attend to Blackie's needs as best she could. As the Parkinson's began to take over and as he became less and less able to cope, Blackie's life was turned more and more into a constant and intense anger against everybody and everything that stood in the way of his perceived needs. He grew progressively self-centered and unable to compromise, this becoming a dominant feature of his personality. Chances are that the nature of the disease was such that he was destined to fight a rear-guard action and finally lose. The battle against the ship owners and the establishment now became the battle against Parkinson's.

When the 1936 strike called for militancy and uncompromising behavior against the ship owners and the political elements on the waterfront whose policies and politics were considered anathema and detrimental to our interests, it was Blackie and people like him who pointed the way. Without them we would have lost the battle.

A case in point has to do with a famous incident that took place immediately after the 1936 strike on the SS *Florence Luckenbach* of the Luckenbach Steamship Co. (known to us all as the "Brokenback Steamship Co."). The Luckenbach ships were all large and carried a "forest of booms," as we used to say. That is, they were all workhorses and the nickname was deserved. In fact, it was the only common carrier freighter company on the West Coast that carried quartermasters. The ship was targeted not only for its bucko mates but also for its steward who was a well-known "belly robber" running a "starvation bucket." Blackie recruited a group of like-minded men and they managed to ship together on her when she called for a crew.

The story of how they educated the bucko mate and skipper was simple. They just applied a "conscientious withdrawal of efficiency" and kept all work to a bare minimum, just enough to bring the ship to and from port. The story of the steward is a little different. Blackie, who shipped quartermaster, took over that problem. Once the ship cleared San Pedro headed for New Orleans, on certain selective nights after the steward's light went out, there was a knock at his door and a committee of three or so sailors "broke him out" for one reason or another relating to food, usually the poor selection of "night lunch" (platters of cold cuts and cheeses to sustain the watches through the night), lack of sufficient coffee, sandwich bread, etc. This was repeated every hour on the hour, on and off, every other day, all the way down to the Canal. When the ship reached the Canal, instead of immediate transit, it docked and the steward, by now half out of his mind, was removed to an ambulance ashore, and all sorts of stores appeared. When the ship reached New Orleans, its homeport, it was in a pretty sad-looking state, so as to "quick fix" the situation, the company removed both the skipper and mate. In most of these instances they switched them to other ships.

As the ship left New Orleans, slowly but surely, things began to turn around. The ice boxes in the mess room stayed stocked, a decent brand of coffee appeared (you will recall some pages back we used to refer to the previous brands as "floor sweepings") and the cooking improved. On deck, the crew turned around and began working in earnest, and when they got to New York, the crew all quit and turned over a clean ship to the new crew. For the next year or so, Blackie engaged in this sort of activity exclusively. The story of the *Florence Luckenbach* spread around and became a model on how to do it.

The point to the story is that it takes a certain type of individual and personality to do such things. They are of utmost importance in the very lives of people. When you can equate your individual needs with the needs of your group, history is made. But when you can't, something has to give.

At the time we were living on our ranch on the West Coast, and so from time to time, about twice a year, Blackie came out to stay with us, once with his two younger children. And on another occasion, while he remained in New York, Mary brought her grandchildren out for a vacation. They were all downright delightful to be with.

Working together around the ranch on the various chores was becoming rather difficult for Blackie. Whereas in his healthier days he could work both quickly and effectively on almost any task, now the Parkinson's slowed him down and made handling tools more arduous. It hurt me to see this happening but it was important for him to prove to himself that he could do these jobs. Apparently, the nature of the disease is such that the mental processes remain intact for a long time while the neurological deterioration marches inexorably on. This was certainly so with Blackie. He always remained lucid, brilliant in his descriptive ability and, at all times, conscious of everything around him.

It was at about this time that Blackie's father died. A few days before, he had gone to be with him and make the necessary arrangements. It is quite possible, and I would love to think that reconciliation might have taken place between them. Neither of his two siblings attended the funeral, even though one of them lived in the same city, so he rode alone in the limousine accompanying the hearse on such occasions.

One day, about a few months after his last visit, we received a notice from the post office to pick up a registered letter. It turned out to be from Blackie and contained a bankbook showing a deposit account under his name only, in the sum of about three thousand dollars. The enclosed note, hastily scrawled on a torn-off piece of paper, asked me to "keep this until I call for it, and don't tell anyone about it." Realizing that if I said anything it would only make matters worse, I reluctantly put it away and didn't think much of it again. Many sailors have a thing they sometimes refer to as their "foxy pocket," that is, they have "an ace in the hole," as it is said. As we later reconstructed it, he was taking a small amount out of each monthly disability check and squirreling it away—a typical survivor's reaction.

I think back now about the many times in life when, willy-nilly, we get thrown into a situation not of our making and must make choices we really don't want to make, as for instance, choices between two "goods" or two "bads." This is not dodging a responsibility. Rather, we accept it as a matter of course, especially from our friends and family. We decided not to tell Mary and honor his request.

About two months after that, I received a call from Mary asking if Blackie was with us. When I said he wasn't, she told me that he moved out of the house and into a hotel, and though she checked him out every few days, he wasn't answering her last few phone calls. I immediately suggested that she get the building manager to open his door. An hour later she called back. They had found him dead on the floor. Within a few days, I called Mary, told her about the bankbook and sent it to her.

When we reflect back on his life, we realize that Arthur Koestler was right when he said that "The rebel's quarrel with society has neurotic roots." But this in no way obviates the validity of the rebel's objective argument. It's just that conditioned as we are by a largely neurotic and highly pressurized environment, family and society, we can't help but interpret what we see through the prism of the resultant neurotic personality. Our attitudes and coping abilities are shaped by a mutual feedback arrangement set in motion between the inner and the outside world. It's what makes the difference in our lives as well as those whose lives we touch.

Through most of our life, both Ann and I have felt a deep and emotional tie to Blackie. For one thing, we owe our meeting to him. For another he was there for us on a number of occasions when it counted. When his compass began to go askew, we felt that we should be there for him. Over a period of a lifetime, he brought much joy as well as sorrow, conviviality as well as pain, enlightenment and intelligence as well as intransigence. Though his "neurosis" drove him in a certain direction, his view of the world remained critical, clearheaded and balanced and was not taken in by establishmentarian thinking. Our union newspaper reported the commitment of his ashes to the deep, northeast of the Bahamas, and all hands came on deck to pay their respects.

> "Do not go gentle into that good night,
> Old age should burn and rave at close of day;
> Rage, rage against the dying of the light."
> **_Dylan Thomas, 1914-1953_**

✳✳✳✳✳✳✳✳✳✳✳

As mentioned earlier on, like in the story of John Francis Nolan, alias Seabiscuit, seafaring men share a conviction with members of the French Foreign Legion that nobody really cares where you come from just so long as you can do your job and be a good shipmate. They didn't usually concern themselves with such things as immigration or country-of-origin problems. They for the most part took the view that all workingmen, regardless of nationality, were equal before the boss, or "employer" (as we finesse it today). At the time our favorite writer was B. Traven whose minor classic, _The Death Ship_ passed among us from hand to hand. Traven preached internationalism and the elimination of all borders and passports, writing at a time of rampant xenophobic nationalism in the Germany of the late 1920s.

Among the many whom I suspected of carrying false papers was a friend of mine, Fred Kocevar. We met as shipmates and although he sailed below in the black gang, we somehow came together off watch and talked; kindred spirits who sort of sought each other out. He was highly intelligent, a good shipmate, and was a pretty good drinking man; that is, he could carry his liquor. And, as I said, I also sensed that Fred Kocevar was not his real name.

Fred and I had a mutual acquaintance named Jim Brady, with whom he did some real serious drinking, and I could never understand why. The

240

contrast between them couldn't be more pronounced. Brady was a stereo-typical hard-drinking Irishman who at a certain point would burst into maudlin sentimentality and start singing about the auld sod. He was voluble, argumentative and downright obnoxious if you didn't agree with him. All the more so when he was drinking. Fred was lean, soft-spoken and fair-skinned with thinning blonde hair, while Jim was short, paunchy, and red-faced with a shock of gray hair. Fred considered himself an anarchist whereas Jim by contrast, was an open communist who worshipped the Soviet Union and believed implicitly any and all claims made by the Stalinist GPU propaganda apparatus. He could very well have been a Party member for all I knew. Fred profoundly disagreed with all his hero-worshiping claims.

One night, after a payoff from a trip to the Orient, when the Cold War was just getting revved up, both of them were drinking at a local bar in San Francisco and as usual the discussion turned political. As the bartender told me some days later, things got a little heavy for Fred and he left and returned to his hotel room. The next morning, two men called at the hotel where Fred was bivouacking, flashed a badge at the clerk, went up to Fred's room, and "took him into custody." From then on, nobody I knew or asked could offer any information as to Fred's whereabouts.

Significantly, Jim Brady also disappeared. It was always assumed in such cases, that if the local shipping hall didn't have him registered, one shipped out from another port until whatever it was had blown over. Our small circle of friends grew increasingly concerned. In those days, when things like this happened, we always checked the jails and hospitals first. Nothing turned up. We asked our union hall to make some discreet inquiries at the FBI office, but they drew a blank.

Approximately one year later, I shipped on an inter-coastal ship and was visiting some friends in New York when some ugly truths came out.

One night a few months before, it was after 10:00 p.m. and they were preparing for bed when there was a knock at their door and there Fred stood, doleful looking, clothes looking like they were slept in, shoes soiled and with a few days' growth of beard. (He was always clean-shaven.) After a fortifying drink the story came out. The two badge-flashers were immigration cops. They hustled him into a car, took him to a detention pen, an adjunct to the county jail. After a few days, they put him on a plane to New York and thence transferred him to a British airliner and deposited him in London. All this after shipping out of American ports for over twenty years! And why did all this happen? Jim Brady was one of the very few who knew that Fred Kocevar's original name was Peter J. Malone of Liverpool, England!

As soon as he got his bearings, he checked out his relatives, decided against staying, and promptly stowed away on the SS *Queen Mary*, a Cunard liner on the steady transatlantic run; a relatively easy thing to do. And so, there he was, ready to start anew and ship out, picking up from when he was so rudely interrupted a year or so ago.

Obtaining a set of papers was not that easy this time. A few days later he thanked our friends for their hospitality and disappeared from our lives forever. As for Jim Brady if he is still "on deck" (that is, if he is still alive), he must deal with his own conscience and may it keep prodding him and reminding him of the dirty work he did to a fine and upstanding fellow human being. From time to time, to this day, I always keep wondering why Fred hung out with him, and my only conclusion was that like some of us, he was constantly on the lookout for intellectual stimulation, and when he met anyone with a point of view, he latched on to him. This particular time he misjudged and paid a price. Also, I reluctantly concluded that Fred didn't hold his liquor too well after all.

❋❋❋❋❋❋❋❋❋❋❋

I had never met anybody who was born on the island of Malta until I met Paul Xerri. In fact when he told me about it, I had to run to my atlas so as to relocate it. It turned out that I had passed it many times in the Mediterranean. His parents, who were fishermen, brought him to America at the age of three when they converted their name to "Sherry."

He went to school long enough to satisfy the state requirements and that was enough schooling for him for the rest of his life. In retrospect, he probably didn't need it for Paul was a mechanical genius. Paul never read instructions; he always knew what to do. He never had to pay attention to the admonition, "When all else fails, read the instructions." To add insult to injury, he could read a blueprint faster than any full-fledged engineer I ever met.

Sometime around the age of eighteen, he managed to get aboard a ship to the Orient and when he returned the 1934 strike broke out. He immediately joined the Sailors' Union and stayed with it to the end of his life.

Paul was a fractious individual, unruly and rebellious. He challenged all authority when and if necessary—and it was always necessary. He was solidly built, five by five and looked a little like Napoleon Bonaparte, who came from the island of Corsica, not too far from and in the general vicinity of Malta.

When the Sailors' Union built and moved into its new building on Harrison Street in San Francisco, they needed a knowledgeable stationary engineer to operate the plant. All hands pointed to Paul who took over the boiler room.

A few years after the war, Paul was visiting somewhere around Lake Tahoe when he happened to spot a pile of wreckage that was once a thirty-foot speedboat. The body was a tangled mess and the engine was rusty and broken into several pieces. As he related it to me, he stopped and asked the owner if he could have it. As a token the owner asked him for five dollars which Paul gave him before piling it into the bed of his pick-up and bringing it down to his machine shop in the boiler room. In his spare time, he rebuilt the engine and the hull. He even ran a special steam line into the shop and bent and molded a new mahogany bow. The entire operation took him six months of work after hours and weekends. When it was completed he took it up to Lake Tahoe and sold it for five thousand dollars. A mutual friend was with him and told me that he witnessed the entire transaction. The story fit him to a T.

Paul lived across the bay over in Marin County where there were some rural areas. One Monday night, returning from a late union meeting close to midnight, he caught a "four-pointer" mature male deer in his head-lights standing in the middle of the street. "And I said right on the spot, I must have that buck," was how he described the incident to me and some friends visiting with him in the boiler room a few days later.

"But, damn it, I didn't have my gun. He was standing there, blinded, right in the middle of the street. So, I backed up and drove straight at him and caught him right in the flank and crippled him. And I backed up again and went straight at him again and caught him in the midriff and he went down. So I jumped out and with my knife, cut his jugular, bled him and made him fast to my trailer hitch and dragged him home. It was a block from my house."

"But why did you have to have him?" I asked. "Do you like venison that much?"

"Nah," he answered, "I gave the meat to the neighbors. I wanted those horns. You should have seen them. Absolutely beautiful. I'm mount-ing them and will hang them right over my fireplace."

A year or two prior to this incident, Paul had met Tanya, a member of the San Francisco Russian community, and they were married. Tanya was an only child of a Russian couple who had come here late in life via

244

Manchuria where many escaped the 1917 Revolution. Her father was a janitor in a big downtown building for a number of years, when one day he lost his job and after a few months became destitute. One day, Paul came home and found Tanya's parents, camped in his kitchen with a couple of old suitcases and nowhere to go.

Paul told Tanya to "give them a few bucks" and tell them to "find someplace else to stay." The next day he came home from work and they were still there, so he told Tanya to "take all the money (meaning their life savings) and do what you want." He then packed a suitcase and moved down to the boiler room where he kept a cot. So much is known by piecing together what a few of us could vouch for. The next morning, the janitor, while opening up the building, checked the boiler room and found Paul's body on his cot with his brains blown out.

The world was full of and the waterfront had its share of Pauls. And as I think back I can identify a number of them among my former shipmates: Emotionally "out of control" with a compulsive, violent streak alongside of a brilliant turn of mind in matters either mental and/or mechanical. When the violent streak took control of the brilliant, mechanical aspect, the world produced a Hitler and a Stalin.

Chapter Twenty-three
The Bill Stops Here

Among the calamities of war may be justly numbered
the diminution of the love of truth, by the falsehoods
which interest dictates and credulity encourages.
Samuel Johnson, 1709-1784

The subject of merchant marine casualties, both ships and human,
remains to this day one of the best kept secrets of World War II,
notwithstanding the fact that within the last few years we have
been officially declared veterans. The following tables attempt to introduce a little order into the conflicting claims:

Table 1: World War Two Armed Forces and Merchant Marine Casualties

	Total Number Serving	Battle and Other Deaths[18]	Casualty Rate
U.S. Army & Air Force	11,260,000	318,274	2.8%
Navy & Coast Guard	4,424,559	64,531	1.5
Marine Corps	669,100	24,511	3.7
Merchant Marine	158,860[19]	5,662[20]	3.6

Table 2: World War II Merchant Marine Casualties and Prisoners of War

Dead	**5,662**
As direct result of enemy action	845
Prison camp	37
Missing	**4,780**
Released prisoners	**572**
Internees unaccounted for	**1**

Military historians to this day are still speculating about these enormous casualty rates, especially those brought about by the German U-boat campaign.[21] Whereas in all of World War I the U-boats sunk 14 million tons of Allied shipping, in World War II that figure was attained by the end of 1942. Most authorities estimate that by war's end, almost 21 million tons of Allied cargo went down, 14.5 million of which were sunk by U-boats. And horrendous as it may sound, the British merchant marine lost 30,000 seamen and over 3,500 ships before VE-Day finally brought the carnage to a halt.

Another example in naval warfare but limited to the human dimension, in the week of May 24-27, 1941, was the sinking of the British battleship *Hood* by the German battleship *Bismark* wherein the *Hood's* complement of 1,420 men was lost with only three survivors. The *Bismark* was then sunk by other elements of the British Navy with only 110 survivors from its crew of 2,200. Between January and April 1942, the first four months after Pearl Harbor, some 228 American merchant ships were sunk, and by the war's end, up to 700. Aside from the human dimension, such damage was worse than Pearl Harbor itself, wherein a number of already obsolete battleships were lost. And in the closing days of the war, the worst and least publicized of all was the German SS *Wilhelm Gustloff* out of Gdynia, sunk by a Russian submarine in the icy waters of the

Baltic Sea, carrying some eight-to ten-thousand passengers, both civilian and military, with 1200 survivors.

At the time, Admiral Ernst J. King was Commander-in-Chief of the U.S. Fleet and responsible for coastal defense. He paid no attention to British advice to organize convoys, and this in spite of the fact that British Intelligence had cracked the German secret code, ENIGMA. However, soon thereafter, convoys and air surveillance were introduced and with the development of radar and sonar technology, allied losses began to drop from 1600 ships in 1942 to 600 in 1943 to 200 in 1944. As Allied successes mounted, service in the U-boats became more dangerous. A U-boat skipper, Captain Reinhard Heidegen, had this to say:

We were expecting the worst but the Americans were totally unprepared. It was unbelievable how many ships we sank. We had our choice of targets. I remember the big Ferris wheel at Coney Island lit up at night ... And then farther down south, the resorts. The ships would be silhouetted against this and we could just fire away. It seemed too easy ... Now I know it was because of Allied errors. If the Americans had listened to the British, I probably wouldn't be here today.[22]

Of the 863 German U-boats that operated, 754 were sunk by the end of the war, and of their 39,000 active service men, only 10,000 remained.

In the Pacific it was the exact opposite. By VJ-Day the U.S. subs managed to destroy some 1200 Japanese merchantmen and 200 warships, which means that their human casualties were in the tens of thousands. In both wars, eighty percent of all ships lost were sunk by submarines. Those days are gone forever.

The military allows us to know that there are two types of submarines; those that destroy other submarines known as hunter-killers and those that destroy civilizations. Today a single U.S. submarine can carry more destructive force than all the fire-power unleashed in both world wars. One Russian sub can do the same. As of this writing, there are thirty-three ballistic missile submarines of which eleven are Tridents; and these vessels carry half of America's long-range nuclear weapons. The Trident D-5 ballistic missile holds eight nuclear warheads with a range of 4,000 miles. Whereas all U.S. subs are nuclear powered, only half of the Russian subs are.

The contrast to the World War II vintage subs is mind-boggling when we consider a then-and-now comparison. The German U-boat was 220 feet in length, did seventeen knots on the surface and some seven knots submerged. The U.S. subs in the Pacific were 311 feet long, did twenty knots on the surface and nine knots submerged. The Trident today, all named after states in the union, is 560 feet long and weighs 18,000 tons. Its speed is classified. I would venture a guess and say that one can double the World War II numbers: approximately 35 knots on the surface and eighteen submerged.[23]

The point to be made of all this is that the casualty rate was awful and the next of kin were treated rather shabbily compared to the regular armed forces. In the last few years, veterans of the merchant marine of World War II have achieved yet another dubious distinction. We have been legitimized. A Certificate of Service has been issued (suitable for framing) attesting to service in World War II. Through the years, I have been asked many times why the merchant marine was never blanketed in under the GI Bill that was signed into law by President Roosevelt on June 22, 1944. Many who did not ask made the incorrect assumption that we were. In 1952, when I left the sea, I returned to school, and the evening I registered, there were over 200 in the room. Of the 200, I was the only one paying my own way. All the rest were on the GI Bill. How did we miss out? Chances are we'll never really know but we can take an educated guess.

For the most part, seafarers never gave return to civilian life much thought. They went about their jobs, working in a civilian industry albeit under military jurisdiction, both in and out of the war zones. Our only tribune was our union. The GI needed no advocacy. It seemed almost axiomatic that a grateful country (maybe a little conscious-stricken) would demand some compensation for time lost for the returning veterans, not to speak of a reactive Congress ever mindful of the ten- to fifteen-million votes they represented.

In very little time, they were well rewarded by a remarkable piece of legislation which effectively educated an entire generation of men and women by mailing them a check every month for tuition and living expenses, extending them cheap loans for buying homes and setting up small business operations, and offering life insurance policies so cheap that almost nobody turned them down. It also introduced a rather unique rehabilitation scheme called the 52/20 Club, which meant that you could use one year to get back into "synch" and draw twenty dollars per week to help you along with some "walking-around money."

The unions, as well as a number of veteran's organizations, began floating trial balloons to the effect that there were some very needy veteran seafarers around, some of them actually basket cases, as well as destitute widows and orphans. In due time, a bill extending the GI Bill to the merchant marine was introduced by Congressman J. H. Pedersen (D-Florida) and referred to the House of Representatives Merchant Marine and Fisheries Committee as HR 2346. Under the chairmanship of Schuyler O. Bland (D-Virginia) during the Seventy-Ninth Congress, First Session, a series of hearings were held on October18 and 19, 1945.

Over this two-day period, as well as a few more later in December of that year, a small army of witnesses gave testimony about their experiences, and the usual amount of experts introduced the requisite amount of exhibits purporting to show that the projected cost of $146.5 million over ten years would not break the Federal Treasury. This fact did not prevent the Administrator of Veteran Affairs, one General Omar N. Bradley, from transmitting a letter from the Director of the Budget informing the committee that the proposed bill "is not in accord with the program of the President."

The biggest bone of contention by far was the perceived discrepancy in take-home pay between the merchant crew and the gun crew. And the biggest grandstanding star of the show was a certain Congressman Alvin F. Weichel (R-Ohio). His principle preoccupation was taking on every witness and by sheer hectoring and bullying, raking him or her over the coals on the pay issue. He was totally obsessed by the fact that the merchant crew earned more take-home pay than the gun crew. Well, the fact is that the U.S. Navy could have done something about it but chose not to.

Various attempts were made to point out to him that the "secret" was in the overtime. Since the base pay and bonus came to about the same, the difference was in the overtime earned while having to work on your watch below. This hard-earned concession was won in bitter struggle in the 1934 and 1936 strikes and we were not about to give it away. As I recall, overtime was payable at somewhere around one dollar per hour and most of it was earned the hard way, as explained somewhere earlier in this memoir. Most gun crews did very little but stand their watches and tinker with the guns. Sometimes, they might paint the gun platform. In enemy action, all hands had stations and were out there without overtime payment for anybody. The strict code of the sea has it that when the safety of the ship at sea is endangered, all hands are called out, as for instance, in enemy action. And to my knowledge, nobody I know ever asked for "overtime" under such circumstances, including the few times it happened to me.

The testimony also showed, via charts and graphs, that the services enjoyed some emoluments unheard of in the merchant marine: free medical care for families, lifetime pensions for widows who did not remarry, mustering-out pay, free uniforms and, last but not least, income tax breaks. And to all this should be added the little "freebies," such as cut-rate traveling and priorities, half-price admissions to theatres and ball games, and lots more which I've since forgotten.

After the congressman got through hassling all the witnesses, and considering the fact that spread over the general population a scattering of votes by seafaring people and their families was meaningless in the big picture, there really wasn't much chance to get anything out of committee, let alone both houses of the legislature. Lastly, it should be recorded for posterity, the all-knowing Congressman Weichel was rewarded for his superb knowledge of the U.S. Merchant Marine with the chairmanship of the Committee on Merchant Marine and Fisheries in the Eightieth and Eighty-third Congresses. With such friends, who needs enemies?

Chapter Twenty-four
Flags Of Convenience

From time to time in the course of this memoir, I have alluded to the dismal state of the American Merchant Marine. The legislative Magna Charta of the American Merchant Marine was HR 8555, signed on June 29, 1936 by President Franklin D.Roosevelt.[24]

Preceding this piece of legislation, a long series of hearings and investigations starting sometime in 1933 were held under the auspices of Senator Hugo L. Black (D-Alabama) having to do mostly with mail subsidies. These mail contracts between the carriers and the Post Office were worth some $26 million a year, a princely sum in those years, in which the U.S. Government paid them to carry mail overseas.

The Black Committee disclosures, comprising nine volumes of closely printed text, found such a dismal heavy-handed record of fraud and extravagance, that it advised the government to abrogate all mail contracts and operate its own merchant marine. One of its more moderate statements was, "Some of the disclosures in which government officials worked hand in hand with private interests, are reminiscent of the scandals of the Harding Administration."

The new legislation created the mechanics for a new government commission, the Maritime Commission, and its first chairman was Joseph P. Kennedy, a well known banker, real estate operator, movie magnate, stock market player and father of the late President and Attorney General of the same name.

The Commission was given broad powers of supervision over American shipping. It then detailed a plan replete with formulas and contingencies for handing out money to build ships in American yards and to run them in foreign trade. For the first time, a new principle in American business enterprise was introduced: the direct subsidy. The theory behind it was that U.S. operators need assistance in competing with cheaper foreign carriers' tariff in reverse. This would allow them to compete for ocean cargo and put them on a competitive par with foreign companies. The act also reaffirmed the Jones-White Act of 1928, which directed that carriage between U.S. ports be reserved exclusively for U.S. flag, U.S. built and U.S. citizen-crewed ships. It was designed to safeguard American economic security, military sealift capabilities and domestic employment. Since foreign ships are prohibited from trading between American ports, American lines in coastal and inter-coastal trade receive no subsidies. The Act also set targeted amounts of ships to be constructed in American yards, but this was soon revised drastically upwards as World War II began.

An interesting anomaly in this whole governmentally regulated world is that the regulation of shipping rates are, to this day, totally set and controlled by the industry itself. Various shipping companies, both domestic and foreign, who service a particular trade route, organize into a "Conference" and agree on what they will charge. They are exempt from anti-trust regulation. These Conferences are in contrast with the trucking and railroad industries, which are tightly regulated by an independent agency, like the Interstate Commerce Commission for the former.

The rise and fall of the American merchant marine is a function of the economics of shipping over water. In short, it is cheaper to ship in a foreign vessel. It all started out sometime at the turn of the century with the idea that "Cargo Preference" was a desirable goal so as to assure U.S. flag ships a minimum share of cargoes produced by U.S. government programs. In point of fact, it is the oldest maritime promotional program around. Historians have tracked this program back to the Spanish-

American War of 1898, probably the first big imperialist power grab outside of our geographical borders. Since our military power, both land and naval, was taking off, it became necessary to insure a merchant fleet able enough to supply it when, where, and if required. Preference laws quoted carrying cargo as a percentage of U.S. vessel use. It started out with one hundred percent, that is to say, one hundred percent of cargo in support of the armed forces had to be shipped in U.S. flag vessels. Congress kept requiring preference statutes to encourage the existence of a U.S. flag merchant fleet to act as a military auxiliary in times of national emergency.

Sometime during the New Deal years, the Reconstruction Finance Corporation (which was formed during the Hoover Administration) and Congress decreed that fifty percent of the exports that it financed must move in U.S. flag vessels. After Word War II, Congress extended the meaning of the fifty percent share to include foreign aid shipments. By about the mid-1960s, Congress extended it further to include all programs including non-military agencies, whether the procurement was for themselves or foreign governments.

The problem is not so much preference for governmental and military cargoes as it is for commercial cargoes. So far, all efforts to apply cargo preference quotas to commercial activity have failed. The reasons for this are well known. U.S. trading partners, that is, foreign countries, want their share of the business since this is one way they can earn hard currency; they have ships too, and can do it much cheaper. Furthermore, their labor unions are either weak, more docile or non-existent.

The second big reason is that U.S. exporters, importers and agricultural interests find it in their interest to also demand cheap rates as part of their own cost-cutting operation. Agricultural interests, especially, lobby continuously and incessantly to have all existing preferences removed from government programs in the belief that they inhibit U.S. farm exports. Likewise, exporters and importers are obsessed with cost, insurance and

freight (c.i.f.) and forever seeking ways and means to bypass cargo preference considerations. Budgetary austerity and the Defense Department's
strict insistence on competitive bidding combine to make for more carrier
dissatisfaction, and from the bottom line viewpoint, it means fewer jobs.

To add insult to injury, there are at least a dozen different agencies
within the federal bureaucracy that deal in cargo preference problems.
There is actually a celebrated case on record whereby a foreign government, Iceland, threatened the future of U.S. military bases on its soil if
the U.S. didn't agree to a departure from the one-hundred percent rule in
regards to its herring trade.

U.S shipping does not take naturally to foreign trade. We are not so
dependent on its imports as most European nations are. Before World
War II most of the European countries had vast empires over the globe,
and a thriving merchant service was a necessity. The United States is largely an inland empire of railroads and highways. Except in times of war,
there is really no reason to carry its own commerce abroad. Even the mail,
which is an export like any other cargo, can and does sail under foreign
flags; that is, if they are still sending mail that way.

It could very well be that the whole exercise is futile. The future of
warfare, our military historians tell us, does not lie in the direction of
large land-based armies engaged in open-country warfare, which must be
supplied by an extensive merchant marine. Rather, the future seems to
belong to "low-level, low-intensity" warfare, that is to say, lightning-like,
small-scale strikes against insurgencies in the Third World (example:
Grenada, Panama, Persian Gulf). A task force can get itself together real
fast and, what with a few large air force cargo transports, can be in "trouble spots" within hours. The few ships needed to bring in the larger stuff
like tanks and field artillery pieces, can get there within a few days. The
U.S. Navy Military Sealift Command does just this and it is more than
adequate for these types of operations. At this writing, with the Persian Gulf

war (Desert Storm and Desert Shield recently concluded) temporarily on hold, the statistics for the use of cargo ships during the last operation is as follows: forty-four percent foreign registry, forty-one percent government (i.e. the armed forces) owned, and fifteen percent privately owned.[25]

Recently, the following announcement appeared in our local press:

The Navy has dropped its Cold War strategy of preparing for all-out war with the Soviets on the high seas and has shifted its focus to potential Third World conflicts .... The new strategy is a fundamental shift from open ocean war fighting on the sea towards joint operations from the sea ... a shift from full-scale naval battles, to smaller quick insertions of military power onto land from the sea.[26]

The Federation of American Shipping, an industry trade association, says that operating costs can run up to four million dollars a year for a U.S flagged ship, as compared to eight hundred thousand dollars for a ship with a foreign crew. Or take another example recently culled from the *Shipyard Weekly,* the newsletter of the Shipbuilders Council of America:

The number of Japanese seafarers declined from 21,000 to 12,000 during the two-year period between April 1986 and April 1988. The annual cost of crewing a 24-man merchant vessel with Japanese seafarers is reportedly about $2.75 million ... Manning the same ship with a Filipino crew costs about $350,000.

Stretching this logic to its ultimate conclusion, by the time they run out of Third World people, they will have returned to sea slavery.

Earlier on, I alluded to the "flags of convenience" ships. That is, many American shipping companies, maybe all of them, keep corporate offices in such exotic places as Panama, Liberia and the Bahamas. For example, that sterling American institution known as Chevron Oil Company, who never quits expounding on the great American values of fair play and love of country, has, as of this writing, forty-three tankers of which exactly seven fly the U.S. flag. And that's because these seven run coastwise, since by law, the Jones Act (as explained earlier) will not allow them to run in the coastwise trade without being registered in the United States.

All these laws and rulings have to do with Cabotage, which simply means to sail along the coast, trade and transport in coastal waters between two points within a country—in other words, to pick up and unload passengers and freight along the coast, i.e., within the American market. Originally passed by Congress in 1886, the Passenger Service Act "prohibits foreign flag vessels from carrying passengers in coastwise trade between U.S. ports." What this all comes down to is that "of the 425 passenger cruise vessels currently in deep-water, overnight cruise trade worldwide, fewer than five are U.S. flag vessels."[27]

As mentioned earlier, all those foreign-flag ships we see in any particular port may use the port facilities during a stopover but may not engage in trade between American ports. In fact, it has recently been reported that the last great bastions of merchant shipping, the Scandinavian fleets of Norway, Sweden and Denmark, are all in the process of changing their flags to something like Liberia or Panama.

One morning recently, in the midst of the Persian Gulf crisis, we were informed that overnight our State Department suddenly decided that there were twelve foreign-flag vessels, Kuwaiti to be exact, that deserved our protection and consequently were converted with the stroke of a pen to U.S. flag ships. And to drive the point home, it was specified that the Kuwaiti crews remain aboard. So now the precedent is set: The U.S. Navy runs protection for a bunch of foreign-flag tankers, masquerading as U.S. flagged ships, thereby opening the door to protecting any old flag-of-convenience runaway anywhere in the world, all on the dubious pretext of a perceived national interest. In the interim, the American merchant marine lies all but dead in the water, also in the national interest. With such friends, who needs enemies?

> Haul up the flag, you mourners,
> Not half-mast but all the way;
> The funeral is done and disbanded;
> The devil's had the final say.
>
> ***Karl Shapiro, 1913-2000***

Chapter Twenty-five
To the Boneyard

The times change and we must change with them

Lothair I, 795-855

Before Pearl Harbor Day, our official entry into World War II, the life style brought about by following a sea-going career in the focsle of a deepwater American merchant ship under union contract had much to recommend it and write home about. Other than an emergency in which the safety of the ship was in danger, once sailing day was overcome, a gentle, steady routine comprising work and leisure set in. With the three-watch system and some required overtime, which at sea was kept to a minimum by cost-conscious skippers and mates, all the necessary work got done. What this means is that a shipload of cargo, entrusted to a crew of some thirty-forty men, worth some untold millions of dollars, was delivered to its assigned destination in a timely fashion, safely and intact, give or take any unusual foul weather.

These ships put into foreign ports which for the most part very few young men and almost no young women would ever have the opportunity of visiting. When you returned to your home port and received your discharge you also received your pay, which was an accumulation of your wages (From $69.50 per month when I started out to $100.00 per month plus an equal amount for hazardous waters after December 1941) less any deductions you allowed like sending money home in the form of allotment checks mailed from the shipping company's front office. Since in most instances there was nothing to spend on at sea and you didn't gamble and if you didn't go hog-wild in the foreign ports, you had a stake.

With your savings you had the wherewithal to stay on the beach for extended periods of time, pursuing whatever dream you conjured up, from writing the great American novel to courting the girl of your dreams, until your money ran out and the whole process started over again.

After Pearl Harbor Day, this process, although remaining in its broad outlines, changed in its details by 180 degrees. The presence of enemy action in and around just about every ocean of the world brought any would-be idyllic life to a screeching halt. From then on until VJ-Day, it was blacked-out ships and zig-zagging convoys, the latter sometimes impossible to follow; invariably carrying various quantities of high explosives or high-octane gasoline interspersed with some general cargo which could be anything you name; in any and every kind of weather, fair or foul; knowing that you are surrounded by wolf-packs of submarines. And on many an old rustbucket with its quarters aft, negotiating the chains and tunbuckles holding down the deckload, trying to get to the bridge to relieve the watch—in total blackout, remember— was many times tantamount to a feat of derring-do. And then you got to repeat this performance the next night and the next night until, hopefully, you got there intact. Sometimes you didn't get there. But for the most part, you did. Those were the times of "ulcer formation."

When the war came to an end, and an attempt was made to get back to where we were, it just didn't, and moreover couldn't, happen. The corporate powers-that-be made the decision that all those Liberty and many of the Victory ships that carried us to victory were now obsolete or "superannuated" as our British cousins had it. Jobs began slowly but surely to disappear, either due to this type of attrition but also, a few years later, to automation. The new pensions for the older members were a partial answer, but the rest of us who still had some years to go, boxed out of the GI Bill by a non-caring Congress and our political inability to exercise any clout, now found ourselves with fewer and fewer options.

Meanwhile, back at the ranch, the Maritime Commission found itself with a few thousand ships on its hands that even the Greek ship owners didn't want. This remark is not meant to be denigrating in any way in that it alludes to an old walnut the old timers used to repeat constantly before the war: The Americans build a ship, use it for twenty years and then give it to the Limeys. The Limeys use it for twenty years and then sell it to the Greeks. The Greeks use it for twenty years and then sell it to the Japanese for scrap. If we change some of the countries' names today, I'm sure it retains its validity.

So what happened to all those ships? Somebody came up with a brilliant scheme to create a "Ready Reserve Fleet." That is to say, put these ships in some pre-chosen backwaters in some out-of-the-way harbors scattered around on both coasts and the Gulf and have them ready to be placed into service on very short notice when the time comes for the next round of killing to start. These out-of-the-way harbors were called the "boneyard." And as fate would have it, I shipped on the very first crew, charged with the task of preparing these ships for their future assignments.

All told, I worked on a dozen ships, preparing them at whatever dock they were and finally depositing them, pulled by two tugboats under dead tow, to their final destination, in this case the mud flats of Suisun Bay, an as far out-of-the-way destination in the greater San Francisco Bay complex as anyone could imagine.

The job itself became routine after the first few ships. You joined it at the dock and it was shut down but for one boiler required for some power. The ship was eerily cold and empty, devoid of all and every sign of previous life. Gone were all the galley equipment and eating utensils, all the mattresses and linens from the crew's quarters, the navigational charts, instruments and flags from the bridge and all the tools from the engine room. In short, a true definition of a dead ship, lying dead at the dock.

Our job was to stow all the deck equipment and lifeboats down in the shelter decks and accompany the ship, under dead tow to its final destination. There were ten of us in the crew, all pre-war sailors, and among the many unanswered questions we asked then and remain unanswered probably to this very day, one still remains: Just what happened to all that expensive equipment, removed from those few thousand ships?

Chapter Twenty-six
To Make the Run

Life can only be understood backwards; but it
must be lived forwards.

Soren Kierkegaard , 1813-1855

As we look back on our lives, we find many unanswered questions. Retrospection and the "what if" game constantly intrude into our thoughts. For instance, how did I know, way back then, that I had arrived and was now an accepted member of the brotherhood? What signals you or tells you these things? There are always the outward manifestations: you have passed all the tests, both technical and social; you have received written confirmation that you are now an equal among equals; you have an equal voice and vote. Your shipmates' attitude towards you is both civil and respectful.

All these things are important milestones, but do they create that inner glow that suddenly flashes on like a great light bulb and arrests that feeling of insecurity that you've been carrying around with you since that first day you stepped aboard your first ship? And long before that ....

There are a few such moments, epiphanies as it were, some already mentioned that come close, such as the night of my induction into the Sailors' Union or the day I outfitted myself with the "uniform" of my in-group. But the one that hit home and made the biggest impression on me was the first time I went aloft in a bosn chair (defined and described somewhere way back at the beginning of this memoir) to the very top of the mainmast some 150 feet above the main deck and strapped myself in with this special knot, accomplishing my assignment with the same expertise and dispatch as every AB I ever saw doing it. And when I got back down on deck, I noticed (or did I imagine?) an attitudinal change all around me that may best be described as an extra little touch of deference from my shipmates. It told me that I had successfully navigated this all-important Rite of Passage.

The very first ship I made after receiving my AB certificate was the already-mentioned SS *Manukai,* a monster of a freighter belonging to Matson Navigation Co. which enjoyed the dubious distinction of having four masts, all over one-hundred feet tall, from the main deck, rather than the two possessed by all other freighters of the day. Each mast had two stationary stays on each side of it, totaling four to a mast, known as shrouds, made of plough steel wire, each some two inches in diameter and placed at forty-five degree angles from below the crosstrees down to the main deck, set back so as not to interfere with the cargo handling operation.

Every few years these masts have to be cleaned and painted and their sets of stays must be slushed down, that is, covered with a concoction of grease and oil applied by hand with a rag. These were two separate operations, but they had one thing in common. One must climb up to the very top of each, some one hundred feet or more from the main deck, and get into a bosn chair and apply the special hitch required for your safety in lowering yourself as you work your way down to the main deck. Although you can practice tying this particular hitch all day long in the comfort of the focsle or on deck, you cannot practice it once you leave the deck. There is no dress rehearsal. You have to know it and you have to do it right the very first time; there is no walkie-talkie communication with anyone. It's strictly hand signals.

There was an unwritten rule that when younger AB's are available, that is those whose age bracket would be their twenties and thirties, they become the chosen instrument, and the one saving grace in all of this is that it must be done in fair weather, since it's stupid to paint in the rain. On the appointed day, the Bosn announced the job and asked me and another younger AB to share it: two masts and eight shrouds each. Dutifully, he asked me if I had ever done this before and I of course said, "Certainly."

So I started up the ladder on the lower mast and got up to the crosstrees, with my chair over my shoulder and a tagline, which will be used to raise my bucket of paint once I'm in position, tied around me. I then tested the block on the very top of the mast that would hold me as I ascended. This was done by attaching your chair to the running line, getting into it and putting your weight on it (my full 130 pounds, wringing wet). You are now convinced that the block on the top will hold you. The bosn and your watch partner are down on deck and you signal them that you are ready to go. Slowly but surely, hand over hand, they raise you the last fifty or so feet to the truck (the very top) of the mast. On a given pre-arranged hand signal you are now at the moment of truth. As your two pullers down below relax their hold, still maintaining contact with the line, you execute that particular hitch which you have been prac-ticing so diligently. Now secure in your chair and in control of your descent, you take a deep breath and begin to clean and paint your way down to the crosstrees.

It's a beautiful day and a gentle breeze is blowing; the sea is calm and the dolphins are playing around the ship's side. The sun is high in the sky and the horizon is limitless. If you get carried away with your thoughts, you may never want to come down, let alone paint the mast. A feeling of exhilaration comes over you. You have just accomplished one of the more dangerous jobs that go along with sea-going janitorial work. And what did my watch partner, one of the iron men from wooden ships tell me when I got down? "Nice work sonny. You should be able to work aloft as comfortably as you work on deck. Let me tell you about the time I was on this square-rigger on our way around the Horn .... This bucko mate sends me aloft to take down the Royal Yard as a gale wind started up .... " And on and on and on ....

The slushing of the shrouds is another one of those dirty jobs that require a certain degree of skill. You go aloft to the crosstrees with your chair and once up there you secure yourself into it with that same hitch and start riding down this forty-five-degree-angled standing shroud. So just as swinging in a bosn chair on the topmast is one of the more danger-ous jobs, there is no job more dirty than slushing the stays while swinging down them in that same bosn chair. The mixture of lampblack, oil and grease (as mentioned earlier on, another one of those concoctions for which many bosns had their own secret formula) is applied liberally by hand with a soft rag, "working it in" to the crevasses of the braided wire, as the bosn advises you to do. And the next time you do this, you had better remember to take a piece of burlap up with you and lay it over your lap because when you get down you may have to consign your dun-garees to the deep.

So, say what you may; I navigated a right of passage, albeit one I set for myself and now qualified me to join that exclusive fraternity which still believed in pride of craft; a phenomenon destined to fight a rear guard battle of eventual extinction just a few short years later and which modern seafaring men today probably never knew existed outside of sea-stories.

****

Sooner or later it began to dawn on me that I would have to face the problem of whether to continue going to sea. There must be many cur-rents that feed into such a decision. Looking back at it, the story of Fred Kocevar left me with an extremely bad taste and was probably one of a number of happenings that steered me in the direction of giving up the seafaring life. At that very time, the U.S. Coast Guard and Maritime Commission were gaining more and more control over our lives. They readily joined Senator Joe McCarthy and his yahoos, supported by a craven Congress and Senate, in persecuting many of our members, some of whom were long disassociated from any political activity. On a ship I was on, they came aboard when we docked and went right down to the focsle and issued a subpoena to one of the crew who hadn't been political-ly active in years. After a drum-head/court martial-type hearing in which he had almost no rights, his papers were yanked and he was forced ashore to fend for himself. And he was a family man like me.

As time went on, I found myself living more and more in two worlds. In one, I was actively engaged in a trade that afforded me a living but clashed with a new and other life. This second life was that of a married man with three children who was becoming disillusioned with the seafar-ing trade and trying to find a way to come ashore.

Like many others before me, I too thought I could bridge the gap by shipping on one of the shoreside stand-by gangs. These gangs, you will recall, relieved the crews when they came into port and picked up the work the ship's crew would ordinarily do. I tried this for a number of months but it wasn't satisfying.

Some time after my trip to the Far East on the SS *Pacific Bear* I took a stand-by job on the SS *Luriline,* a first-class passenger ship running to and from the Hawaiian Islands. Shipping in a stand-by capacity on this ship usually meant one thing: over the side on stages with buckets of white paint, two men to a stage. It is usually not hard to find a partner in almost any crew. But this particular day, as fate would have it, although I knew some of the gang, they were all partnered up by the time I got there, so I wound up with an old Swede whom I used to see up at the hall, in a terribly hung-over condition. His hands were shaking and his voice was hoarse. He could barely get on the Jacobs ladder needed to get on and off the stage.

To make matters a little more interesting, it so happens that this ship had what we call a modified clipper bow. That is to say, the bow curves inward as in an hourglass manner and flares back out again as you descend to the water line. Since the stage descends from the main deck in a straight line and the ship curves inward, the stage moves further and further away from the ship's side as it descends. This particular situation calls for bringing the stages in against the ship's side, a process called tricing (i.e. the stage must be pulled or triced in). What with five stages on both sides of the bow, a line is passed all around the bow so as to include all the stages and the ship's winches pull in all the stages together, against the ship's side.

Though my newfound partner was an old-time sailor, he was not up to any such work that day. As the stages are pulled in, you have to hold on so as to maintain your balance, and the upshot of the whole thing was that he neither could stop vomiting nor hang on to the stage. So he took a nosedive (fell over the side) and a passing tug fished him out of the water and put him on the dock. He took off uptown and I never saw him again. Since we were about thirty feet out of the water and on the offshore side, he was lucky. Had we been on the inshore side, it would have been his end.

I sat on the stage working alone for the rest of the morning, since no replacement arrived until the noon break, jumping from side to side as best I could, with the bosn coming down the Jacobs ladder to help me lower the stage. And as I was painting, I began an internal dialogue. It was now fully twelve years since I set foot aboard my first ship, and other than the two years that I tried to run the credit union, I had made my living exclusively on West Coast ships for the most part, sailing deepwater. I further reflected on the fact that I had been awfully lucky, in that other than some enemy action in the South Pacific, I never had to run for the lifeboats and made it through the war intact. As a survivor, to this day, I am obsessed by the fact that so many of my old shipmates did not make it through.

My former stage partner showed me where I could possibly land twenty years downstream. Of course, this was the extreme situation, a worse case scenario. But even at its best, it was a future devoid of a future. The more I thought about it, the more my head began to ache. What with the feast or famine philosophy of the American Merchant Marine, shipping would be going straight downhill over the long term. More and more talk was heard about the mechanization of cargo handling, so the future of longshoring looked equally bleak. The ranks of the old timers who were my mentors were thinning out with frightening regularity. In short, it was time to end a beautiful friendship. It is interesting to note that years later, as I sit and pen these lines, when my monthly copy of the union newspaper, *West Coast Sailor,* arrives in the mail, the first page I turn to is the obituaries. For a while I recognized many names, but in recent years, I notice that the names listed all came into the union some years after I did. By now, none of the names are familiar.

When a ship is being moored and snaked into position alongside the dock, the last signal on the ship's telegraph from the bridge to the engine room is "Finished With Engines." It is usually done by swinging the telegraph handle back and forth a number of times across the spectrum of commands, accompanied by a ringing of bells. I should like to think that working that day on the bow of the *Luriline* was the "Finished With Engines" to my sea-going career. Making the decision was half the battle. It was then just a matter of doing it.

I grabbed a freighter on the Hawaiian run, which brought me home every three weeks for a few days. After six months I had saved a little stake and decided to retire my book and what's more I had better chop it off cold turkey. The morning I went down to the union hall to retire my book, I had a lump in my throat and as I went around and shook hands, I received lots of good luck wishes, slaps on the back and offers of enough drinks to float a passenger ship. A chapter in my life had closed and another was about to open.

Many of the young men who went to sea during World War II for the duration and then went back to the farm, had the opportunity of knowing and working with the seafaring men who survived sea slavery—the iron men from wooden ships—and lived to see a better day. These men made their mark in the decade of the 1930s, an era, it will be remembered, which saw the radicalization of the working man in America, moved him a little closer towards center stage and allowed him a place in the sun thereby empowering him to lead a better life. This era has never been repeated and probably never will. It was my supreme good fortune to have met them, known them, warts and all, and learned my own place in the sun. I had learned to make the run.

To Make The Run

Epilogue

PART ONE

There is one more story to tell. Another type of my many shipmates was the ex-Navy man who had a "Bad Conduct Discharge." These men, for the most part, were rebels without a cause who for some personality reason or another could not accommodate to shipboard life a la U.S. Navy. All I can say is, you couldn't prove it by me. Except for some excessive drinking habits and some poor judgments ashore, at sea they were, to a man, the finest and most competent of shipmates in every way. When World War II broke out, the U.S. Navy, recognizing their experience and ability, offered them a return to the service for the duration with no questions asked in exchange for a "Good Conduct Discharge" and full GI Benefits. Many of them accepted and performed admirably.

Such a person was Clarence L. Clarence, the son of a coal mining family from somewhere in downstate Illinois who at an early age decided he wasn't going to uphold family tradition and go down to the mines. He later explained to me that all the males in his family—father, uncles, cousins and in-laws—were coal miners. When his eighteenth birthday came around during the depth of the Depression when even "soda-jerk jobs" were at a premium, untrained in anything and getting madder at the world as each day passed, he went up to Chicago and joined the Navy. After boot camp, he was sent to San Diego and shipped out on a destroyer to join the Pacific Fleet.

Clarence's tour of duty, as he described it to me, was a merry-go-round of work ("as little as possible") and as much drinking, fighting and whoring ashore as his limited pay could buy, which in those days, in the Orient, was considerable compared to what the natives could buy. It didn't take long for the Navy to decide that they had an "incorrigible" rebel aboard so before his four-year enlistment was up, they parted company with him, issuing him a BCD, a "Bad Conduct Discharge."

When he got back to the States, he visited his family and used up what little mustering out pay he had for a round robin of parties. On one such occasion, his mother took him aside and suggested that she didn't approve of his younger sister's choice of a boyfriend, whereupon Clarence sought him out and beat him up just enough so as to eliminate his mother's imagined threat to his sister and end his sojourn in Southern Illinois. He drifted back to the West Coast and got his shipping papers just as the 1936 strike erupted. And as he tells it, he immediately joined the Sailors' Union and became one of the chief "enforcers" on the picket line. The rebel had found his cause.

Some years later, as my watch partner on the MV *Willmoto*, he unfolded his story during the course of that long trip to the South African coast. After listening, I recognized a dominant theme you might call the "alpha male syndrome" running through his stories. Wildlife biologists the world over have identified this behavioral concept in many species. To the best of my limited knowledge, there is a certain individual, usually a male, in all animal groups who comes forward to take charge of the group, winning his position by fighting his way to the top. Clarence L. was such a person and on the MV *Willmoto* he did just that. He got into a number of fights while ashore and managed to dominate them; that is, he was left standing.

One of my counterparts, the ordinary seaman on the 12:00 to 4:00 watch, John "Sarge" Kollence, decided that he wasn't going to allow this to happen without a showdown. Sarge, originally from Great Falls, Montana, was orphaned at an early age and landed in Father Flanagan's Boys School. He told me his greatest thrill of a lifetime came in June 1932 when as a twelve-year-old he was chosen with a few other boys to attend the Sharkey-Schmeling World Heavyweight Boxing Championship at Madison Square Garden in New York City (a match Sharkey won in a controversial decision).

When Sarge reached the qualifying age he went directly into the Army and was shipped to Schofield Barracks in Hawaii where, he said, he won every fight in his class. When I knew him, he was about 190 pounds, six feet tall and looked like Charles Atlas of body building fame. (The name Sarge, it should be explained, is given to all those who put in a hitch in the Army. In most instances they never rose above the rank of Private, First Class.)

Although Sarge and Clarence never came to a showdown, an undercurrent of animosity between them was palpable throughout the trip. Clarence, however, was smart enough to realize that this state of affairs would not last forever. When we got home, as luck would have it, some uniformed U.S. Navy officers came aboard and offered him another opportunity. The fleet was expanding (this was the lend-lease days in late 1940) and the Navy needed him. They offered a raise in grade, elimination of the BCD and a few other goodies if he'd come back for the duration. He made the right decision and they got an excellent teacher for the new recruits.

After VJ Day, he came up to the union hall, still in uniform and told me he was leaving for Honolulu where he was promised a job in the local fire department. And as we parted, he couldn't help but tell me about the "chicken-shit officer" in charge of his PT boat who refused to attack a Japanese destroyer during a certain battle. In a sense it was still the same old Clarence L. and then he mentioned one last question before we parted. "Did you ever run into Sarge Kolence by any chance?

PART TWO

Once upon an evening in 1994, I sat down in my living room with a copy of a video documentary, *The Men Who Sailed the Liberty Ships,* created and produced by Maria Brooks of Oakland, California. As the title indicates, it proceeded to show some footage of the war while interviewing various characters and personalities associated with the war effort on the American waterfront.

As it unfolded, the subject of PQ 17 and PQ 18 came up. This was the code name of two convoys, probably the largest in maritime history, made up of some fifty merchant ships each, with some naval escort. Its destination was Murmansk, Russia, via the North Cape, that is, over the top of the Scandinavian Peninsula into the Barents Sea that empties into the Arctic Ocean, all well within the Arctic Circle.

The convoys brought with them every possible type of material of every size, shape and description that could be used to help the Soviet Union fight the war while she was under siege and attack ... if they got through. For while the combined resources of the fearsome German military machine was now trying to cope with a rejuvenated Russian Army, it was also doing its utmost to devastate and sink as many of these convoys as possible, denying them the possibility of getting to their destination.

The narrator's voice described the unfolding situation. Ships torpedoed by German subs and attacked from the air by the Luftwaffe were exploding and going down while crews were struggling with any remaining rafts and lifeboats lowered into the frigid sea. A familiar voice emanated over the narrator's, and proceeded to pick up the story from the point of view of the lifeboat. A voice immediately got my attention; firm and self-assured with a certain propulsive vitality, it matter-of-factly told the rest of the story and nobody hearing it would ever forget it. For me, the voice was unmistakable. It belonged to "Sarge" Kolence (who now went under the name of Ransome) with whom I was shipmates on the SS *Willmoto* on my first trip to sea in the spring of 1940, some fifty-four years ago!

I thought of this as I reached for the phone and started tracking Sarge down. Luckily he was still on deck. And as I introduced myself and began explaining it all, the silence broken only by my elevated heartbeat, he slowly began remembering and talking, pronouncing every syllable succinctly and concisely: " ... fifty-four fuckin' years ... *fifty-four fuckin' years* ... ," the second one, one decibel higher. And he proceeded to name every one of our shipmates as well as every ship in Table Bay, the harbor of Cape Town, and which berth it was in, both port and starboard sides on our day of arrival!

And this was no ordinary feat, since Table Bay was the rendezvous point for the entire passenger fleet of the British Merchant Navy. There converged every available Cunard, White Star and Pacific and Oriental liner (or P. and O. as the passenger buffs would have it) having been pressed into service, carrying the first consignment of the Australian-New Zealand Expeditionary Force up to England immediately after Dunkirk and who eventually found themselves in the African desert chasing Rommel's Afrika Corps. We estimated at the time, as I recall, that there must have been about a dozen or more of these world class liners, such as the Queen Mary for instance, converted hurriedly to troop ships, all told carrying many thousands of troops.

As we wound down and were ready to say goodbye, Sarge had one last question, posed rather hesitatingly, "Did you ever, by any chance, run into Clarence L.?"

And we have been in touch ever since, reminiscing about the crew, the ship, the trips and sailing ships all over the place. And stranger yet, it turns out that we had both quit the sea at approximately the same time!

****

I have been speaking of a world we may never see again. Nevertheless, I leave a little room for hope that some day soon the requirements of life will turn things around and the will of our body politic will assert itself and resuscitate the once proud American Merchant Marine now lying buried in the deep.

> Life is short, the art long,
> Timing is exact,
> Experience treacherous,
> Judgment difficult.
>
> ### *Hippocrates, c. 460-400 BC*

Endnotes

[1] The term "focsle" is a contraction for "forecastle," a term coined when sailors lived in the front of the ship, albeit below the main deck. *(Page 5)*

[2] *San Francisco Chronicle,* March 21,1989, p. B3. *(Page 70)*

[3] See *Knights of the Road* by Roger A. Bruns for an excellent discussion of hobos and a glossary of their terminology. *(Page 78)*

[4] A good discussion of this era may be found in *The Barbary Coast* by Herbert Asbury, Chapter 9. *(Page 82)*

[5] A more detailed discussion of this subject as well as some excellent background on the economics of the industry may be found in *Maritime: A Historical Sketch-A Workers Program,* by Fredrick J. Lang. *(Page 93)*

[6] In fact, the original may be traced back to Eugene V. Debs, the great American Socialist who in a speech delivered sometime in 1910 said, "If you are looking for a Moses to lead you out of the capitalist wilderness, stay right where you are. I would not lead you into the Promised Land if I could, because if I could lead you in, some one else will lead you out. You must use your heads as well as your hands, and get yourself out of your present condition." *(Page 103)*

[7] *West Coast Sailors,* January 11,1952. *(Page 108)*

[8] For information on the accidents in this and subsequent paragraphs see Noel Mostert's *Supership,* Chapter 7, p. 130, et seq. *(Page 115)*

[9] See *Pollution, Politics and International Law: Tankers At Sea,* by R.M.M'gonigle and M.W.Zacher, p. 15. *(Page 117)*

10 Compiled from *World Almanac,* 1991, p. 546. *(Page 117)*

11 This story, as well as much of the factual information I have used on Liberty ships, is told by John G. Bunker in his book *Liberty Ships:The Ugly Ducklings of World War II. (Page 146)*

12 The measurement from the keel to the upper deck. *(Page 148)*

13 Internal capacity measured in units of 100 cubic feet per ton. *(Page 148)*

14 *Fortune Magazine,* September 1937, is the source of most of this information. The entire issue is devoted to the pre-war merchant marine as well as the Merchant Marine Act of 1936. *(Page 148)*

15 For those who wish to pursue this subject a good start may be made with *Merchant Seamen's Law* by Silas Blake Axtell, Proctor in Admiralty. *(Page 196)*

16 Literature on this period is scarce. However a definitive study on the whole subject is *The Government of the United States vs. Wilhelm Reich* by Jerome Greenfield. *(Page 233)*

17 *Fury On Earth* by Myron Sharaf. *(Page 233)*

18 The official numbers for the Armed Forces are government figures and easily found in the *World Almanac,* 1989, p. 756. *(Page 246)*

19 The figures for the merchant marine are controversial. Scattered throughout the literature are various claims mostly from 200,000 to 250,000. I feel that these type of figures are rather inflated, since they probably count everyone and anyone who ever made a trip within the given time frame, December 7, 1941 to August 15, 1945. Also, it should be kept in mind that various writers and publicists picked up this figure and used it for various promotional reasons not the least of which was for Congressional testimony. The official Maritime Administration figures may be found in the *U.S. Statistical Abstract,* 75th Edition, p. 595, table # 695. *(Page 246)*

20 U.S.Coast Guard, July 1,1950. The casualty figure of 5,662 is also controversial. Various students of the subject such as Captain Arthur R. Moore in his book, *A Careless Word, A Needless Sinking,* lists over 6,000 names and in a phone conversation with me, he claims that the revised listing is now in the vicinity of 6,800. *(Page 246)*

21 Authentic figures are hard to come by. The few that I use may be found in *Convoy,* by Martin Middlebrook. *(Page 247)*

22 Interview in *St. Petersberg Times,* March 4, 1992; quoted in *West Coast Sailors,* June 19, 1992. *(Page 248)*

23 The material on Trident Subs was taken from the TV program, *Nova,* broadcast January 21, 1992. *(Page 249)*

24 One of the better studies of the entire subject may be found in *Fortune Magazine,* September 1937. The entire issue is devoted to U.S. shipping. *(Page 253)*

25 Quoted by Congresswoman Helen Bentley (R-Maryland) in *West Coast Sailors,* June 19, 1992. *(Page 257)*

26 *San Francisco Chronicle,* October 1,1992 *(Page 257)*

27 *San Francisco Cruise Passenger Terminal Assessment,* May 30, 1990. *(Page 258)*

List of Images

List of Images

Image	Credit	Page
• Joe Gladstone *photo*	Jay Saucedo	**viii**
• A voyage begins *illustration*	Tom Carey	Facing page 1
• Hog Islander *illustration*	Tom Carey	10
• Joe in 1940 *photo*	Photographer unknown	48
• Hog Islander *illustration*	Tom Carey	63
• Captain Ahab *illustration*	Rockwell Kent in Herman Melville, *Moby Dick*, 1930	76
• MTWIU 510 *sticker*	Charles Kerr Publishing Co.	88
• Harry Lundeberg Stetsons *illustration*	Tom Carey	106
• Disaster at sea *illustration*	Bits Hayden in Mike Quinn, *The Big Strike*, 1949	118
• Neptune's Court *illustration*	*Coast Seamen's Journal*, masthead	127
• Scoping out the news *illustration*	*Voice of the Federation* column, December 5, 1935 – LARC-SFSU files	141